CREAM

the legendary sixties superg

BILL GRAHAM PRESENTS IN SAN FRANCISCO
THE
DELICATE
HANDLE WITH CARE
Goodbye
CREAM

CREAM

the legendary sixties supergroup

Ginger Baker

Jack Bruce

Eric Clapton

by Chris Welch

A Balafon Book
AN IMPRINT OF THE OUTLINE PRESS

Cream

By Chris Welch

A MILLER FREEMAN BOOK

First British edition 2000

Published in the UK by Balafon Books, an imprint of Outline Press Ltd,
115J Cleveland Street, London W1T 6PU, England.

ISBN 0-87930-642-6

Printed in Hong Kong

Art Director: Nigel Osborne
Design: Paul Cooper
Editor: Tony Bacon
Production: Phil Richardson

Origination by Global Colour (Malaysia)
Print by Color Print Offset (Hong Kong)

00 01 02 03 04 5 4 3 2 1

INTRODUCTION

"THEY WILL BE CALLED CREAM"

Cream caused a sensation when they burst on to the scene in 1966. Eric Clapton, Jack Bruce and Ginger Baker unleashed a dazzling blend of musical styles, played with unrivalled skill, energy and panache. The very name of their band seemed bold and uncompromising. Yet it was a legitimate choice. Cream were simply the best.

When the band was launched with a formal announcement by their manager, Robert Stigwood, it was proudly proclaimed: "The first is last and the last is first, but the first, the second and the last are Cream. They will be called Cream..."

Cream in action. Left to right: Jack Bruce (bass, vocal); Ginger Baker (drums); Eric Clapton (guitar, vocal).

It sounded egocentric. Certainly the new group brought together some of the most gifted musicians of the day. Although the band's roots lay in the traditions of jazz, blues and rock'n'roll, their energy and vision ensured that Cream's music was new, fresh and individual. It wasn't long before they achieved a remarkable success with a series of highly distinctive hit records and blistering concerts that set new standards of excitement.

At a time when rock music was rapidly changing, Cream broke down musical barriers. Among their admirers was trumpeter Miles Davis, whose celebrated switch to a jazz-rock policy with *Bitches Brew* in 1969 was heavily influenced by the groundbreaking work of Cream. The British group also introduced the concept of the "power trio" which laid the foundations for the entire heavy rock genre.

Cream inspired and set standards for countless young players who followed in their wake. Between them, Baker, Bruce and Clapton helped to

redefine the arts of playing rock guitar, bass and drums. And Cream proved that it was possible to retain musical ideals while achieving huge commercial success. It was a pattern that would be repeated in the future by such trios as The Jimi Hendrix Experience, Rush, and The Police.

During their brief career of two years plus a few months, Cream released a relatively small number of records. So it should not be a surprise that the bootleg industry has attempted to provide alternatives, often well packaged but containing an infuriating mix of gems and rubbish.

Yet Cream were never just "a heavy rock group". Their dynamic live shows emphasised long, improvised solos and impressive instrumentals like 'Stepping Out', 'Traintime' and 'Toad', but the group also played with keen attention to dynamics and displayed a harmonic and rhythmic sophistication far in advance of their contemporaries.

Developing their songwriting skills with lyricist Pete Brown, Cream devised material that often combined poetry with cinematic imagery. Surreal tone-poems and hook-laden chart hits took their place alongside ballads, music-hall ditties, rock tunes and down-home blues. Cream took risks and experimented. Not every idea succeeded, but at least the band was never predictable. There was no great master plan to make them pioneers of progressive rock. As Ginger Baker cheerfully insists, "We were a pop group!"

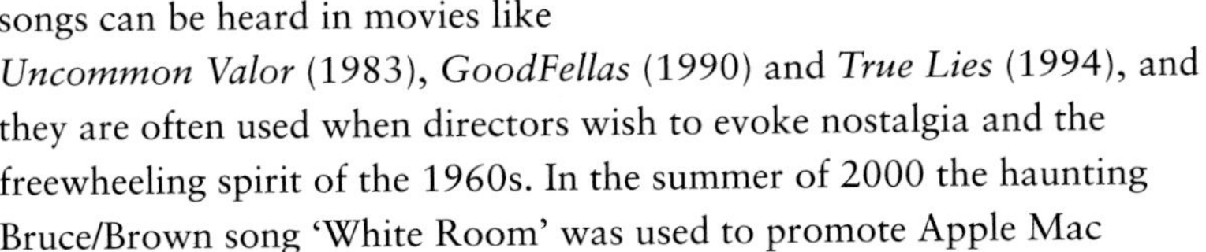

Often thought controversial or avant-garde at the time, Cream songs like 'I Feel Free', 'White Room', 'Strange Brew', 'Politician' and their biggest hit 'Sunshine Of Your Love' are now revived on innumerable soundtracks and in TV ads. Cream's songs can be heard in movies like *Uncommon Valor* (1983), *GoodFellas* (1990) and *True Lies* (1994), and they are often used when directors wish to evoke nostalgia and the freewheeling spirit of the 1960s. In the summer of 2000 the haunting Bruce/Brown song 'White Room' was used to promote Apple Mac computers in a major TV advertising campaign, bringing the sound of Cream into the 21st century.

During their brief, fiery career the group made just four albums: their 1966 debut *Fresh Cream*, followed by *Disraeli Gears* (1967), *Wheels Of Fire* (1968) and *Goodbye* (1969). Virtually their entire recorded output was collected on the long-overdue four-CD box-set *Those Were The Days* (1997) together with some demos and alternative versions. Anyone who heard these tracks for the first time must have been struck by the richness of the material, the spontaneity and the intensity of the performances.

"Cream was a success... despite the music industry."

Cream's recordings seem amazingly diverse compared to the output of today's bands who tend to stick to one style, usually on the advice of

producers who prefer a uniform approach to album-making. This has probably been a reaction against the post-Cream "prog rock" years when eclecticism went too far and often resulted in stylistic confusion. But Cream were focused in their own way, with a personal, well-defined sound. Their search for new territories away from basic blues-rock fare was hardly surprising, given their backgrounds in art-school and music-school. The need to explore, to learn and to keep an open mind was an important part of their training. A sense of humour and a taste for anarchy was also considered an asset in the 1960s. All these attitudes and influences took their place in formulating the music of Cream.

In the midst of the acclaim for their achievements, it's easy to forget that this so-called supergroup was formed in humble circumstances with a minimum of publicity, investment and equipment. The sensation they caused was largely confined to the cognoscenti, a few music critics and those eager fans who queued up in the rain to pay a few shillings to see the group play their first few gigs in London pubs and clubs.

Despite the esteem in which Baker, Bruce and Clapton were held, when the fledgling group had the temerity to ask a promoter for an extra £5 (about $7.50) for a sold-out gig, it was refused. When they wanted to record songs that weren't just recycled R&B standards, they were greeted with blank incomprehension and even hostility. Demo tapes were "lost" and sessions sabotaged. "Cream was a success, despite the industry," is how Jack Bruce describes it.

Cream changed the lives of each of its founder members. They were all three powerful yet intensely different characters. In many ways Ginger Baker was the driving force. He came up with the idea for the group, got them together and brought them to the attention of their manager, the impresario Robert Stigwood. Baker was regarded as one of the finest rock and jazz drummers in Europe. He had established his name and achieved

Composing the image: a Cream photo-shoot in 1967.

cult status while playing alongside Jack Bruce in the Graham Bond Organisation. As a result of Cream's success, Baker's status was transformed, and the hard-hitting extrovert became a star, the epitome of the wild-eyed rock drummer.

Jack Bruce, the band's singer, bass-player and co-composer, found his wings with Cream after many years of struggle and hard work. In the aftermath of Cream's acceptance he was able to launch a busy solo career, leading his own groups and working with a vast range of musicians, from Tony Williams to Frank Zappa.

Eric Clapton devised the name Cream and was also a prime motivator in forming the group. After his previous experience with The Yardbirds and John Mayall's Bluesbreakers, Clapton found that Cream gave him the chance to play with complete freedom and to experiment and develop a more mature guitar style. The tempestuous trio was a highly competitive musical environment, and the Cream experience wasn't always a happy one for Clapton. But it was like a finishing school that honed his talents and paved the way for a tremendously successful solo career. He was and remains the finest blues guitarist of his generation, a warm and sensitive singer-songwriter, and the creator of many of pop's most moving and memorable themes, from 'Layla' to 'Wonderful Tonight' and 'Tears In Heaven'. He has never forgotten his Cream years, and songs like 'Badge', 'Sunshine Of Your Love' and 'White Room' remain regular constituents of Clapton's live performances.

In their heyday Cream were at the forefront of a musical revolution that overlapped with and followed on from The Beatles. Together with The Who, the Jimi Hendrix Experience and Pink Floyd, Cream raised expectations and, for many of their adherents, delivered the musical equivalent of an acid trip. The sheer intensity of Cream shows remained locked in the memories of eager audiences for years afterwards. Whether wowing hippies at the Fillmore Auditorium in San Francisco or delighting fans at London's Saville Theatre, Cream became icons of the Flower Power period and an integral part of the psychedelic experience of the 1960s.

Cream managed several important visits to the tailor and to the coiffeur during their busy schedule.

With fame, money and success came problems. It was a heavy responsibility for any band to be expected to turn on their fans night after night on endless tours. Each member of Cream had his own ego and temperament, and eventually the strain took its toll. The band had begun as brothers, but came to an end with abrupt finality after only a little over two years at the top. There was a huge sense of disappointment and loss among fans as Cream broke up at the end of 1968. When they completed their final recordings for their *Goodbye* album and played their farewell concerts in the US and at the Royal Albert Hall in London in November they left their fans in limbo.

Yet this was probably their wisest move. The complete break ensured that Cream split at the top of their game. They are remembered today only for great shows, hit singles and groundbreaking albums that left their audience wanting more. There was no attempt to drag out their career together, no legacy of failed albums or less-than-successful comeback tours – often the fate of bands who never give up trying. In the light of subsequent developments during which pop and rock have undergone big, fundamental changes, it is unlikely that Cream in its original form could have survived and prospered into the 21st century.

Pete Brown, the poet and singer who co-wrote many of Cream's hit songs with Jack Bruce, is today amazed that such a musicianly band was so acceptable. "Looking back now," he says, "it seems extraordinary that it

should have been such a success worldwide. It was a case of being in the right place at the right time. If you look at anything remotely comparable now, you just know it's not going to be the same. There are a couple of young bands around today that are terrific, including a rock trio called Ether from Cardiff. But you just know they're not going to be another Cream. The music business nowadays just wouldn't know what to do with them."

Of course, the business back at the time didn't know what to do with Cream either. "Luckily they were all strong people and managed to motivate themselves," Brown continues. "At first people thought Cream were going to be just a Chicago-style blues band playing a few clubs. Indeed the whole operation was initially club-orientated and based on percentages of the venue's door income. The British music business has always been terribly blinkered. Very few people could see that Cream were going to make it in America and around the world."

"Very few people could see that Cream would make it in America."

Brown says that in America people are educated about music and appreciate those who can play. It's very different in Britain, he reckons, where the attitude is more to do with fashion. "Take the most anarchic punk rock bands in America," he suggests. "If you listen to them, they can really play. It's quite unlike the anti-musician attitude people have here in

Unofficial recordings of Cream concerts are plentiful: this one (left) is typical enough, snatched at gigs in Oakland and Los Angeles during 1968. Such bootleg recordings are still, of course, illegal.

the UK, which is partly based on an inferiority complex. If you mention Cream to Green Day or Henry Rollins or any artist in the States who has come up in the last ten years, they'll say, 'Oh, Cream were fantastic. They were great musicians and I listen to their stuff.' Even Miles Davis liked Cream. What greater tribute could you ask?

"Yet in Britain," concludes Brown, "young bands will say, 'Who the fuck were Cream?' Or they'll say, 'Oh, they're just a load of old musos who got lucky.' Everything gets superseded so rapidly. It's a process that started in the 1970s. Now, instead of 15 minutes of fame, you only get three minutes. So everything gets forgotten and traditions don't get passed on."

"Cream was a nice little trio. And it certainly was an influence – on the whole future of rock music."

But the memory of Cream is strong enough to ensure a stream of Cream tribute bands. Among them is a band called Cream'd, led in England by blues guitarist Ray Minhinnett. Meanwhile, the real Cream have resisted many million-dollar offers to reform. They only came together for old time's sake when they performed at The Rock & Roll Hall Of Fame awards ceremony in New York in January 1993. Once again Ginger Baker, Jack Bruce and Eric Clapton launched into 'Sunshine Of Your Love', 'Crossroads' and 'Born Under A Bad Sign'. As Jack Bruce says, "The magic was still there."

Tears were shed, and there's no doubt Eric Clapton too regarded the old group as important. But he had to move on and create a musical environment more conducive to his tastes and temperament. Clapton has never been keen on a full-scale revival, despite those offers, and there are surely aspects of his life as a young musician in the 1960s he would rather not revive. It was left to Baker and Bruce to team up with guitarist Gary Moore in the 1990s to create a new group that they hoped would re-ignite the flames. But the original trio proved a hard act to follow.

Says Jack Bruce: "Cream showed that rock musicians could play. That was a double-edged sword, because it became very unfashionable to be able to play, didn't it? But Cream was a nice little trio. And it certainly was an influence – on the whole future of rock music."

Bruce, Baker and Clapton stepping out for the last time at the Royal Albert Hall, London, in November 1968.

CHAPTER 1

BLUE CONDITION

Each member of Cream came to the group with a formidable reputation for musical excellence, hard-won on the thriving British R&B scene. Eric Clapton was regarded as a young veteran from his work as lead guitarist with The Yardbirds and John Mayall's Bluesbreakers. At a time when most pop guitarists could barely manage a rhythmic strum and a few erratic solos, Clapton's authentic blues style and effortless soloing seemed like a revelation. His reputation spread rapidly and Clapton was held in high esteem – even in America, the land of his idols.

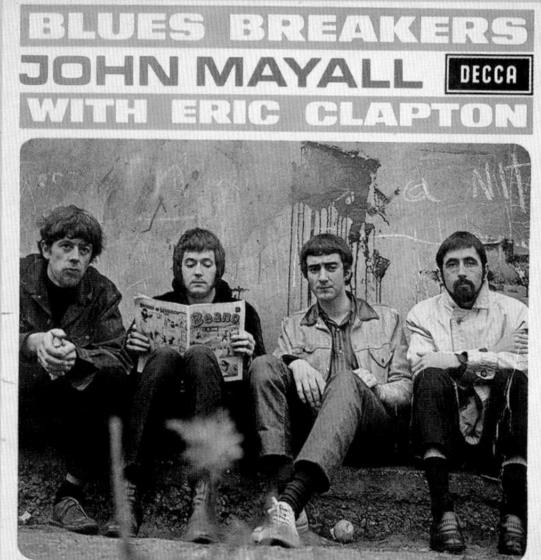

The "Beano cover": Clapton and the funnies, 1966.

He was born Eric Patrick Clapton on March 30th 1945 in Ripley, Surrey, just south-west of London. He was brought up by his grandmother Rose Clapton and her second husband Jack Clapp. Eric's mother Pat Clapton was 16 and unmarried; his father, a soldier called Edward Fryer, returned to Canada after the war. Pat left England to live in Germany, leaving Eric in the care of her mother and stepfather. It would cause the youthful Eric some confusion and stress as he gradually became aware of these tangled relationships. Playing music gave him a sense of identity and self-esteem... as well as pleasure.

While at primary school, young Clapton began playing the recorder in the school band, fuelling his growing ambition to become a musician. He discovered rock'n'roll in 1957, along with the rest of the British teenage population. His stepfather gave him his first guitar, a Spanish-style acoustic.

His musical career really began during his time at Kingston art college, which he entered in September 1961, intending to study stained-glass design. Rock'n'roll and the blues took precedence over art as Clapton began listening to records by BB King, Muddy Waters, Chuck Berry, Big Bill Broonzy, Robert Johnson and Buddy Holly. He spent hours practising guitar, trying to play what he'd heard on record. But he was no mere copyist. "I knew after a while I had to develop my own style," he said later. "I would do something I'd heard on record, then add something of my own. Gradually, more of my own stuff took over."

Clapton began playing at local folk clubs. He was expelled from college in July 1962, having failed to convince the authorities that he was taking the art course seriously. He was disappointed at having to leave, but became more determined to succeed as a musician. He embarked on a bohemian lifestyle, living in squalid flats with friends, drinking, visiting jazz clubs and sitting in with bands. In September 1962 he obtained his first electric guitar and soon formed a blues duo with guitarist Dave Brock.

Clapton's first proper band was The Roosters, formed at the start of 1963. The line-up included Clapton and Tom McGuinness on guitars, Robin "Ben" Palmer on piano, vocalist Terry Brennan, and drummer Robin Mason. They played John Lee Hooker's 'Boom Boom' and the Muddy Waters song 'Hoochie Coochie Man' among others, appearing at pubs, clubs and parties in and around the Surrey towns of Kingston and Richmond, hotbeds of R&B revivalism. The Roosters only lasted from January to September, but it was a lot of fun and a useful first step. Tom McGuinness remembers that the band never recorded. "And we couldn't find a bass player," he says, "which illustrates how few people there were wanting to play R&B in 1963."

"Clapton decided to become a wandering minstrel."

Clapton began using his first electric guitar, a Kay, with The Roosters. He fitted light-gauge strings that enabled him to bend notes and imbue a "singing" quality to his playing. It might be imagined that Clapton was a rather ordinary player, perhaps no better than the average young amateur guitarist of the period, given his youth and lack of experience. Not so, says Ben Palmer, a friend and confidante who was immediately struck by the brilliance of Clapton's musicianship, even at that early stage in his career. Palmer would become an important figure in the story of Cream. He was to be their first tour manager, and experienced the highs and lows of life on the road during the early years. He also worked with Blind Faith and remained part of Clapton's team when the guitarist toured with his own bands during the early 1970s. Palmer was also a prime mover in the famous 1965 expedition to Greece with The Glands when Clapton decided to become a wandering minstrel – and ended up held captive at the hands of modern-day brigands.

A keen fan of blues, R&B and modern jazz in his youth, Palmer has clear views on the development of rock music and is refreshingly honest and candid about both the music business in general and Cream in particular. After spending much of his early life working in the music business, today he is a skilled craftsman, living far away from the raucous sounds of live music in the heart of the Welsh countryside. He retains his sense of humour, once so necessary to cope with the tantrums of some of the most powerful and egotistical characters of the rock era. Yet his involvement with Clapton and Cream came about through a series of chance meetings and the shared love of original American music forms.

"The Roosters' first drummer had a car, so he was forgiven a great deal."

Ben Palmer was born in Berkshire on February 8th 1937. He had piano lessons as a child and later took up the trumpet to play in a trad-jazz band. He was a fan of jazz revivalist Ken Colyer and shared that generation's fanaticism about the purity of jazz and blues. "I picked up a secondhand trumpet which I started playing at home along to records," says Palmer. "I met a chap in the army who had friends in West London who were starting a band, so I used to play with them every weekend. Then the first Muddy Waters records started to arrive in Britain in the late 1950s. Until then we had only heard Leadbelly and there wasn't much else available. I worked for Esquire Records for a long time which was run by Carlo Kramer, and there was a chap there called Ron Atkins who lived at home with his mother. Anyway, I left Ron this *Muddy Waters At Newport* LP and he played it in his room, and when he came out his mother said, 'Oh, I'm glad you're all right. I heard such a row I thought you'd fallen down and hurt yourself.' That's how this music sounded to people in England at the time."

Palmer was living in a flat in Oxford when he put a classified advertisement in *Melody Maker* asking musicians to contact him with a view to forming a blues group. Tom McGuinness was the first to answer. Palmer hitchhiked to West London to meet McGuinness, and between them they started The Roosters. "Our first drummer was Robin Payne. By virtue of being a drummer he had a car, so he was forgiven a great deal," laughs Palmer. "He wasn't all that keen on blues but he was a pretty reliable drummer. I was playing the piano by then. Living in Oxford at the same time was Paul Jones, or Paul Pond as he was then. So ostensibly we put the group together for him to sing in front of. At this point Clapton wasn't in the band. The first guitar player I can remember in the band was Brian Jones from Cheltenham. He came along a couple of times, but by then Alexis Korner was going and he felt more attracted to Alexis's club in Ealing than a semi-pro band in Oxford."

Then McGuinness's girlfriend told them that there was someone at Kingston art college who was a decent guitar player. "He turned out to be

Eric," says Palmer. "Once he joined we went out on the circuit. I remember playing the Ricky Tick Club at Windsor." McGuinness was keen on Chuck Berry; Palmer more into Chicago blues. "So Tom could be persuaded to play some Muddy Waters numbers in exchange for me playing Chuck Berry numbers. I think we both did it with pretty bad grace at times. Paul Jones didn't stay with us as he wanted some more professional experience. He went to sing with a house band in a cinema in Slough that just covered chart songs. We had to get another singer, and we never saw Paul again. The next thing we knew, he was with Manfred Mann. But we had a new singer called Terry Brennan, and we had Eric.

"It was instantly clear that Eric was better than anybody else, on any other instrument," Palmer recalls of The Roosters. "It seemed like a miracle at the time. He got lots of solos, and he could carry them too. Oh yeah! In those days people would say, 'Well, give me a solo but don't make it too long.' But you could leave Eric playing away and light up a cigarette. And he wouldn't mind, because he could solo endlessly, and he really got people excited. Pretty deafening, too, with his 30-watt amplifier."

"People would say, 'Give me a solo – but not for too long.' But Eric could solo away endlessly."

Eventually The Roosters broke up, allegedly due to lack of money and little commitment. Clapton occasionally sat in with Alexis Korner's group at the Ealing Club, an R&B stronghold in west London. Then Clapton and McGuinness joined Casey Jones & The Engineers, run by Brian Casser, the former singer with Liverpool group Cass & The Cassanovas. Cass had left Liverpool to seek his fortune in London, where at the height of Beatlemania anybody with a Liverpool accent was guaranteed an audience and a record contract. He arrived in the capital in October 1962 and briefly formed a backing group called The Nightsounds, which included Albert Lee, another fine guitarist, who years later would work extensively with Eric Clapton.

Cass recorded a single for Columbia called 'One Way Ticket' in 1963 under the name of Casey Jones & The Engineers. The Engineers didn't actually exist, so the singer began looking for backing musicians. His regular drummer Ray Stock met Clapton at The Scene club in London's Soho. Clapton told Stock that he was an unemployed guitarist, and Stock revealed that Casey Jones was looking for musicians to form a backing band. Clapton said he'd join if he could bring along his ex-Roosters pal Tom McGuinness.

In October 1963 Casey Jones & The Engineers were formed with Brian Casser (vocals), Eric Clapton (guitar), Tom McGuinness (bass guitar) and Ray Stock (drums). Clapton lasted just seven gigs before stomping off in a

"I was watching The Yardbirds one week and playing with them the next."

temper. It seems that The Engineers were expected to back a female pop singer on the night of their first gig in Macclesfield, Cheshire. The group drove all the way from London expecting to play the blues. Neither McGuinness nor Clapton knew the chords to the lady's cabaret songs and they were highly embarrassed by the experience. It transpired that Casey had taken many more such unsuitable bookings all over the country, from Reading to Manchester. McGuinness and Clapton enjoyed their first taste of life on the road, away from home. But the music was getting on their nerves and one day Clapton decided to quit, without telling McGuinness.

Clapton didn't turn up for the next gig and McGuinness went looking for him. He was informed by Clapton's pal Guy Stevens that the guitarist wasn't going to do the Casey Jones gig any more. McGuinness remembers thinking: "Well sod that, I'm not doing it either." Clapton recalled later: "Casey Jones & The Engineers was a heavy pop show, and I couldn't stand that for very long. At that time I was such a purist, and they were playing real Top-20 stuff, which was disastrous."

Ben Palmer loyally went to see Clapton with The Engineers and feels in retrospect that they weren't quite as bad as reports have suggested. "They were a bit like Jackie Lomax & The Undertakers. It was that sort of band: quite exciting and professional, and they played well together. But I lost contact with Eric completely for some time after The Roosters broke up. He lived at John Mayall's house in south London for a while, so other than John Mayall and his wife Pam, nobody else saw much of Eric."

After the Casey Jones adventure, Tom McGuinness went off and joined Manfred Mann's highly successful pop group, now of course fronted by Paul Jones. McGuinness later formed McGuinness Flint with ex-John Mayall drummer Hughie Flint (and had a number-2 chart hit with 'When I'm Dead And Gone' in 1970). Brian Casser apparently had boundless enthusiasm, forming a new band called Casey Jones & The Governors. They took up residence in Germany, where they had several hit records and became a popular act.

Back in London, the various blues purists assembled in search of the ideal band. Among them was Brian Jones, his brief tenure with The Roosters long forgotten as his new group The Rolling Stones rapidly became popular in the fledgling British R&B movement. The Stones had been resident at the Crawdaddy club in Richmond during 1963. When they gained their first hit records and set off to rival The Beatles they were replaced at the Crawdaddy by a Kingston-based R&B group, The Yardbirds. The group's original guitarist Anthony "Top" Topham decided

to leave, following parental opposition to being in a beat group, and singer Keith Relf phoned Eric Clapton, whom he'd known at art college. He asked Clapton if he would be interested in joining The Yardbirds.

Clapton watched a gig, then came to a rehearsal. He immediately fitted in with the band's style. "I was watching them one week and playing with them the next," he said later. Clapton's arrival in October 1963 gave The Yardbirds a terrific boost. For a year or so he was happy to play with the band, which consisted of Keith Relf (vocals, harmonica), Chris Dreja

Eric Clapton (far left) with The Yardbirds, serenading BBC TV scriptwriter Lord Ted Willis in 1965, somewhere in England.

(guitar), Paul Samwell-Smith (bass) and Jim McCarty (drums). The Yardbirds seemed to be going places. They had a residency at The Marquee club, a record contract with EMI, and a dynamic manager, Giorgio Gomelsky. They began to record material in the studio and also cut a live album at The Marquee. These mid-1960s recordings reveal Clapton's developing guitar work. His playing at this time was ideally suited to the band's "rave up" style, employing fast boogie riffs and improvised solos on tunes like 'Smokestack Lightning' and 'I Wish You Would'. He broke guitar strings so often that the impatient audience would give the band a slow handclap, earning Clapton his first nickname of Slowhand – bestowed on him by the band's equally impatient manager.

As part of his duties, Clapton was expected to back visiting American blues singer Sonny Boy Williamson on his UK tour with The Yardbirds. It was a daunting prospect. Sonny Boy, armed with a whisky bottle as well as his harmonica, could be an erratic performer, and he apparently terrified the band. He altered tunes, changed keys and never let them know what he planned to do next. This was a learning experience.

The Yardbirds on Ready, Steady Go! in May 1964: Paul Samwell-Smith (bass), Chris Dreja (guitar), Keith Relf (vocal), Jim McCarty (drums) and Eric Clapton (guitar). Note Clapton's skinhead haircut.

The "most blueswailing" Yardbirds, clad in their smart mod suits, set out on a seemingly endless string of one-nighters. It was hard work, but they built up a devoted following. It was clear that The Yardbirds might go on gigging forever. However, they needed a hit record. The group released their first single 'I Wish You Would' in June 1964. They appeared regularly on ITV's *Ready Steady Go!* pop show and were showcased at the Richmond jazz and blues festival. It looked like The Yardbirds could be as big as the Stones. Before too long their records were in the charts and the fans began screaming.

The group's second single 'Good Morning Little Schoolgirl', released during September, was in a blues and soul groove, while their debut album *Five Live Yardbirds* reflected their regular live set, based on tunes like 'Boom Boom' and 'Too Much Monkey Business'. That was fine so far as

Clapton suspiciously eyes up Yardbirds manager Giorgio Gomelsky (left) and Ted Willis as they plan his future in showbusiness.

Eric Clapton was concerned, but The Yardbirds were also being promoted by Giorgio Gomelsky as a pop group. They even shared billing with The Beatles at the Liverpudlians' Christmas show. That was quite an honour, and Ben Palmer remembers seeing The Yardbirds on the bill. "But you couldn't hear anything," he laughs. "The Beatles audience was up and screaming straight away and continued to do so long after The Beatles left, so I couldn't say I really heard The Yardbirds. I had gone to hear Eric play, and I didn't have any interest in that sort of music."

Amid all the deafening screams of the teenage girls, Clapton had begun to worry about the group's commercial leanings. Matters reached a climax over the choice of the band's next single. Clapton voted for a cover of an Otis Redding song. The rest of the group wanted to try an original Graham Gouldman item called 'For Your Love'. It turned out to be a Top-Five hit and has since been hailed as a classic of 1960s pop production, thanks to its atmospheric use of harpsichord and bongos.

The b-side of that 45, 'Got To Hurry', has Clapton playing a great solo, but the guitarist was unhappy with the a-side, which the group had to try to reproduce on stage. Clapton decided to quit the band in protest. During the weeks before his departure he became increasingly detached from the group. At a Yardbirds gig at the Bromel club in Bromley, south London, shortly before his departure, he looked particularly unhappy on stage.

"You noticed?" said Clapton with a wry smile when the matter was raised by a *Melody Maker* reporter reviewing the show.

Although Clapton's departure was a shock, the consequences were good. The Yardbirds gained a new guitarist, Jeff Beck, who was keen on experimenting and didn't mind moving in new directions. And it wasn't long before Clapton found himself in a much more blues-oriented touring band. Within days of his departure being announced, Clapton received a call from John Mayall inviting the guitarist to join Mayall's group, the Bluesbreakers. The result would be a highly beneficial association. Eric Clapton was established as the first great British guitar hero since Hank Marvin and The Shadows, and the Bluesbreakers became one of the most popular bands on the club-touring circuit. Such was the power of Clapton's playing that fans began chalking on pub walls "Clapton is god". It was flattering, and confirmed that Clapton had taken the right decision to walk away from pop success. Now he had taken up a blues crusade.

John Mayall had come to London in 1962 from Manchester. He was several years older than Clapton, and played organ, piano, harmonica and guitar, as well as singing. He did not drink, and was a strict disciplinarian, not afraid to hire and fire at will. These were hard-headed, business-like attributes. The Yardbirds tended to operate as pals, with any change in the line-up a personal wrench. They also regarded boozing and carousing as essential to the life of a real bluesman.

The Yardbirds played R&B on their live 1965 debut album, before indulging in the pop experiments that led to Clapton's departure.

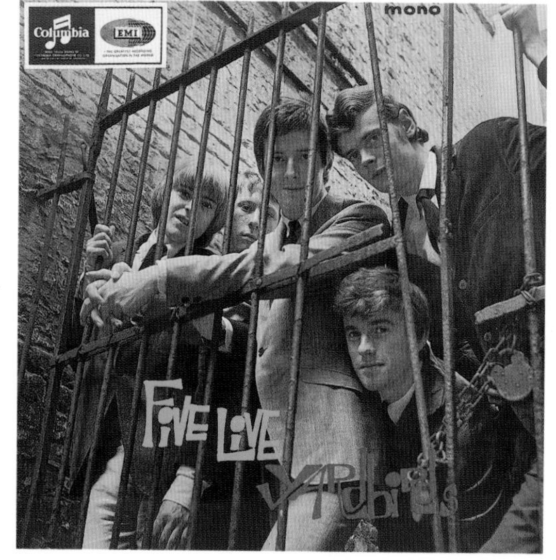

At first Clapton seemed ready to accept the rather glum strictures of working with Mayall and stayed in the bandleader's south-London house for a while, listening to the boss's collection of ancient blues recordings. But Clapton was still a restless young man, keen to experience what the world had to offer. Playing smaller gigs for less money than The Yardbirds began to pall.

One night in August 1965 Clapton decided to quit Mayall and go off with a group of friends, including pianist Ben Palmer, for a trip around the world. It was going to be a bit like Cliff Richard's film *Summer Holiday*. They would take an old London Transport bus to serve as their mobile home, stopping off at various points to play. In the event, they couldn't get a bus, so four of them set off in a station-wagon and headed for Greece.

The Bluesbreakers in 1965, left to right: John Mayall; Hughie Flint; Eric Clapton; and John McVie.

Calling themselves The Glands (later known as The Greek Loon Band) they found a gig at an Athens hotel. Without work permits or money they soon got into trouble with the local authorities. At first all seemed well. They met a club proprietor who hired Clapton and his friends to support a local Beatles-covers band who played at the hotel's club.

Ben Palmer recalls how the adventure got underway. "Don't forget The Glands! It's the dark secret of Eric's climb to fame," he laughs, explaining that when Clapton first left Mayall he came and stayed at Palmer's place in Oxford for a while. "Then we made our disastrous attempt to tour the world. By now we were all living in Covent Garden in London, and during a drunken evening someone suggested the idea. Eric was going to leave John anyway. He was pretty fed up with the routine of it all. We said, 'Come in the car with us and we'll go round the world!'"

So off went this unlikely group in an old American Ford Fairlane, driven by Bernie Greenwood, sax player from Chris Farlowe's band The Thunderbirds. "He's now a GP, but he still plays the sax," Palmer explains. "We also had a singer called John Bailey – who's now a musicology professor in Belfast – and a bass player called Bob Rae who was also a trad trumpeter. He had to learn to play the electric bass in the back of the car on the way to Athens. And finally," says Palmer, "there was me on piano and Eric on guitar."

John Bailey went on ahead to Athens, because he had friends there, and he assured the group that by the time they arrived work would be waiting. "It wasn't, of course," smiles Palmer. "It came eventually, but Eric found himself having to play his old Yardbirds hits again because that's what they'd heard. We didn't get a chance to play any blues at all. Instead we covered numbers by The Kinks and The Beatles. We ended up playing in a nightclub called The Igloo, one of those places where it costs £8 for a whisky. It was full of Greek footballers and rich Arabs spending money. The draw from their point of view was that we were fresh from London and they had just heard about the Swinging Sixties. That made it different from other nightclubs which all had Greek bands."

"The Greek club boss had us surrounded by heavies, in a state of kidnap."

The club also had its own Greek band called The Juniors, but unfortunately after The Glands had been in town for a few weeks The Juniors were involved in a car crash and several of the members were killed. "We had to take over all the playing," recalls Palmer. "We'd play from 8pm until the Greek footballers had had enough." When it turned out that the group's enormous hotel bill wasn't being paid as promised, and that there was no money coming in for all their hard work, the musicians decided to quit. The club boss then pointed out that he had omitted to get them work permits, so they were soon arrested by the police.

"The club owner used strong-arm tactics," says Palmer. "We were supposed to have deposited a bond on all the amplifiers when we entered the country, but of course we hadn't done that. By now we were virtually prisoners. The club boss insisted that Eric move into his house, and we weren't allowed to take the instruments away. Eventually we were forced into playing two concerts in a cinema in the docks area on a Sunday morning, after ten hours of continuous playing on the Saturday night. We were surrounded by heavies and we were in a state of kidnap."

Just to make matters worse, there was a near riot at the end of the second concert. This was mainly because the audience liked the band so much that they didn't want them to stop. It may also have been due to the fact that the band, by way of protest, had played the Stones song 'Satisfaction' continuously for the whole concert. The cumulative effect led to a mini riot. In the confusion the group managed to get some of the crowd to help them with the instruments, and they escaped, leaving Clapton behind. He was locked in the office – the club boss had begun to realise that he was the key figure. In the meantime Palmer sold most of the amplifiers and got a train ticket back to London for him and Clapton, who had to make a break for it and meet Palmer at the station.

Clapton managed to get out of his room by claiming he needed to buy new guitar strings. He and Palmer hid in the station toilets until the train pulled in. "Isn't that ridiculous?" says Palmer. "Anyway, we got back to London. When Eric got off the train at Victoria station he said, 'Hang on a second.' He went into a phone box and came out looking quite cheerful for the first time in weeks. He'd been on the phone to John Mayall asking if he wanted him back, and John had said yes. So within seconds of putting his foot on the platform, he was back in the Mayall band. He got into a taxi round to John's and left me there with no future, as I saw it.

"There is a strong ruthless streak in Eric," continues Palmer. "It's one of the flaws in an otherwise delightful man. He is very ruthless. I don't think he blamed us for the events in Greece, but he was certainly looking out for himself when we got back."

The returned Clapton found that John Mayall's Bluesbreakers had picked up a new bass player since he last worked with the band. Jack Bruce, who had left the Graham Bond Organisation after a row with Ginger Baker, was now doing dates with Mayall. But not for long. Shortly afterward Bruce left to join the Manfred Mann group, and was replaced by John McVie. During the brief period in which they played together in the Bluesbreakers, Clapton gained an idea of Bruce's skills as a bass player and singer, and made a mental note to work with him again, some day.

"The Blues Breakers album established Clapton as a giant among contemporary guitarists."

Putting the Greek disaster behind him, Clapton plunged into serious work with the Bluesbreakers. The band recorded for the Decca label, and produced two tracks at this time which featured Clapton: 'The Lonely Years', and 'Bernard Jenkins' – a taster for a full album that would become one of the cornerstones of the British blues-rock movement and which established Clapton as a giant among contemporary guitarists.

That album was *Blues Breakers With Eric Clapton*, recorded in April 1966 and released in July. The striking cover picture still raises a smile. It shows the band including their leader sitting in front of a paint-daubed concrete wall, staring rather glumly at the camera. All except Clapton. He is engrossed in a copy of the children's comic *The Beano*. Eyes averted, he is clearly enjoying the cartoon exploits of Dennis The Menace, which seem rather more important than living up to his status as "god".

The album sold well, sparking a blues boom and enhancing Clapton's personal reputation still further. He replaced the nervy, agitated guitar sound he'd displayed on the live Yardbirds recordings with a much more positive, masterful approach, revealing a maturity beyond his 21 years.

Clapton's guitar exuded power and authority right from the opening numbers on the Mayall album, 'All Your Love' and 'Hideaway'. He followed these with a virtuoso display of guitar pyrotechnics on his showcase number, 'Stepping Out'. Even better was the slow blues, 'Have You Heard'. Here Clapton constructed a truly remarkable solo, perfectly conceived, timed and executed, and one that today still sends shivers down

A young and bearded Peter "Ginger" Baker (right), in about 1958, at London's Top Ten club.

the spine. Fortunate indeed were those who saw Clapton live at the Bluesbreakers' intimate club gigs, when the fans hung on every note and shouted at Mayall: "Give god a solo!"

Although a lot of playing time was devoted to the leader's vocals, Mayall made room among the album's 12 tracks for Clapton's first vocal performance, on the Robert Johnson tune 'Ramblin' On My Mind'. But despite the Mayall band providing a sympathetic and unpretentious musical platform for Clapton's burgeoning skills, once again the guitarist began to feel restricted, even a little bored.

Clapton (below) at the Decca studio in West Hampstead, London, in 1966, cutting the legendary Blues Breakers album that consolidated his reputation as a brilliant blues guitarist.

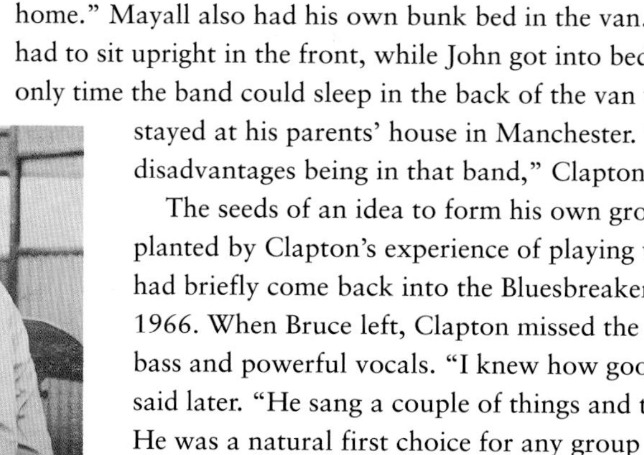

Apart from the fact the Mayall wasn't the greatest singer in the world, band members also had to put up with his quirks on the road. "John was an amazing man," recalled Clapton. "No one was allowed to drink. John McVie got slung out of the band's van half way between Birmingham and London one night because he was drunk, and he had to make his own way home." Mayall also had his own bunk bed in the van. Clapton and the rest had to sit upright in the front, while John got into bed in the back. The only time the band could sleep in the back of the van was when the leader stayed at his parents' house in Manchester. "So there were disadvantages being in that band," Clapton noted.

The seeds of an idea to form his own group had already been planted by Clapton's experience of playing with Jack Bruce, who had briefly come back into the Bluesbreakers again during April 1966. When Bruce left, Clapton missed the Scotsman's driving bass and powerful vocals. "I knew how good he was," Clapton said later. "He sang a couple of things and they were really great. He was a natural first choice for any group I might dream about forming. I hit it off with Jack really well. Then he left to go with Manfred Mann, and John Mayall got John McVie back on bass. I decided that playing with Jack was more exciting. There was something creative there. Most of what we were doing with Mayall was imitating the records we'd got, but Jack had something else. He had no reverence for what we were doing, and was composing new parts as he went along. I thought well, if he could do that, we could get a drummer and I could be Buddy Guy with a composing bass player..."Clapton was

therefore keenly interested if somewhat surprised when Ginger Baker approached him at a Mayall Bluesbreakers gig in Oxford one night in May 1966. Baker sat in with the band, and his playing transformed the session. Clapton knew right away that he could play with this wild drummer, and they had a drink together. Baker typically seized the moment and said to Clapton bluntly, "How about getting a group together?"

It seemed like a great idea. Clapton thought they could form a trio, but with one proviso. He wanted Jack Bruce as the third member. Baker would have to think about this, as his last meeting with the bass player had been somewhat fraught. But once a few problems had been sorted out, there was nothing to stop Clapton making his move. The *Blues Breakers* album was at number six in the UK charts, but Clapton told Mayall he was leaving. There was no time to argue. The guitarist's new band had already started rehearsals. However, it would not turn out to be quite the down-home blues-based trio that Clapton had in mind. He would have to contend with two very fiery characters. Jack Bruce and Ginger Baker would become his musical partners for the tumultuous two-and-a-bit years that followed.

Baker on drums with Tony Archer (bass), John Mumford (trombone) and Ray De Milo (alto sax) at The Phoenix, Cavendish Square, London in 1962.

Peter "Ginger" Baker was born in Lewisham, south-east London, on August 19th 1939. The red-haired youth of Irish extraction grew up in New Eltham, a suburb to the east of Lewisham. As a teenager Baker was a highly competitive racing cyclist. This kind of exercise later gave him the extraordinary strength and stamina which he needed for his highly personal style of drumming.

Baker's first instrument was the trumpet, which he played with an Air Training Corps band. The outfit's drummer also played kit drums in a trad-jazz band, and this led Baker to switch from trumpet to drums. It seemed a much more satisfying mode of expression, and was better suited to his explosive and mercurial temperament. Baker listened to New Orleans

Baker jamming at The Phoenix in London with Pete Shade (vibes), Tony Archer (bass) and a young Dick Morrissey (tenor saxophone) in 1962.

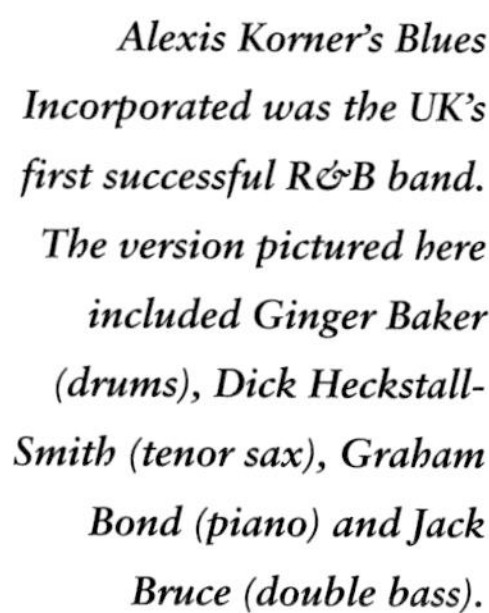

Alexis Korner's Blues Incorporated was the UK's first successful R&B band. The version pictured here included Ginger Baker (drums), Dick Heckstall-Smith (tenor sax), Graham Bond (piano) and Jack Bruce (double bass).

drummers like Baby Dodds and Zutty Singleton and later turned on to modern jazzmen such as Max Roach and the British drummer Phil Seamen, who became a close friend and mentor.

Baker had started out banging knives and forks on the kitchen table before he got his first kit. He sat in with a band on another drummer's set-up before he was finally convinced he should become a drummer. A toy drum kit costing £3 (about $5) was all he could afford, having blown most of his money on an expensive racing bike. He got jobs with a signwriting company and an advertising agency to raise the money for a proper kit. His mother then had to put up with the sound of endless drum practise. At the age of 16 he joined Bob Wallis & His Storyville Jazz Men, quit his day job and spent the next year touring. During his trad-jazz days Baker played with Acker Bilk and Terry Lightfoot, although they doubtless found his aggressive, extrovert style alarming.

Unhappy with his existing kit, Baker set about building his own set of drums from Perspex, a clear plastic. "I bent the shells and shaped them over a gas ring," recalls Baker. "I cut them all out and pieced them together with metal drum fittings. I used that kit until 1966 when I bought my first Ludwig kit." Baker played his home-made drums on two Graham Bond Organisation albums, *The Sound Of '65* and *There's A Bond Between Us.*

Although Baker was adept at New Orleans-style drumming, he became increasingly influenced by Max Roach. Terry Lightfoot complained about

Baker's "bebop drumming", demanding that he stick to playing a steady four-to-the-bar on the bass drum. Baker's answer was short and to the point. As a result he lost his job and in 1959 went off on a trip to Copenhagen, Denmark, with guitarist Diz Disley. He also played on a three-month Scandinavian tour with blues/gospel singer-guitarist Sister Rosetta Tharpe. On his return Baker was unemployed, and his mother insisted he got a day-job loading trucks. At the same time he learned to read drum parts so that he would be able to play arrangements with professional bands.

Baker hung out in Archer Street, the musicians' haunt in central London where work was picked up and gigs exchanged. He got a job playing with an Irish showband in north London, playing some interesting big-band jazz arrangements. He was resident at an Irish ballroom in Kilburn, north-west London, for over a year, and then joined pianist Johnny Burch's Octet. Baker desperately wanted to break into the modern-jazz scene which was based in Soho, central London, primarily at The Flamingo club in Wardour Street and at Ronnie Scott's in Gerrard Street. Some of the beboppers appreciated Baker's brash enthusiasm. When Phil Seamen heard him play at the All-Nighter club at The Flamingo, he invited Baker to practise drum rudiments with him, as well as just to talk about the philosophy of drumming.

Others found Baker just too loud and were not keen on his use of a heavy off-beat. Baker's argument was that if it was good enough for Art Blakey, it should be good enough for them. Instead, he found himself being frozen out. He came to find a looser, more appreciative atmosphere on the burgeoning R&B scene. He bumped into several other renegade modernists, including alto saxophonist Graham Bond, tenor saxman Dick Heckstall-Smith and double-bass player Jack Bruce.

All these musicians had been encouraged by the example of two crucially important bands, Alexis Korner's Blues Incorporated and The

Page 18 JAZZ NEWS — Wednesday, May 2nd 1962

R & B AT THE MARQUEE

opening on MAY 3rd is the new R & B band BLUES INCORPORATED, formed by ALEXIS KORNER featuring CYRIL DAVIS on HOHNER HARMONICA.

The harmonica Cyril plays is one of a wide range. There is a leaflet describing them all.

HOHNER 11/13 FARRINGDON ROAD LONDON EC1

More line-ups of Alexis Korner's ever-changing Blues Incorporated, pictured (below) with drummer Charlie Watts, Jack Bruce on bass, and harpist Cyril Davies, and on the sleeve (left) with bearded Dick Heckstall-Smith on sax.

Cyril Davies All-Stars. These charismatic bandleaders had shaken up the local music scene in the early 1960s by showing that there was an exciting alternative to rock'n'roll which, by that time, had become increasingly commercialised and debased. Strongly influenced by Muddy Waters's Chicago-style electric blues, Korner and Davies helped tear down the perceived barriers between blues, jazz and rock.

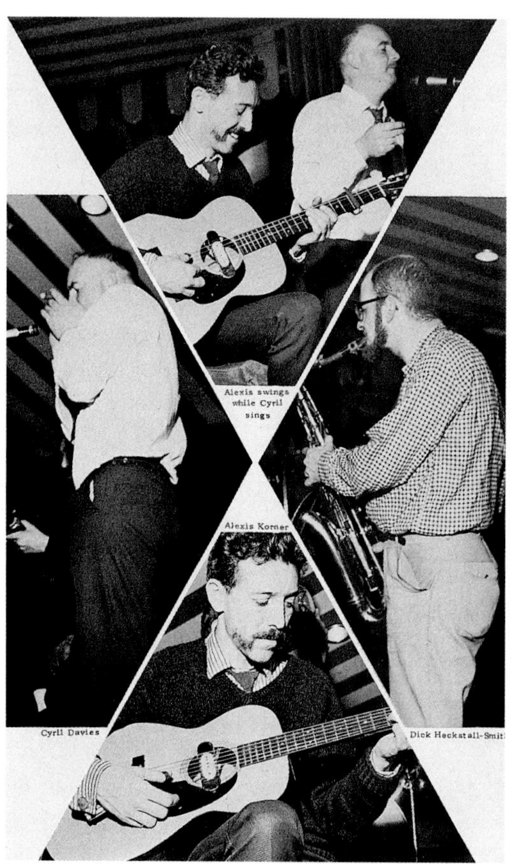

Korner loved boogie-woogie and modern jazz as much as he liked pure blues. Some of his recordings featured jazzmen Phil Seamen and Dick Heckstall-Smith, and the results were actually closer in spirit to Ronnie Scott's jazz club than the blues-oriented Ealing Club, which Korner had founded. The moustachioed singer and guitarist, who became a major influence, was a cultured, charismatic figure with a smouldering voice, fired with enthusiasm and among the enthusiasts responsible for setting the important British R&B revival in motion.

Korner was born in Paris, France on April 19th 1928 of Austrian and Greek parentage. At the start of World War II in 1939 his family fled to England. They had many adventures en route, not least when their refugee ship was chased by submarines and their train was bombed on the way to London. During the war young Alexis amused himself by listening to imported American boogie-woogie records, which started his lifelong devotion to jazz and blues. He joined trombonist Chris Barber's band at the age of 20, and played guitar in Barber's offshoot skiffle group.

Blues Incorporated at the Marquee in 1962 with founder/guitarist Alexis Korner, plus Cyril Davies (left) and Dick Heckstall-Smith (right).

In 1955 Korner started a blues and skiffle club in Soho, and formed Blues Incorporated with harmonica player Cyril Davies in 1962, the first white blues band in the world. That same year Korner opened the R&B-based Ealing Club in a basement in west London, and it soon became a magnet for fledgling artists such as Mick Jagger, Paul Jones, Charlie Watts, Art Wood, Ginger Baker and Jack Bruce.

Cyril Davies left to form his own group, The All-Stars, and Blues Incorporated eventually broke up in 1967. But Korner continued playing and performing. Always keen to help new talent, he encouraged the formation of the blues band Free and even suggested their name. He often played and sang in duo settings with artists like Robert Plant and Victor Brox. In 1970 Korner and singer Peter Thorup formed the big-band CCS which enjoyed a hit with their version of Led Zeppelin's 'Whole Lotta Love', and in 1981 Korner formed Rocket 88, a boogie-woogie band with Charlie Watts, Jack Bruce and original Stones pianist Ian Stewart. Korner was still playing and singing the blues as ill health took its toll, and he died from throat cancer in London on January 1st 1984.

Ginger Baker joined Korner's Blues Incorporated in August 1962, taking over the drum stool from Charlie Watts. Then in February 1963 Baker left with Graham Bond and Jack Bruce to form The Graham Bond Organisation. Bond, a poll-winning jazzman from Ilford, Essex, became a star personality on stage, singing as well as playing alto saxophone, Hammond organ and, soon, the newly invented Mellotron. With Baker on drums, Bruce on bass and vocals, and Dick Heckstall-Smith on tenor sax, the band became well known for excitement and innovation. Two of their most popular numbers were 'Wade In The Water' and 'Spanish Blues', along with 'Traintime', a Jack Bruce song featuring the composer on harmonica and vocals and Baker playing a stomping rhythm on wire brushes. When Baker switched to sticks he developed a contrapuntal style, involving the snare drum, tom toms and bass drum in a climactic thunder of swirling triplets.

Baker stayed with Graham Bond for three-and-a-half years until the formation of Cream in 1966. Just as Clapton was a hero to all aspiring young guitarists, so Baker was the most influential drummer of his day.

While Baker was bringing new vigour to the art of drumming, Jack Bruce was developing a powerful new sound on his six-string bass guitar. He radically transformed the role of bass within a band, often playing it like a lead instrument. He anticipated the kind of fusion playing introduced later by players like Jaco Pastorius. Bruce was a much better singer than Graham Bond, who relied on a rather hoarse interpretation of the Ray Charles style. Bond clearly recognised this and encouraged the fiery young Scot to sing more often.

Bruce and Baker created a unique rhythm section that became a draw in its own right. In addition to the thunderous bass guitar playing, Bruce's harmonica blowing and intense vocals were formidable. This didn't stop Baker regarding Bruce as a rebellious spirit to be crushed, often by the simple expedient of bouncing a stick off his head during a solo. The clashing of their Scots and Irish temperaments didn't help when it came to

ALEXIS KORNER
★ BLUES ★
IN CORPORATED

MARQUEE
7.30 — 11.00 p.m.
165 OXFORD STREET
EVERY MONDAY
and THURSDAY

DISCOTHEQUE
11.30 — 2.30 a.m.
17 WARDOUR STREET
EVERY WEDNESDAY

XMAS EVE ★
NEW YEARS
★ EVE
AT THE MARQUEE

KORNER

Alexis Korner's datesheet at the end of 1962: jamming at The Marquee, then based in London's Oxford Street, and at La Discotheque, in nearby Wardour Street.

CYRIL DAVIES
R & B
ALL - STARS

TUESDAY
RAILWAY HOTEL
Harrow, Wealdstone.
7.30 p.m.

WEDNESDAY
PICCADILLY J. CLUB
(Opp. Windmill Thtre)
7.30 p.m.

THURSDAY
MARQUEE JAZZ CLUB
165 Oxford Street,
7.30 p.m.

FRIDAY
ROARING TWENTIES
Carnaby Street,
7.30 p.m.

EVERY WEEK

settling arguments about tempos and volume. Yet most of the time they got on well enough – and they certainly respected each other's abilities. The sheer strain of living frugally as itinerant musicians on the road was bound to cause friction, added to which they were both strong-willed and ambitious. The two had first met in 1961 when Baker was with Bert Courtley's band. Bruce on double-bass had sat in with them at a gig in Cambridge. Whether they got on or not didn't matter. Both musicians knew they had to play together.

Rare recordings made by Cyril Davies (harmonica) and Alexis Korner (guitar) at the Roundhouse pub in London's Soho in 1957 were reissued on this LP (below). The datesheet for Davies (right) is from late 1962.

Jack Bruce was born John Simon Asher Bruce on May 14th 1943 in Bishopbriggs, just to the north of Glasgow, in Scotland. His parents travelled extensively in Canada and the United States, and as a result Bruce attended some 14 different schools, finishing his formal education at an academy in Glasgow. He played piano as a child and sang in the school choir. He also performed Schubert as a boy soprano soloist in music competitions, with adjudicators checking his performance. Although he suffered stagefright during these ordeals, the vocal training helped him a great deal in his professional career.

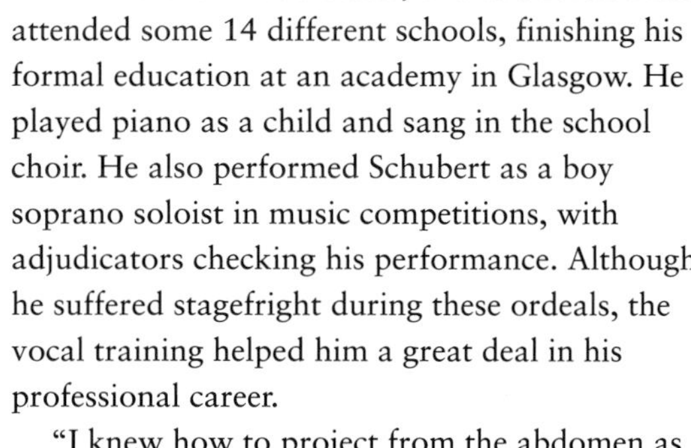

"I knew how to project from the abdomen as opposed to most pop singers who sing from the throat," says Bruce. At 17 he won a scholarship to study cello and composition at the Royal Scottish Academy Of Music in Glasgow. He didn't stay long as they neither understand nor appreciated his interest in composers like Stravinsky or his enthusiasm for The Modern Jazz Quartet. He was upset that none of his tutors appreciated his ideas and he thought them hidebound and narrow-minded. He quit college and decided to leave Scotland and head south in search of work.

In 1961 Bruce answered an advertisement in *Melody Maker* for a job with the Murray Campbell Big Band in Coventry, in the Midlands. He went for an audition at the Mecca Ballroom and played as his test piece 'One Bass Hit', a double-bass feature written by Ray Brown for the Dizzy

100 CLUB
100 OXFORD ST., W.1
7·30 to 11 p.m.

Thursday, September 3rd
THE GRAHAM BOND ORGANISATION
THE KING B FOUR

Friday, September 4th
THE MIKE DANIELS BIG BAND
THE DELTA JAZZMEN
JOHN CHILTON'S QUARTET

Saturday, September 5th
ALEX WELSH and his BAND
JOHN MADDOX TRIO

Sunday, September 6th
TERRY LIGHTFOOT'S JAZZMEN

Monday, September 7th
THE BIRDS
THE BLUES BY KNIGHT

Tuesday, September 8th
THE PRETTY THINGS
BRIAN KNIGHT'S BLUES BY SIX

Wednesday, September 9th
Wednesday Night Beat Session
THE KINKS
DANNY AND THE TORINOS

Thursday, September 10th
THE GRAHAM BOND ORGANISATION
THE KING B FOUR

Full details of the Club from the Secretary
100 Club, 8 Great Chapel St., W.1. GER 0337

Britain's most innovative and exciting R&B outfit, the Graham Bond Organisation, featured Ginger Baker (left) Dick Heckstall-Smith (top), Graham Bond (bottom) and Jack Bruce (right). They were regulars at London's 100 Club, confirmed by the ad from September 1964.

Gillespie orchestra. As he could sight-read the difficult piece he got the job immediately. The band then reduced in size and went to Italy for a tour which turned out be almost as traumatic at Eric Clapton's experience with The Glands in Greece.

Being mainly Scottish the group were expected to wear kilts while playing gigs at Italian variety theatres. Then a promoter ran off with the band's money and they were left stranded in Milan for six weeks, living off carrot stew until they could be repatriated back to Britain. Bruce returned to London and, like Ginger Baker and many other unemployed musicians, he went to Archer Street in the centre of town to search for a gig. He got one right away, but it meant returning immediately to Italy, to play at an American air base.

Although only 17 years old, Bruce was expected to drive the band from France to Venice, towing a trailer loaded with equipment. "I'd only just got my driving licence and I had to drive a 1940s Mercedes over the Alps. But we made it, and we stayed there quite a while." After this more successful adventure Bruce came back to the UK and joined Jim McHarg's Scotsville Jazz Band under rather curious circumstances. "Jim McHarg was the bass player," Bruce explains, "but he got fired by his own band, and I got the bandleader's gig." This was at the tail-end of the trad-jazz boom, and Bruce was really more interested in playing modern jazz. "But at least we didn't have to wear kilts," he points out.

Bruce was playing with the Jim McHarg band at a May Ball in Cambridge when he first saw Ginger Baker jamming with a pick-up group which included Dick Heckstall-Smith. He was knocked out by their musical prowess and managed to sit in. Bruce's nifty bass work impressed Heckstall-Smith in particular, who later managed to get him a gig with Alexis Korner. Bruce in turn was most impressed by the sight and sound of the drummer. "Ginger looked just like a demon," he remembers, "sitting there with his red hair and the kit of drums he'd made himself. I'd never heard a drummer like him and I knew that I wanted to play with him."

Bond and his boys sounded better with the instruments.

Once ensconced with Korner's band, Bruce and Heckstall-Smith campaigned to get Baker in as well. The group with the Baker-Bruce rhythm section and Graham Bond on alto played regularly at The Marquee and the Ealing Club, as well as at many society parties thanks to Korner's upper-class connections. They played at Lord Rothschild's polo parties, attended by the Duke Of Edinburgh. At one particular high-society ball the band included Alexis Korner, Jack Bruce, Charlie Watts, and *the* Benny Goodman on clarinet.

All went well until one day Korner was hit by the mass defection of his best sidemen. Bruce recalls: "We were with Alexis for a long time, until Graham resigned – for us. Alexis got really upset and thought I had left him in the lurch. But it was Graham who handed in our resignations, without even telling us."

The Graham Bond Trio was established with Bond on alto and Bruce still on double-bass. John McLaughlin also joined the group on guitar for a while, and when he was replaced by Dick Heckstall-Smith the four-piece Graham Bond Organisation was born. It was February 1963. Around the same time Bruce made the switch from double-bass to electric bass guitar. Jamaican jazz guitarist Ernest Ranglin had booked Baker, Bond and Bruce for a London recording session. "He wanted bass guitar," says Bruce, "so I went and borrowed one from a music shop and immediately fell in love with it. I'd been a snob about bass guitar, but it was great. It was loud and easy to play. To get a slapping effect I applied my double-bass technique."

The new Graham Bond Organisation was managed by entrepreneur Robert Stigwood. He had come to Britain from Australia in the early 1960s and had successfully managed pop singer John Leyton. Although his latest signing was clearly an R&B band with solid jazz leanings, he tried to make them a little more commercial. This resulted in the Organisation recording a single of the pop ballad 'Tammy'. The track also appeared on their otherwise sensational debut album *The Sound of '65*. A dreary tune, 'Tammy' seemed out of place alongside such driving performances as 'Got My Mojo Working', 'Hoochie Coochie Man' and Baker's drum feature 'Oh Baby'. The album was cut in just one three-hour session, but the hasty recording captured the band's spontaneity, and most of the numbers had already been well played-in on gigs.

Cream lyricist Pete Brown was a huge fan of the Graham Bond Organisation. "It was my favourite band," he remembers. "It was a mixture of Muddy Waters, Charlie Mingus and Roland Kirk – all the things I loved rolled into one, and becoming something else. They were the most exciting band ever. In fact I preferred them to Cream live. Some of the studio things Cream did were wonderful, but I was more into the Graham Bond band live. It was less guitar-oriented and more horn- and organ-driven.

"Graham Bond was a unique person," continues Brown. "He was my mentor, and very inspiring to everybody. He certainly did a lot for Jack and Ginger and I'm sure they'd be the first to say so. It wasn't an easy ride, but musically he was tremendously inspiring. He drove them and they responded. When they were playing, it was like a house on fire, there was nothing else happening – they were it! They understood the concept of the groove, which very few on the local scene did. Their take on jazz and R&B was extraordinary. At the time people like Jimmy Smith were fantastic, of course, but much more predictable and conservative, except perhaps in individual solos. They wouldn't take risks in the way that Graham did."

Jack Bruce (below left) switched from upright double-bass to electric bass guitar during his time with Bond's Organisation.

Jack Bruce agrees. "That was quite a band," he says. "It also provided the start of my songwriting career." The Bond band had its own fan club secretary, Janet Godfrey, who co-wrote songs with Bruce including 'Baby Make Love To Me' and 'Baby Be Good To Me'. Janet and Jack later got married, and one of the reasons

Bruce eventually joined the more successful Manfred Mann group was to ensure he had enough money to buy a place for the couple to live.

Although the Bond Organisation proved highly popular on the club circuit, despite the experiment with 'Tammy' they couldn't get a hit single. It seemed impossible to break from their local popularity into a wider success. Bond himself suffered from drug problems and, even more

Two fine albums from the "Organization" included Baker's first recorded drum solos and Bruce's earliest version of 'Traintime', later revisited with Cream.

alarmingly, became obsessed with the occult. None of this helped his general well-being or his capacity to run a band. Ginger Baker took over the day-to-day running of the outfit and its financial affairs. Amid this increasing pressure, Bruce and Baker began to fall out, on stage and in public. One such outburst led to the bass player's abrupt departure.

Bruce confirms that he was sacked from the group and that he and Baker often had acrimonious arguments. "I was being very difficult myself," says Bruce. "We had one famous and awful punch-up. It happened in a club in Golders Green in north London. I was playing, and Ginger was playing too loud during the bass solo. He was making fun of it, probably. I kind of looked round and made a face at him. He did his famous 'lobbing the drum stick off my nut' trick. So I just picked up my double-bass and threw it at him! I completely demolished him and the drum kit. It was my double-bass, too. He didn't like that, of course, and we started fighting. We ended up rolling all over the floor. The audience really got into it too. They probably thought it was better than the gig. The rest of the band came and got us apart and took us out of separate doors. I was leaving the band, anyway."

Baker also recalls the arguments and fights. "In the early days there were several upsets with Jack, all along the line. I called him Doctor Jekyl and Mister Hyde. Apparently he's been Doctor Jekyl for the past few years, because Jack can be the most charming, wonderful bloke, then he'll suddenly turn into this awful person. It started happening when we were with Graham Bond. I fired him from that band. That's another story that gets all mixed up. It's like: 'Ginger fired him off his own bat.' It wasn't like that. It was in agreement with Graham and Dick, but I got the job. It was because he'd turn round and start shouting at me on stage. He'd start playing something really clever, and then he'd come out on the wrong beat. Well, I don't do that. He'd turn round and start shouting 'No, no!' through the mike on the stage and really upset everybody.

"We had one famous and awful punch-up. The audience probably thought it better than the gig."

"The final straw was at Golders Green when I went into my drum solo," says Baker. "Jack was playing some bass guitar things and I was sort of phrasing with him on the bass drum. And he turns round and shouts into the mike, 'You're playing too fucking loud!' in the middle of *my* drum solo. He did that to me again when we were playing together in the States about ten years ago, he pulled the same number."

The dispute between Bruce and Baker stemmed from the way Bruce was trying to expand the role of bass guitar in the rhythm section. For years bassists had been content to plod away, while drummers had more freedom to extemporise. "Once I started to experiment with more melodic lines on bass guitar," explains Bruce, "Ginger felt that was wrong. He felt I should be playing in a much more simple style. That's why we fell out."

The band had played a TV show with visiting American soul singer Marvin Gaye, who vigorously approved of Bruce's more ambitious bass style. "He came round to my place in Hampstead and we spent the whole night talking," says Bruce. "Marvin actually asked me to go back and join his band in the States. But I couldn't do it while I was still with Graham." That encouraged Bruce to go on with a style that had originally been influenced by James Jamerson, bassist on many Motown records. "Meeting Marvin Gaye was a real turning point. If it hadn't been for him, I might have given up bass guitar and gone back to playing acoustic bass in a jazz context, where I could get away with a lot more."

Because of his impending marriage to Janet Godfrey, Bruce had to turn down Gaye's offer. After the bust-up with Baker he joined John Mayall's Bluesbreakers instead, which led to the meeting with Eric Clapton. This was followed by Bruce's stint with Manfred Mann. Baker stayed on with Bond for a while until he too left. Bond would recruit new players and struggled on for a few more years. He even lived and worked in America for a while, but never regained the popularity he'd enjoyed while playing with Bruce and Baker. Tragically, Bond died under the wheels of an underground train at London's Finsbury Park station on May 8th 1974.

Bruce suggests that, while the Bond band was frighteningly good, people weren't ready for it. "The public really wanted a good-looking young group, like The Beatles," he says. "I was with John Mayall for a short while before Manfred Mann, but to be honest it wasn't one of John's finer bands and he didn't have any outstanding lead players. Eric Clapton was

A wild night at the Marquee in early 1966 when Eric Burdon of The Animals sat in with Manfred Mann. Mann plays the organ (left) with Jack Bruce (bass), Burdon (vocals), and Paul Jones (harmonica).

there very briefly before he left to go on that abortive world tour. He got as far as Greece and the story goes that he saw all this meat hanging up in a butcher's shop with flies crawling over it and said: 'I'm going home.' I joined the Manfreds for a while, which was kind of interesting. I'd never been in a pop band before. Paul Jones left at the same time that I did. I did get to do some arranging for a Manfred Mann instrumental EP which became quite successful."

Tom McGuinness relates an amusing incident involving Bruce while they were both with the Manfreds, though it wasn't so funny for their esteemed bass guitarist. "We were running late for a gig in Scotland and stopped the car to ask a local Scotsman the way," says McGuinness. "When we all laughed at his completely incomprehensible reply Jack got quite angry and said, 'These people are the salt of the earth.' We eventually got to the gig and it was very late, almost midnight. As we went on stage we were pelted with pennies and shouts of abuse. We went off and the promoter told the audience, 'If you throw any more stuff at the band, there'll be no music tonight!' We came back on – and were pelted again. This time the crowd began to jump on the stage and knock the amplifiers over, so we fled to the dressing room. "The audience followed us and began to batter the door down, so the whole band began climbing out of a tiny window to escape. Meanwhile the roadie got the car and drove it down the alley up to the dressing room window. We all piled into the car, but Jack was the last one out. Just at that moment the mob came running round the corner. Jack was still hanging by his fingertips from the window-ledge and as we drove off we shouted: 'They're the salt of the earth!' We heard later that he had to be smuggled out in a flightcase."

"Forming a blues band in England is like banging your head against a brick wall."

Apart from these dramatic incidents, the life of a travelling bluesman could be isolating, and would deepen the sense of frustration felt by a sensitive musician like Eric Clapton. In an interview with *Melody Maker*'s Nick Jones in March 1966, Clapton said that he had thought about going to America to realise his ambitions. "Forming a blues band in England is like banging your head against a brick wall. Nobody wants to record it." Clapton explained that he felt that using his guitar as a medium for communicating with people was more important to him than technique alone.

"I think I have a power and my guitar is a medium for expressing that power," said Clapton. "I don't need people to say how good I am. I've worked it out by myself. It's nothing to do with technique and rehearsing. It is to do with the person behind that guitar who is trying to find an outlet. My guitar is a medium through which I can make contact to myself. It's very lonely."

It wasn't long before three lost musicians in search of the ultimate band would finally make contact. There would be an end to loneliness amid a glare of publicity. Cream was about to churn into action.

CHAPTER 2

STRANGE BREW

Cream was planned as a group with the best: Ginger Baker on drums, Jack Bruce on bass guitar, Eric Clapton on guitar. Before Chris Welch continues the story of Cream's formation, three top musical experts – Geoff Nicholls, Jim Roberts and Dave Gregory – discuss in this chapter exactly what it was that made Baker, Bruce and Clapton such outstanding instrumentalists.

GINGER BAKER: DRUMS

Cream have been criticised for their musical self-indulgence, but this ignores the spirit of the 1960s, a truly innovative decade when rock players purposefully abandoned musical boundaries. A Cream concert was a very exciting experience. Audiences could hardly believe what they heard. For the first time, musicians who were both young and cool employed the improvising skills of jazz but with a rock attitude – and at megawatt volume. The fact that every half-arsed band for the next decade would extemporise in public was hardly Cream's fault.

Ginger Baker and Jack Bruce: rock's finest rhythm section of the 1960s.

Cream are remembered as a jazz-blues improvising trio, but they were also probably the earliest progressive rock band. Jack Bruce's classical training and Ginger Baker's facility meant that Cream's original songs were littered with sly syncopations and occasional odd time signatures. The result was strange but beautiful songs like 'As You Said' and Baker's famous 5/4 bolero timpani intro to 'White Room'. Perhaps the best fun is had with the dastardly 'Politician', who stumbles along like a giant with a limp. It is possible actually to count four-time through 'Politician' – but it's a struggle.

The result of all this was that Cream's virtuosity encouraged the musically-inclined youth of Britain to push rock to its limits. The brightest,

Ginger Baker, with bebop haircut, pounds a huge riveted ride cymbal as he evokes the spirit of Art Blakey and Elvin Jones.

most adventurous young musicians were soon bewildering their parents and abandoning long-held desires to go to the classical academies. Instead they were growing their hair long, and throwing their creativity into rock music – which in turn led to jazz-rock, folk-rock, heavy metal, and almost every other cross-fertilisation imaginable.

Cream pointed to the future of two-hour concerts, away from the 20-minute slots on package tours and on to the art rock of the 1970s that would flourish until 1976, when punk called a halt. What an irony, then, that it was Johnny Rotten who in 1985 brought Ginger Baker back in from the wilderness when he invited the drummer to play on PiL's *Album*.

To assess Baker's importance we must go back to the mid 1960s, when British rock came of age. Three very different musicians changed the face of rock drumming, by virtue of their style, originality and brilliance. They were The Who's Keith Moon, Jimi Hendrix's Mitch Mitchell, and Cream's Ginger Baker. These three led the most important flowering of drumming talent in British rock history.

Moon was an amazing player, a one-off showman with unconventional technique, while Mitchell was a lighter, sparkling technician. But Baker was a colossus. Although equally wild in appearance, he exuded the air of a master drummer. This mastery had been hard won as he diligently practised the rudiments in long sessions with his mentor, the jazz great Phil Seamen. Of his first meeting with Seamen, Baker recalls coming off stage at London's Flamingo club to be confronted by "God himself". Says Baker: "We ended up at Phil's flat, where he played me his entire African drummer collection and opened the door to drum heaven."

This appreciation of drumming's ultimate roots gave Baker authority and a directness of purpose. Every beat counted. With Baker, there was none of the chaos of Moon or the fussiness of Mitchell. He was as fiery as either of them but appeared to be in control, where Moon was unstable and Mitchell a psychedelic swirl.

When Baker formed Cream in 1966 he quickly became the most revered drummer in Britain. He denies any influence by other mid-1960s rock drummers. "No rock contemporaries whatsoever, ever, ever," he stresses. "Being jazz players we considered them, to quote Phil Seamen, 'wankers who don't know a crotchet from a hatchet'. My influences were Seamen, Max Roach, Elvin Jones, Philly Jo Jones, Art Blakey. My most important influence before meeting Phil was Baby Dodds, who I first heard in 1956. Other musical influences were Bird, Dizzy, Coltrane, Ornette Coleman, Monk, Duke and Basie."

It's ironic, then, that Baker became the first true virtuoso drummer of British rock, and one of the most important rock drummers ever. He was the first to successfully integrate double bass-drums into rock and he redefined the extended drum solo – which would become a feature of jazz-rock, prog-rock and heavy metal. Baker laid down the guidelines for the next generation of power rock players. He completed the transformation, started by Keith Moon, from the beat music of the early 1960s to the mature playing which formed the basis of album rock – and which in turn would lead to the blueprint heavy drumming of John Bonham with Led Zeppelin in the 1970s.

"Baker was a colossus. Although wild in appearance, he exuded the air of a master drummer."

Bonham would later usurp Baker as the archetypal British power player, but Bonham's was a funkier, soulful approach. Baker's vibe was more individual, African and bluesy. Baker was the Art Blakey of rock, with a healthy dose of Max Roach's melodic toms. His beats were razor sharp, predating the stripped-down brutality of metal players, and as such Baker gave us our first intimation of a stadium-playing mentality.

A couple of years before Cream emerged, The Who had crossed the boundary from pop to rock. They had the technique and the ideas to extend their guitar-riff-fuelled bluesy-based jams into tours de force of rhythmic and sonic mayhem. But it was Cream – as their name implies, the three best players around – who showed that rock could be a true virtuoso music. No other band had their instrumental prowess, which allowed them to improvise on songs for 15 minutes and (on a good night) maintain the excitement. Each member was capable of sustaining interest and taking the initiative.

This is perhaps best heard on the amazing March 1968 live recording of 'Spoonful', first heard on the *Wheels Of Fire* album. What starts as a fairly typical mid-1960s blues cover is transformed into an epic 16-minute rollercoaster. Baker smoothes the initial plodding blues shuffle into a flowing 12/8, allowing all three musicians to experiment with phrases in three, four and six time. The piece also beautifully illustrates the empathy (on stage if not off) between Baker and Bruce as the bass cuts across the drums from every direction imaginable.

Prior to Cream, Baker used a drum-kit that he had made himself. He took green Perspex which he bent into cylinders over his gas stove – an early indication of the drummer's single-minded pursuit of his own sound. Throughout Cream, Baker played a silver-sparkle American-made Ludwig drum-kit. Although Ludwig drums were the choice of most British rock

Baker considers the toms before launching into his showcase drum solo 'Toad' at London's Royal Albert Hall in November 1968.

drummers who could afford them following Ringo Starr's conversion in 1964, Baker says his adoption of Ludwig came about differently. He and Phil Seamen met Bill Ludwig Senior in London's Drum City store. "Phil and I used to go down and play on a couple of kits," says Baker. "One day we arrived to find this grey-haired old bloke sitting on a bass drum in his underpants sewing up a tear in his trousers. Having finished his repairs, he sat there and boogied while Phil and I played duets. He was such a cool old geezer that I decided that if I ever could afford a new kit it would be a Ludwig. As it happened, they gave me the kit."

"The dramatic potential of the big drum kit is apparent from the start of Cream's career."

What was special about Baker's kit was its double bass-drums, plus two "mounted" toms (12-inch and 13-inch diameters) and two floor toms (14-inch and 16-inch). For the time, this was a monster set. Keith Moon appeared with double bass-drums just prior to Baker. "Moony did get his before me," Baker admits. "But I'd told him I was getting one – so he got two British Premier kits and joined them together."

Baker had to wait a bit longer because his kit was American and had unusually shallow bass drum shells (11 inches deep as opposed to the standard 14). And Baker's two bass drums were of different diameters – one was 22 inches, the other 20 – which he says was to provide different tonalities. "I didn't use a lot of damping," he explains. "I seem to recall a couple of folded towels in each drum, on the bottom inside of the shells." With his formidable bass-drum technique, Baker's pedals were a crucial element in his set-up. He used Ludwig Fleetfoots with leather drive straps, rather than the metal-link Speedking models which most Ludwig drummers tended to use.

The dramatic potential of the big kit is apparent from the start of Cream's recording career, not only in the long multi-tom rolls of 'NSU' but also in the way that Baker creates widescreen drama during the guitar solo of 'Sweet Wine'. For all Clapton's later massive commercial success he would never sound as exciting as when Baker was pushing and goading him with his syncopated double-fisted toms and double-booted kicks.

The double bass-drum kit had been pioneered in big-band jazz by Louie Bellson as early as 1946. Bellson introduced the double bass-drum solo into the jazz orchestra of Duke Ellington with his own composition 'Skin Deep' in 1951. But it was another Ellington drummer who had the greater influence on Baker. Sam Woodyard appeared with Duke at a London gig in 1966 playing a double bass-drum Premier kit. "He blew me away," says Baker. "One simple fill opened my eyes to the possibilities involving toms and bass drums."

Baker's outfit also mirrored Bellson's in his use of double-stacked cymbals, although he was unaware that Bellson had done this. The cymbals were all Zildjian. "I'm still playing the 22-inch riveted ride and hi-hats that I got from the Avedis Zildjian factory in Boston in 1966," he said in June 2000. Baker used several snare drums live and in the studio, all made by Ludwig except for a 1940s-vintage American wood-shell Leedy Broadway. "I bought the Leedy from Alton Red, the drummer with Kid Ory, in the early 1960s," he remembers. "I've still got it and use it occasionally, especially when I'm in the studio. It's a little battered but still sounds cool. I'm afraid I can't recall what Cream tracks I used it on, but for sure it's in there somewhere."

Baker's distinctive, warm tom tom sound led many drummers to suspect that he used old-fashioned calf-skin heads on his drums. In fact he used Ludwig heads everywhere. "Plastic heads were a great invention!" he says. And, unlike most drummers who just tension the heads until they feel right, Baker would always tune his toms to the band. "When they tuned up, so would I," he says. Unused to such fastidiousness from a mere drummer, Bruce and Clapton would moan at him. "They would say, 'Oh man! We're trying to tune up!' It always happened." But the result of this care can, for example, be heard on 'We're Going Wrong' where Baker's fine phrasing and beautifully tuned drums sustain the entire song.

> "Baker's emphasis on the toms was a revelation, right from the opening of I Feel Free."

Baker's emphasis on the toms was a revelation, starting right from the opening figure of 'I Feel Free'. And then the driving on-beat assault of 'NSU' is like a statement of intent, that Baker is the boss. A similar tom introduction reappears famously in 'Sunshine Of Your Love', this time as a "backwards" half-time figure, and once again as a significant hook in the song. Even in the company of great up-front players like Bruce and Clapton, Baker offered drum patterns that regularly became equally important components of Cream tunes.

Such hooks, written down, often appear quite simple. For all his undoubted technique and mastery of the rudiments, Baker never tires of playing straight 16th-note fills in a clockwise direction around the kit. Now, virtually every rock drummer has resorted to this with almost moronic insistence. Yet Baker somehow made it his own. Right from 'NSU' where the thundering rolls are a featured riff in the song's structure, it could only be Baker playing them. There's a warmth and breadth of sound that makes such a simple statement carry the whole track, and when Baker fills in there is no apparent drop in dynamic. His kit compensates for the whole band.

> "Baker could play the simplest fills… but with such authority that it could be no other drummer."

How did he achieve this? First, he struck the drums loud and true. He set his two small toms horizontally. If he'd tilted them towards him, he says, "I'd have put the stick through the head on the first hit." The horizontal layout also enabled him to strike rim shots off the toms. A rim shot is where the player deliberately catches the metal rim of the drum at exactly the same moment that the tip of the stick strikes the centre of the head. This produces a resonance which makes the beat much louder. It's a technique which drummers have always used to make snare drum back-beats cut through, but is much less common on tom toms.

The tom rim shots are perhaps most startlingly evident in the climax to the studio recording of 'Toad' where Baker achieves a stunning helicopter-taking-off effect. The use of rim shots is one clue as to why Baker's patterns are so clear and distinctive. But although he always used this technique, he says it was only in the latter period of Cream, when the amplification became huge, that cutting through became a problem.

Although he had a thorough grounding in jazz, Baker always sounded like the ultimate rock-blues drummer. He's a master of blues shuffles, whether it's the Mayall-flavoured 'Take It Back' or the almost Buddy Holly-like light swing of 'Four Until Late'.

He also played great double (or "cut") time, particularly exemplified by his brush work on 'Rollin' And Tumblin'' and the awesome live 'Traintime' where Baker and Bruce are as tight as they ever got. Throughout much of 'Traintime' Baker also plays a fast and super-light "feathered" bass drum with admirable control. This technique was a feature of the trad and big-band eras and was lost by the later heavy-footed rockers. On many of the live recordings that Cream made the drummer keeps up a rapid double bass-drum ostinato for minutes on end – both loud and soft – with apparent ease. Doubtless he gained stamina from his serious teenage passion for cycling.

Cream's career was so short that the studio albums only give a glimpse of Baker's range. He always played just what the song needed while still imposing his personality. He could be inventively funky, as on 'Born Under A Bad Sign', but the in-concert recordings occasionally reveal other areas of his repertoire, such as the start of the live 'Sitting On Top Of The World' from *Goodbye*. Here Baker revisits his early-jazz roots with Baby Dodds-like press rolls on the snare drum, accompanied by a left-foot shuffle on the hi-hat pedal.

Although 8th-note rock rhythms abound, closer listening reveals there's often a lilt in Baker's "straight" beats. Take the funky verse rhythms of

'Strange Brew' or 'White Room', where the syncopated snare-drum beats have a hint of triplet swing against the back-beat. Now check the apparently straight 16th-note tom rolls. On both tracks these actually have a slightly staggered "dumpty-dumpty-dumpty" phrasing.

Baker's jazz roots are not in question. What was new was his rock player's directness. No jazz-steeped player before him had played rock with anything like such power. And when he did incorporate jazz roots it was rarely in the busy, toppy style commonly expected of conventional jazz drumming. Instead, it was more often in a flowing 12/8 fashion that recalls nothing short of a tribe of African master drummers.

Baker squares up to his hero Elvin Jones for a memorable "drum battle" at London's Lyceum ballroom in 1970. Ever the true gentlemen of percussion, they declared the event a draw.

This tribal exoticism was most famously apparent in Baker's mammoth drum feature, 'Toad'. More than anyone else, we have Baker to thank for the drum solo in rock. Others had attempted it before him, but mostly these were sporadic novelties. Baker's solos were altogether more weighty. Whereas something like 'Little B' by Brian Bennett in The Shadows can be traced back to Gene Krupa through Sandy Nelson and the rest, Baker's 'Toad' owes directly to the story-telling melodicism of Max Roach, the earthiness of Art Blakey, Elvin Jones and Baby Dodds, and to those late-night sessions listening to Phil Seamen's African albums.

The studio version of 'Toad' is a model of clarity, with repeated melodic motifs. Whereas previous pop drum solos had tended to feature swing-band triplets, Baker creates a hipper, tougher, post-rock vibe by sticking almost entirely with 8ths and 16ths right up to the "helicopter" climax. Here the bass drums pound away in 16ths while the hands interject double beats that create triplets in between. This climaxes at the only place where he plays continuous snare-drum triplet 16ths: the cue for the band to come back in. And even then the triplets are played straight, without the Buddy Rich-like accents to which all other jazz drummers aspired.

The live recording of 'Toad' from *Wheels Of Fire* is an heroic effort, but less satisfying as a structured piece. It's overlong on record – though maybe not if you were in the audience – and reaches a few too many climaxes

Baker in cheerful mood during Cream's excursion into the highlands of Scotland in 1967.

before dropping back and starting all over again. Some of the most impressive playing occurs early on where Baker's left foot keeps a jazz drummer's off-beat hi-hat going though some very tricky co-ordinations, including paraddidle variations between snare drum and right bass foot, then a right-hand jazz ride cymbal against post-bop figures with the other limbs. Baker's integration of toms with the double bass-drums would influence every rock drum solo and fill right to this day. He would weave them into his patterns, making them an equal voice rather than simply a lumberingly heavy foundation. The result in 'Toad' was a solo with a new grandeur previously unheard in rock. Here was a solo for grown-ups, and not simply a novelty feature for "the non-musician" in the band.

All these elements – the double bass-drum kit, the cymbals, the heads and tuning, Baker's touch, and most importantly his unique style with those trademark fills and groove – made Ginger Baker one of the most distinctive drummers of all time. He would play the simplest of fills and stamp such an authority in sound, attitude and phrasing that it could be no other drummer. To be instantly recognisable is the true mark of an original voice and a great musician. ● *GEOFF NICHOLLS*

JACK BRUCE: BASS GUITAR

When Cream was formed in the summer of 1966, Jack Bruce was working on a new approach to his instrument. It was simple enough, really: "I was trying to play the bass guitar like a *guitar*, as opposed to a bass." That's how he summarised it when I interviewed him for *Bass Player* magazine in 1993. Bruce's development of that concept in Cream proved to be a watershed in the history of the electric bass, and it established a new standard of creativity for an entire generation of bassists.

For Bruce, playing the electric bass "like a guitar" was not merely a matter of cranking the volume, flinging out lots of notes and bending strings – although he certainly did those things. He believed that basslines should be melodic and contrapuntal as well as supportive, and in asserting this concept in Cream he elevated bassists to a new position of importance in rock bands. After Bruce, just standing in the back and thumping out quarter-notes wouldn't do.

Jack Bruce sings Jack Bruce (below). In addition to his brilliant bass work, Bruce was and is one of the finest vocalists in rock music.

To appreciate his concept of bass playing, you need to know something about his background. He had studied composition at the Royal Scottish Academy Of Music, so he understood counterpoint and knew how to develop a theme. He had also acquired a deep appreciation of the melodic basslines of JS Bach, whom he has called "the greatest bass teacher I ever had".

Added to this is his knowledge of swing and improvisation, which he acquired playing upright bass in R&B and jazz bands and listening to the great jazz bassists of the late 1950s and early 1960s – especially Charles Mingus, Charlie Haden and Scott LaFaro. His other key influence was James Jamerson, whose brilliant session work for Motown had demonstrated the expressive capabilities of the electric bass. "Listening to those records, I began to see the possibilities of the bass guitar," said Bruce. "It could actually be a melody instrument."

All of these influences began to coalesce in Bruce's playing with the Graham Bond Organization in the mid 1960s. When guitarist John McLaughlin left the group, Bruce adopted the Fender VI six-string bass so he could try to combine the functions of guitar and bass in his parts. The VI has a 30-inch scale-length and is tuned like a guitar but one octave lower. Because of its tight string spacing, it is usually played with a plectrum, but Bruce used his fingers. Ginger Baker, the de facto leader of the band, was so moved by Bruce's unusual approach that he fired him. And thus the stage was set for their ironic reunion in Cream, where Bruce would find the perfect setting for his "guitar-like" concept.

Bruce with Fender VI six-string bass guitar. The instrument was later hand-painted – though it was a pity the paint wouldn't dry.

The Fender VI was still Bruce's primary instrument when Cream was formed, and he used it during the recording of *Fresh Cream.* The album was split almost evenly between re-workings of blues tunes and originals (most of them written or co-written by Bruce), establishing a duality that would continue throughout the band's history. It was issued in different UK and US versions, with 'I Feel Free' missing from the British album and 'Spoonful' left off the American release. But it's these two tracks that are crucial to understanding Bruce's bass style in the early days of Cream.

'I Feel Free', with its clever mix of pop and blues elements, illustrates the ingenuity that would characterise Cream's finest studio efforts. Not insignificantly, it is a Jack Bruce tune with lyrics by Pete Brown, and Bruce brought it to the studio with all the parts written out. "Because of my classical background, it was easier for me to just write things down," he has explained.

The choruses contrast floating call-and-response vocals with a bassline distinguished by two important characteristics of the Bruce style: relentless forward motion, and creative use of the blues scale. The verses have a blues-like feel, but Bruce's urgent vocals are answered with fills from the bass rather than, as might be expected, the guitar. The recording doesn't do justice to Bruce's sound, and the bass is rather far back in the mix – but it's clear that something very interesting is going on.

If 'I Feel Free' shows the band leaning toward pop, then 'Spoonful' is a complete immersion in the blues. A quintessential Willie Dixon lament, it's based on just two notes: the root (E) and the blue third (G bent). With so little harmonic material with which to work, Baker, Bruce and Clapton had to rely on rhythm and dynamics to create an effective arrangement – and their spirited, freewheeling interpretation foreshadowed the Cream to come. Bruce's bass is farther forward in the mix on this one, and we can really hear that nasty, distorted tone that became his trademark.

Like all of the great jazz musicians, Bruce has developed a personal sound. This is not an easy trick with an electric instrument, and it's especially hard with bass guitar. One of the great virtues of Fender basses – some consider it a vice – is their consistency. Recording engineers love them because they are so easy to set up in the studio: plug in a Fender Precision or Jazz Bass, make a few minor adjustments, and away you go. As a result, many recorded bass parts sound similar; distinguishing one electric bassist from another is often a matter of listening carefully for rhythmic nuances and characteristic note choices. Not so with Jack Bruce. He established his sound in Cream, and it has stayed with him throughout his career – even though he has played many different bass guitars through a variety of amplifiers.

Working on the Disraeli Gears sessions at Atlantic studios in New York, 1967, with a Danelectro bass.

Asked about this, Bruce said: "The sound comes from your brain and then from your fingers… It's touch. It's what you *do* with the instrument." The first key ingredient of the Jack Bruce sound is indeed his touch – which, in his case, is perfectly described by the word "attack". Bruce has always hit the strings hard, which tends to push the pickups to their sonic limits. No doubt his days playing double-bass in R&B bands contributed.

So, to begin with, Bruce stresses his instrument excessively. He then pushes his signal through the amplifier at near-peak levels, with plenty of midrange for punch, and drives his speakers until they begin to distort. In Cream, he used 100-watt Marshall heads driving 4x12 cabinets, a set-up renowned for its distortion capabilities. Constantly driving the gear to the edge is perilous, but it's perfectly in keeping with the risk-taking attitude that has always defined Bruce's musical personality. His playing is on the edge, and so is his sound.

The Jack Bruce tone has been described in various ways. Fellow bassist Jeff Berlin has called it the "fart sound", albeit with considerable affection. However described, it was far from the smooth, deep tone considered the "ideal" electric bass sound in 1966 – and that's one reason why Bruce deliberately chose not to play a standard Fender bass. "They had a wonderful sound, but I thought well, that's a bit limiting," he said. "I was trying to find different sounds and different approaches to the bass guitar."

In Cream, that quest led Bruce to a flirtation with a Danelectro Long Horn Bass, noted for its unusual "twanging" tone, before he settled on the Gibson EB-3 that became his main instrument from *Disraeli Gears* onward. The EB-3 was the perfect choice: a short-scale bass with a raw, biting tone (further enhanced with electronic modifications) and light-gauge strings that were easy to bend.

Bruce blows a harp for 'Traintime' (left) at Madison Square Garden, 1968. He made wide use of a Gibson EB-3 bass, and is pictured with it (opposite) during Cream's final US tour.

Bruce says his EB-3 had an unusually wide neck that made string-bending easy, although Gibson has denied ever making such a version. The Gibson bass was also a good visual match for the custom-painted SG that Eric Clapton often played, and it was about as non-standard as a bass could be in those days. Just holding it made a statement about Bruce's approach to bass playing. But of course he did much more than hold it.

Bruce's full-blown bass style began to emerge on *Disraeli Gears*. With Felix Pappalardi producing, Bruce's potent sound was pushed to the foreground and his contrapuntal approach became bolder. Rather than outlining chords, he constructed melodic lines that complemented – and challenged – Clapton's increasingly complex guitar parts. Bruce often used minor thirds (or, more precisely, blue thirds) against major chords, which deepened the blues feel on even the most overtly psychedelic pop tunes. His parts were, quite literally, becoming more "guitar-like" while still providing a solid foundation.

Bruce has often cited the "blues feeling" as an important element of his style. Traditional American blues is, of course, one source of this, but he says he has found it in much other music, from traditional Scottish folk songs to Pakistani qawwali music. This is undoubtedly why he found a blues-based contrapuntal approach so appealing in a band with Eric Clapton, who offered him a wealth of bluesy ideas to complement and contrast. And Ginger Baker's fluid, jazz-inflected drumming gave him the freedom to do just that.

"Risk-taking has always defined Bruce's musical personality. His playing is on the edge, and so is his sound."

Many of Bruce's basslines are founded on the blues scale: the pentatonic minor scale (in the key of C this would be C, E-flat, F, G, B-flat) with the second (D) and the flatted fifth (G-flat) inserted strategically. The flatted fifth is usually heard either as a leading tone going to the fourth or a "blue" replacement for the perfect fifth – but in the most famous Bruce riff of them all, 'Sunshine Of Your Love', it is played chromatically between the perfect fifth and perfect fourth. Bruce also uses other chromatic notes with telling effect, either as leading tones or deliberately dissonant elements, which sets his use of the blues scale apart from its usual limited (and clichéd) role in rock.

For its bass playing, 'Tales Of Brave Ulysses' is one of the most interesting tunes on *Disraeli Gears*. Perhaps surprisingly, it is not a Bruce-

Brown composition – Clapton wrote it, with lyrics by Martin Sharp – but that may have given Bruce more time to focus on his part. It's built on a descending D, C, B, B-flat line, which Bruce plays by sliding down the G-string during the intro. He repeats it an octave lower beneath the verse, but then his jazz instincts kick in and he drops from D to low F and ascends to G and B-flat – a neat change of direction (and register) that kicks the song forward. Under the guitar solo at the end he plays some ascending riffs that develop this contrapuntal idea further. To hear how far he later went with this, listen to the March 1968 live recording of 'Tales' that was originally heard on *Live Cream Volume II*, with its world-weary vocal and bone-crunching bass sound.

"His playing was intoxicating at the time, and can still be a source of encouragement and inspiration today."

Bruce has asserted that Cream was two bands – a studio band and a live band – and noted that the live band was actually a jazz group ("…we just didn't tell Eric"). This dual identity was fully expressed on *Wheels Of Fire*. Its nine studio tunes are the apex of the band's efforts in the controlled environment of the studio, while the four live tracks still rank among the finest concert recordings made by any rock band of any era. The same can be said of Bruce's bass playing, which reached creative maturity during the period when this landmark album was recorded.

'White Room' is Cream's studio masterpiece. It's no coincidence that this is a Bruce-Brown tune featuring a strong Bruce lead vocal and a powerful bassline that rises to new levels of improvisational inspiration. The D, C, G/B, B-flat descending progression echoes 'Tales Of Brave Ulysses', and Bruce once again uses contrapuntal ascending lines with telling effect. (In fact, the compelling D-minor lick he plays near the end of the tune later became the basis of an entire song, 'Life On Earth', on his 1989 album *A Question of Time*. Bruce does a fine job demonstrating this lick on his 1998 instructional video, *The Cream Of Cream*.)

There are many other studio delights to savour. On 'Sitting On Top Of The World' Bruce is at the top of his game: his tone is a mile wide, and his riffing "guitar-like" concept has been perfected. In fact when you compare this track to the studio version of 'Spoonful' on *Fresh Cream*, it's hard to believe they were recorded only about a year apart. Bruce's unique personal vision of the blues is perfectly expressed on 'Politician', with its oddball half-step bassline and the beautiful co-ordination between the guitar and bass parts (listen to the guitar solo, especially).

Bruce's jazz and classical influences, which would come to full flower in his later solo work, are evident on 'As You Said', boasting an angular melody and unusual textures. And everything converges on 'Deserted Cities

Of The Heart' – a tune surely underrated among the recordings in the Cream discography – with its dramatic rhythm shifts and underlying tension. Bruce plays a tremendous bass part here, using his full complement of runs, string-bends and octaves to underscore the tune's complex emotional message.

Then there are *Wheels Of Fire*'s live tracks. The four-and-a-half minute version of 'Crossroads' was a revelation in 1968, and it is no less compelling today. First and foremost a classic blues tune, it has the improvisational vigour of jazz, the thematic development of a classical composition, and the sheer power of high-volume rock. Clapton's guitar solo has long been admired, but Bruce's contrapuntal bass part is every bit as inventive.

'Spoonful' is even more impressive. A staple of the band's repertoire from the early days, it had become an improvisational tour de force by the time the *Wheels Of Fire* version was recorded in 1968. Beginning with just that root and blue third, the three musicians created more than 16 minutes of free-flowing improvisation that showcased the full range of their powers. The dynamics are especially notable. While many of the bands that came along in the wake of Cream tried to emulate this style by blasting through long blues jams start-to-finish at full volume, they missed the point, which was that the power of the best of Cream's improvisations always relied upon careful control of dynamics.

"Jack transcended the bass guitar's traditional role and made it something new."

The finest example of Cream's dynamic control in a jam – and maybe their finest live recording – is 'Sweet Wine', which was recorded at the same monumental March 10th 1968 Winterland gig as 'Crossroads' and 'Spoonful'. Once again, the melodic material is simple: a Baker tune based on a five-note riff. The bass playing is especially inventive, and Bruce finds dozens of ways to augment and manipulate the melody, working in most of the chromatic scale along the way. One of the most memorable sections occurs near the eight-minute mark where Bruce and Clapton reverse roles, with Bruce playing "lead" high on the neck and Clapton laying down bass figures. Later, Bruce drives the music with powerful bass chords – playing rhythm guitar/bass, for want of a better name – as the band builds toward the final statement of the theme. By this time, there's no doubt that Bruce has mastered the concept of playing "like a guitar".

Cream was a band of ironies, so it is probably not surprising that many of their finest jams (the recorded ones, anyway) were done as the band was coming apart. That was probably painful for them, although the tension may have contributed to the intensity of the playing. There's nothing like a

Baker, Bruce and Clapton face off the competition at the height of their fame.

little one-upmanship in music. The downward spiral played itself out on the studio tracks for *Goodbye*, which were well done but sounded decidedly like afterthoughts. Bruce's 'Doing That Scrapyard Thing' is certainly one of his lesser compositions, although it is notable for his effective use of wah-wah bass.

In addition to all these creative elements, with their roots in different aspects of Bruce's experience, there's one overarching element that united them all: joy. More significant than his classical training or jazz chops, more important than his technical innovations or distinctive tone, it was Bruce's ability to transmit pure emotion that made it so exciting to hear him in Cream. His playing was intoxicating at the time, and can still be a source of encouragement and inspiration today.

It is not an overstatement to say that Bruce's bass playing in Cream was heroic, in the true sense of that word. He tried hard to overcome the limitations of his instrument and, in doing so, transcended its traditional role and made it something new. In his quest to "play the bass guitar like a guitar", Jack Bruce took the electric bass guitar somewhere else – and it's never returned. ● *JIM ROBERTS*

ERIC CLAPTON: GUITAR

To appreciate fully the impact of Eric Clapton's guitar playing in Cream, it's first necessary to understand the nature of popular music as it was in the late summer of 1966. The Beatles had set seemingly impossible new standards of writing and production with the recent releases of their *Rubber Soul* and *Revolver* albums, and inspired a growth of songwriters within self-contained, free-spirited groups. The British music scene was awash with some truly original and exciting new music.

While the electric guitar was still very much the catalyst for this new revolution, it remained in essence a twanging machine. Players had begun overloading their amplifiers to create crude distortion and feedback, and were plugging into the new fuzz-boxes to try to bring a new energy and edge to their playing. Jeff Beck, Clapton's replacement in The Yardbirds, had built on his predecessor's innovations with a new awareness of the instrument's potential, using whatever devices were at his disposal. Hampered by the group's often lightweight pop material, he was nonetheless making significant progress in the development of the electric guitar's sound – and was getting it into the Top 20.

Clapton communes with his beloved Gibson Les Paul on Ready Steady Go in late 1966. The guitar was stolen around early March 1967; after a few trials, Clapton settled on a Gibson SG.

Eric Clapton couldn't have cared less about the pop charts. He wanted something far more serious than the confines of the three-minute single. Having teamed up with John Mayall, Clapton too had discovered an extraordinary sound and technique, the result of endless one-night stands playing the music he loved – blues.

The sound was delivered with an out-of-production solidbody Gibson guitar, the Les Paul Standard, powered by a modest 60-watt Marshall combo amplifier cranked until it hurt. The technique, which incorporated an expressive left-hand vibrato and smooth legato phrasing, was Clapton's interpretation of the styles of American blues players such as Freddie, Albert and BB King, and Buddy Guy, of whom few people in Britain had ever heard. Therein lay a problem; there simply weren't enough fans of pure blues to make any of its purveyors wealthy or famous. Burning with talent and ambition, Clapton was restless.

He had sought out the Gibson Les Paul after seeing his hero Freddie King holding a mid-1950s "gold-top" model on the sleeve of an early-1960s compilation album, *Let's Hide Away And Dance Away*. Later versions of the Les Paul would feature a sunburst top and twin-coil "humbucking" pickups, though after little more than two years of those improvements, falling sales forced Gibson to cease its production in 1960.

"Eric wanted something far more serious than the confines of the three-minute single."

Second-hand examples were especially rare in Britain, though Clapton was fortunate enough to find a sunburst Les Paul at a shop on central London's Charing Cross Road. By marrying his new acquisition with the Marshall amplifier, and employing his rapidly blossoming technical skills, he was about to invent a completely new concept in guitar sound, which would be as much equipment-dependant as it was musically innovative.

Late in 1965, Jim Marshall had designed a 100-watt version of his new amplifier at the behest of The Who, in constant need of more volume for their literally explosive stage shows. Marshall could scarcely have imagined how successful his product would become once placed in the hands of an agent like Clapton who, together with Jack Bruce, had acquired one just prior to forming Cream.

Cream's odd debut single 'Wrapping Paper', released in October 1966, raised barely enough steam to coddle an egg. But the b-side was very different, thanks in no small part to the new amplifiers the group were using. 'Cat's Squirrel', a largely instrumental update of a traditional blues riff in an unusual rhythmic meter, was the perfect overture. Blasting off the turntable for a little over a minute before grinding to a halt with a soulful scat vocal from Bruce, it paused just long enough to allow the real Eric Clapton to deliver his opening address to the faithful. Obviously recorded at very high volume, the overdriven amplifier lent energy and sustain to the notes, which formed a perfectly-worded musical prognosis of what Clapton had in store. Neat, fluid blues phrases were played with a butter-smooth tone. Here was a new voice in the universe of the guitar, spoken with assertive eloquence. Mixed with a large, Spector-like hall reverb, the overall effect was spectacular; nothing so huge had ever been heard from a three-piece group before.

The debut album, *Fresh Cream*, was released in time for Christmas 1966, together with a second single, the psychedelically-tinged 'I Feel Free'. With its opening E7#9 power chord setting up a ten-bar a cappella vocal introduction, a bar of tom toms and two huge guitar chords enter the picture and launch the track on its dizzy trajectory into the acid ether. At 1:14, The Solo is served: a sweet sound, somewhere between a flute and a kazoo, cuts through the maelstrom like a siren on the rocks.

Unbelievably, it's a guitar. Supported by chanting voices, it weaves its way through the mix; a slight stumble at 1:30, where it narrowly escapes missing the change to D, before the sound changes subtly as a switch is thrown at 1.40 for the last two bars of the performance. A fluffed high F-sharp adds a little angst, and the solo ends on a painfully-squeezed G-searching-for-an-A before Bruce's vocal re-entry arrives and guides the song back to earth.

"Here was a new voice in the universe of the guitar, spoken with assertive eloquence."

Unhappy with his performance, Clapton requested he do the solo over again. As a 4-track recording, this would not have been possible without erasing permanently the part he'd just played. Thankfully, Bruce was able to convince him that it was fine as it was. But it was more than fine; the sound, the phrasing, the choice of notes and the attitude in the delivery made it fantastic. It provided ample evidence that here might be the very best guitarist of his generation, leaving the competition for dead at the impossibly young age of 21.

The new album was terrific. The simple, uncluttered production was necessitated by budget and the limitations of working on 4-track tape, resulting in a minimum of overdubs. It was an astounding showcase of the group's prowess as instrumentalists, and in particular Clapton's skills. For the first time on a pop record, most of the songs served chiefly as vehicles for the players to show off, an indulgence that was previously only accorded to jazz musicians.

Closing side one, the six-and-a-half-minute live-in-the-studio reading of Willie Dixon's 'Spoonful' is an exercise in power and restraint, Clapton's dynamic guitar responding to Bruce's wailing vocal in an articulate exchange that drips with passion. The song is simply a basic two-note riff in E minor, yet the sympathetic interplay between the two musicians creates a masterpiece of a performance. Clapton's tone is sublime. His left-hand vibrato – first developed during his Yardbirds period – has evolved to a virtuosic degree. It's this facility that gives his tone its unique quality, and remains at the heart of his sound to this day.

Vibrato is a technique used chiefly by singers and orchestral musicians to create emotion and expression in their voices and instruments. It's a controlled wobble, slightly raising or lowering the pitch of the note, and is the most honest communicator of how players are "feeling" the music they're performing. Every musician has a unique vibrato, or none at all, and it's as individual as handwriting. On the steel-string electric guitar, vibrato is particularly difficult as it involves an unnatural "wrist-rotating" action and a degree of physical strength. Gut or nylon strings will produce a vibrato tone if the fretting finger is rolled gently as the string is depressed; steel strings, however, do not respond in this way and need to be pushed sideways across the fret to alter the pitch. Pushing or pulling the string and releasing in quick succession creates the vibrato – and this is a technique that can take a long time to perfect. It is this god-given talent that separates Eric Clapton from the pack. T-Bone Walker, Buddy Guy, Muddy Waters and the Kings may have done it first, but Clapton did it – and still does it – best.

Fresh Cream demonstrates a number of extraordinary guitar techniques. String-bending, a central characteristic of the blues style, is exemplified brilliantly. Clapton's pitch-perfect phrasing adds authority and power, as does his natural skill at playing loud, an art in itself. At such volume levels, the electric guitar is super-sensitive, introducing dynamic and harmonic characteristics that call for complete control by the player.

The attack of the player's picking hand will dictate the energy behind the note – or, if the amplifier is driven to the edge of feeding-back, "hammer-ons" and "pull-offs" can negate the use of the pick almost entirely. Clapton's solo on 'I'm So Glad' uses this to great effect, "hammering" the strings on to the frets with the fingers of the left hand alone, gripping the note, and "pulling" the string as the finger is released.

Clapton on the beach during a short tour of Scotland in the summer of '67.

Feedback, so often the guitarists' bête noire, is presented both on 'I'm So Glad' and 'Sweet Wine' as an exquisite musical experience thanks to the young master's consummate skill and control. The staggering rendition of Muddy Waters's 'Rollin' And Tumblin'', featuring a blistering guitar riff played in unison with Bruce's vocal and harmonica, is an exciting tour de force that recalls Clapton's sound from the Bluesbreakers period, mixed dry for maximum impact.

These new styles, so faultlessly displayed throughout the album, would have a huge effect on guitarists everywhere. Before very long, a phenomenon known as the British blues boom would sweep the UK, as hordes of Clapton imitators armed with second-hand Gibson Les Paul guitars and Marshall 100s sprang apparently from nowhere in a bid to become the next blues guitar hero.

With the ghost of Jeff Beck having been laid to rest for now, a new challenge presented itself almost immediately in the form of Jimi Hendrix, newly arrived from the United States. Comparisons between Clapton and Hendrix were inevitable in that the American too played dazzlingly brilliant blues guitar very loudly, and led a trio. Hendrix had taken blues and soul influences, hijacked Beck's flashy wizardry and Pete Townshend's violent delivery, added fuzz, vibrato, volume and sheer nerve, and proceeded to burn a trail across the British music scene in the early months of 1967.

Bruce and Clapton had their guitars hand-painted with psychedelic designs (left), probably in March 1967. Clapton's Gibson SG Standard (below) is today owned by Todd Rundgren. It has been modified and restored over the years, but retains its period charm.

Hendrix was a showman and a singer-songwriter, and he had a high visual profile. What he didn't have was Ginger Baker and Jack Bruce, or Eric Clapton's purist dedication to absolute perfection. Still, Hendrix had a profound effect on Clapton, who was not about to sit back and coast as long as the fiery American was around and making a name for himself.

Songs for Cream's second LP were recorded in two short bursts in Atlantic's studios in New York City in April and May 1967. *Disraeli Gears*, arguably their best-known album, wouldn't surface for another six months, though it contained all the hippie psychedelic trappings of the period, its Day-Glo coloured sleeve perfectly complementing the music within. In May a single was released in Britain.

'Strange Brew' was a spooky 12-bar sequence featuring Clapton's vocal/guitar duet. It was backed with his first composition, 'Tales Of Brave Ulysses'. Here, the Hendrix threat was met full-on. A new effect unit had just arrived in the form of the Vox Wah-Wah pedal, a trip to Manny's store on 48th Street having placed one in the guitarist's possession. This remarkable unit boosted the high and low-midrange frequencies of the guitar signal as the pedal was rocked up and down. That it should have made its debut on the world's stage with this performance was as fortunate for Vox as Clapton's choice of amp was for Jim Marshall. Playing what sounds suspiciously like a Fender Stratocaster, Clapton blows delicate bubbles of sound over a simple, descending bass riff behind Bruce's unearthly vocal. Each verse is separated by four bars of some lunatic improvised noodlings, and the track climaxes and fades with an extraordinary rush as the blues is launched into yet another dimension by the agitated guitarist.

Having lost his beloved Les Paul guitar to a thief during the early months of 1967, Clapton had replaced it with a Gibson SG Standard, equipped with similar pickups and wiring scheme but with a re-designed slimmer body and neck. Sporting a colourful psych-pop paint job, it's the instrument most readily associated with Clapton during his Cream period. He used the SG both in the studio and on tour for about 18 months.

A Dutch husband-and-wife team, Seemon and Marijke Posthuma, artists on the London scene known collectively as The Fool, painted the guitar in groovy pastel colours, portraying a red-haired winged cherub sitting on a cloud beating a triangle, against a backdrop of rainbow hues and yellow stars, rising above a fiery furnace. A white base undercoat was brushed directly over the Gibson's original cherry lacquer, followed by the oil paint which initially covered the entire body front and back, the pickup surrounds and the upper fingerboard. Only a small area beneath the pickguard was left untouched.

> "Eric made the guitar produce a sound more akin to a wind instrument than somethnig with strings."

The engraved nickel-plated cover plate for the original vibrato bridge was removed in order to reveal more of the artwork. Almost immediately, Clapton had the paint on the back of the neck scraped off, presumably because it was flaking into his left hand as he played. Shortly after the *Disraeli Gears* sessions, the sustain-compromising vibrato was ditched, though the basic trapeze mounting was left in place, its front edge drilled to accommodate the strings which were now pulled downward across the bridge at a steeper angle. As a result of this, the guitar's tone, sustain and playability would have been much improved.

In June1968 Clapton had left the guitar with George Harrison, who passed it on to guitarist Jackie Lomax. Lomax still had it late in 1971 when he met Todd Rundgren. Short of money, Lomax agreed to hock the guitar to Rundgren in exchange for a $500 loan. Lomax later called on Rundgren with 500 bucks for the guitar, but was sent away. Rundgren continued to use the SG both in the studio and on stage for the next 20 years or so.

Back in 1967, Clapton used the SG to develop the sound he'd introduced with the 'I Feel Free' solo. This was the much-celebrated "woman tone", so-called because of its apparent resemblance to the female human voice. Rolling the tone control of the neck pickup back to zero and playing with a sensitive touch through the overdriven Marshall amplifier, the guitar produced a sound more akin to a wind instrument than something with strings.

The technique was especially effective when the guitar was played in the upper area of the neck, particularly with its wound strings. 'Sunshine Of Your Love', which would eventually become Cream's biggest hit, showcased the sound perfectly. Its central riff soon became every aspiring player's favourite lick. The languid solo, developing from a theme loosely based on the Rodgers & Hart song 'Blue Moon', is delivered with graceful panache, notes dripping like little pearls into the turbulent mix.

'World Of Pain' features more of the same, this time double-tracked to dizzying effect, against a sombre wah-wah backing and some powerful, exhilarating rhythm guitar in the choruses. 'Dance The Night Away', a nod in the general direction of America's West Coast music scene, features Clapton's only appearance to date on electric 12-string, perhaps another trophy from a Manny's music-store trip. Bruce's pleading vocal in 'We're Going Wrong' is given a sympathetic counterpoint by soulful kazoo-like guitar lines, while 'Outside Woman Blues' gives the Clapton tonsils an outing on a back-to-basics blues romp, laced with more woman-toned hooks. On its release in November 1967, *Disraeli Gears* was an instant success on both sides of the Atlantic; in the UK it shot straight into the album chart where it remained for almost a year.

Flower power, as Clapton enjoys rest and a moment's meditation during Cream's Scottish expedition, a time for peace and friendship.

In late August 1967 Cream began their first full concert tour of the United States. For the next twelve months the band remained almost constantly on the road. Lacking the time to write or rehearse, shortage of song material soon became an issue, and as a result they developed improvising in live performances.

In order to gather enough material for a 90-minute show, the songs were fleshed out with extended solos. Audiences were more than happy to hear these three musical giants playing so perfectly together, albeit on simple blues structures that would often last for 20 minutes at a stretch. There was a magical chemistry between the musicians, who listened to and clearly inspired each other as they played. Bruce's bass-playing went way beyond the standard role, encouraging, stimulating and urging Clapton to greater musical heights, while Baker's relentless yet creative drumming drove things forward with tireless energy.

In live performance, the guitar sound was not as refined as on record, though no less expert. The woman-tone effect was notably absent for most of the time, Clapton reverting to his less-fussy tone of the *Fresh Cream* era.

Armed with a "brittle-sounding" Gibson Firebird, Clapton sings and plays at New York's Madison Square Garden in November 1968.

Recordings that emerged from their San Francisco concerts of March 1968 demonstrated how the band extemporised and elaborated upon the basic blues format.

Just four songs made up the 45 minutes necessary to fill the two live sides of the two-disc *Wheels Of Fire* set, released in August 1968. Of these, Robert Johnson's 'Crossroads', at a digestible 4:13, remains a high-point of Clapton's playing career to date. Within the standard I/IV/V chord sequence in the key of A there are two solos, the first of 24 bars, the second 36 bars long, separated by a verse of vocal. The solos are outbursts of pure joy, demonstrating not only Clapton's intuitive melodic mastery but also the support, vision and focus of his colleagues Bruce and Baker.

The studio half of *Wheels Of Fire* consolidated Cream's unassailable reputation. 'White Room', the album's opener, begins with long feedback guitar notes doubled with producer Felix Pappalardi's viola, in a ghostly 5/4 preamble to a rewrite of 'Tales Of Brave Ulysses', complete with complimentary wah-wah guitar. The wah-wah reappears in 'Sitting On Top Of The World', though set stationary at a honking mid-point to lend a sorrowful edge to Clapton's almost tearful playing.

Baker's whimsical 'Pressed Rat And Warthog' ends with a landscape of guitars fighting their way through the mix, the gorgeous closing solo lines resembling some fabulous songbird warbling in the psychedelic twilight. 'Politician' sees no fewer than three lead-guitar tracks playing simultaneously on what was soon to become a live crowd-pleaser, Bruce's bass hook doubled by Clapton an octave above it.

Baker's 'Those Were The Days' breaks into a euphoric 'Crossroads'-style solo section, all three musicians locked into a different groove yet somehow creating magic from the chaos, before regaining their composure in time for the final verse. 'Born Under A Bad Sign' is more straightahead call-and-response blues-guitar-and-vocal over a gently-swinging 12-bar sequence. The album closes with Bruce's barmy 'Deserted Cities Of The Heart', Clapton's excited solo marred slightly by the unfortunate studio trick of vari-speeding the guitar track.

"Clapton's solos on Crossroads are outbursts of pure joy, showing intuitive melodic mastery."

Even before *Wheels Of Fire*'s release, rumours began to circulate that the group was about to break up. Plans were put in place to record more live material on Cream's final US tour in the fall of 1968. Three songs from their show at the Los Angeles Forum on October 19th formed half of what would become their last album, *Goodbye*, released in March 1969 following the inevitable split.

Clearly, the spirit of the band was beginning to burn out, despite some high-energy playing, particularly by Jack Bruce. A brutal, pedal-to-the-metal version of 'I'm So Glad' and a perfunctory 'Politician' revealed them playing to the gallery, much to the delight of the crowd, though Clapton excels on this version of 'Sitting On Top Of The World' where his florid bursts of incendiary guitar bounce off Jack Bruce's rasping electric bass in a frenzy of aggressive emotion, before finally breaking down in tears at the song's finale.

A significant change to the guitar sound became evident on *Goodbye*'s three studio cuts. Clapton was by this time favouring a Gibson ES-335 and a brittle-sounding Gibson Firebird, though the big Marshall amplifiers remained. The super-heavy overdriven effect began to thin out, and he'd taken to feeding the guitar through a Leslie cabinet, a rotating set of loudspeakers normally used to amplify and colour the tone of the Hammond organ.

Working with The Beatles on George Harrison's 'While My Guitar Gently Weeps', and having recently discovered Robbie Robertson and The Band, Clapton began to crave a more melodic, song-orientated forum for his playing. A collaboration with Harrison provided just that in 'Badge', Clapton's chiming arpeggios setting up one of his finest, most yearning solos and providing the band with a hit song into the bargain. Both Bruce's 'Doing That Scrapyard Thing' and Baker's 'What A Bringdown' are saturated in Leslie-fied guitar: the former has tastefully-written hooks decorating some neat modulation; the latter a rare slide-and-wah-wah work-out as mad as the song itself.

In 1970 the first posthumous concert album, *Live Cream*, was released. Largely consisting of recordings from the San Francisco dates in March 1968 not included on *Wheels Of Fire*, it makes an interesting comparison with the somewhat world-weary Oakland performances of seven months later. There's a jaunty, joyful version of 'Rollin' And Tumblin'', Clapton's perky guitar motoring effortlessly behind Bruce's harmonica solo, taking liberties with the riff for four-and-a-half minutes without once dropping a stitch. Clapton's impressive skill as a rhythm guitarist is so often overlooked; it is neither funky nor rhythmically complicated, yet always in the pocket, never out of tune, and played with an extremely powerful, driving attitude.

Perfection: Eric Clapton, a Gibson ES-335, and two Marshall stacks.

Another live album, *Volume II*, followed two years later, and contained a marathon 13-minute version of 'Stepping Out', the solo guitar accompanied for the most part by Baker's sympathetic drumming. After blowing faultlessly in G for seven minutes, Clapton's sound changes briefly to recall a hint of the delicate woman-tone of yore. Then a dynamic shift of gear occurs as he breaks into some aggressive rhythmic chord-work, he and Baker bringing the song to a glorious climax with a final resolving change to E major.

The 'Stepping Out' solo illustrates the musical DNA from which Clapton's work within Cream was created: the fluid, legato phrasing; the vibrato; the note-perfect accuracy and delicacy of touch; phrases beginning with strings bent up to pitch before they're struck, then released; phrases ending in exaggerated glissandi; the tone, the aggression, the power; but most of all the feeling. These are all classic Clapton trademarks.

By the age of 23, Eric Clapton had done it all. He inspired guitar players young and old alike. He took the lead guitarist from the passenger seat of the singer's Morris Traveller and placed him in the cockpit of a Ferrari. He sold more Gibson guitars and Marshall amplifiers than any other musician, ever. And any guitarist who uses distortion and finger vibrato to shape their sound owes a debt of inspiration to Cream's lead guitarist. It is no exaggeration to say that the roots of what we recognise today as heavy rock can be traced back to Clapton and Cream.

Cynics might argue that Clapton has been guilty of under-achieving in recent years. But so what? If he'd not played another note after 1968, history would still record that he remains one of the most important musicians of the 20th century. ● *DAVE GREGORY*

CHAPTER 3

STEPPING OUT

Ginger Baker picked up the phone and called me at *Melody Maker*. He had exciting news for the British music press. "I've left Graham Bond and I'm forming a group – with Eric Clapton. And Jack's gonna do it too!" The *MM* hailed this unprecedented new "group's group" with a small story on an inside page. Baker had called on a Tuesday morning, just missing the weekly paper's news day. If there had been more time, and the edition hadn't been about to go to press, it would have been on the front page. Nevertheless, the brief item caused a stir among blues fans and those music-biz people who knew nothing about Baker's plans.

Within a few months of being formed, Cream were in front of the TV cameras.

"Eric, Jack & Ginger Team Up" was the headline on the story in the *MM* dated June 11th 1966, pictured opposite. It put three cats among the pigeons. There was a flurry of phone calls to the paper from the groups' managers. But a subsequent item in the following week's edition confirmed that the proposed outfit wasn't just a figment of the paper's imagination. This time the headline read: "Bruce-Clapton-Baker Group Debut". The story followed: "The all-star group's group consisting of Eric Clapton (guitar), Jack Bruce (bass) and Ginger Baker (drums), announced exclusively in the *MM* two weeks ago, has been signed by Robert Stigwood. 'They will be called The Cream,' Stigwood told the *MM* on Monday. 'And they will be represented by me for agency and management. They will record for my Reaction label and go into the studios next week to cut tracks for their first single. Their debut will be at the National Jazz And Blues Festival, Windsor in July, when their single will be released.' In the meantime Jack Bruce will continue with Manfred Mann and Eric Clapton with John Mayall. Ginger Baker leaves Graham Bond's Organisation on July 20th, to be replaced by modern jazz drummer Johnny Hiseman."

Melody Maker, the first weekly music paper in the world, was founded in 1926, and long since championed the best sounds of the day, whether it was dance-band music, jazz, swing or bebop. In the late 1950s trad-jazz was regarded as important as rock'n'roll. By the mid 1960s the paper was enthusiastically embracing the new era of The Beatles and The Rolling Stones. It may have been a long way from Bing Crosby to Mick Jagger, but the *MM* was always there, with its finger on the pulse. The pulse of the music business certainly quickened when news broke about Cream. Some managers at first denied the band's existence, and wanted to hang on to "their" star sidemen. But there was a row within the group about the way the story had been leaked.

ERIC, JACK & GINGER TEAM UP

● CLAPTON

A SENSATIONAL new "Groups' Group" starring Eric Clapton, Jack Bruce and Ginger Baker is being formed.

Top groups will be losing star instrumentalists as a result. Manfred Mann will lose bassist, harmonica player, pianist and singer Jack Bruce; John Mayall will lose brilliant blues guitarist Eric Clapton, and Graham Bond's Organisation will lose incredible drummer Ginger Baker.

The group say they hope to start playing at clubs, ballrooms and theatres in a month's time.

It is expected they will remain as a trio with Jack as featured vocalist.

Breaking news: Melody Maker's story by Chris Welch announced the formation of the world's first supergroup in June 1966.

"I got into trouble with Jack for telling the *MM* about my idea for forming Cream," Baker recalls. "Things were going badly with Graham Bond. I was trying to get straight, and Graham was trying very hard to get fucked up, and succeeding. I had been running Graham's band for over three years. I was the guy who was in the office all the time and so I thought, well… I'll get my own thing together. Eric had sat in with the band a few times, but I was unaware at the time that Eric had this huge following. I just dug his playing. So I phoned up Johnny Gunnell [John Mayall's manager] and found out where Eric was playing. Johnny told me the Bluesbreakers had a gig in Oxford. I had just bought my first car and I drove down there.

"In the interval Eric said, 'Come and play a number with us.' I played with the band and it really took off. I said to Eric afterwards, 'Look, I'm getting a band together. Are you interested?' He said yes straight away, and then he suggested Jack as the bass player. Well, Jack is a very good player, so I went round to see him and he was very surprised to see me. We had a chat and he said OK – and that's when I phoned the *Melody Maker*. I then got an irate phone call from Jack. He said, 'I haven't told Manfred Mann yet!' Oh God, I'd made a blunder."

Despite this glitch, Bruce thoroughly approved of Baker's plans for an exciting new group. "Ginger always wanted to play with Eric," remembers Bruce, "as many people did. He approached Eric, who said yes. But Eric wanted me to be the singer in the band, which was a bit tough for Ginger to swallow, because we had really fallen out. So Ginger came to my then wife's parents' flat in St John's Wood [north-west London], a council flat I hasten to add. He had to come and eat humble pie. But, of course, I was very excited. I was beginning to write and already fancied myself as a songwriter. I'd written a couple of things with Graham Bond, which appeared on the *Sound Of '65* album. I had also started singing, although I hadn't quite found where my voice was and used to sing very low. It took a while to discover that I had a higher voice."

Straight away Bruce could see the possibilities of putting together a band that would be much more than just another blues jamming outfit. "I was very excited about the idea of being able to write some things for the new band," he says. "As for being the lead singer, well, Graham Bond had this reputation for being a very difficult guy, but he was always most encouraging. It was probably his idea that I started singing with his band. Then Ginger and I agreed to bury the hatchet. The next step was to go to Ginger's house in Neasden [north-west London] and have a play with Eric. The magic was there from the word go."

"I was unaware that Eric had this huge following. I just dug his playing."

Baker remembers that first rehearsal. "It was in the living room of my maisonette in Braemar Avenue in Neasden. There were a whole load of kids out on the Welsh Harp [an open space opposite nearby Brent Reservoir]. We looked out the window and they were all up on this bank behind the garden, boogie-ing to the music. As soon as we played, it was total magic, immediately. I remember we played a few of Eric's things like 'Cat's Squirrel' and 'Lawdy Mama'."

Clapton has also recalled that first session, not so much for the music as what happened during the meeting. "We had our first talk during the rehearsal at Ginger's house," said Clapton, "and those two had an argument, right away, about the press story that had leaked out. It went along the lines of, 'There you go, you've done it again.' I thought there was something, going back, that I wasn't aware of. 'You've done it again' implied there was a pattern. But it calmed down after a while."

The next step was to organise management. Bruce was not keen on the idea of having a manager and would have preferred an agent to book the band. However, Baker wanted Robert Stigwood to be their manager as he had previously looked after the Graham Bond Organisation. Stigwood would eventually become one of the most successful pop impresarios in the world. Brought up in Adelaide, South Australia, he had planned to be a Catholic priest before eventually working for an advertising agency. He emigrated to Britain in 1956 and later worked for a theatrical agency. One of his clients was John Leyton, whose echoing ballad 'Johnny Remember Me' had topped the UK charts in August 1961. Leyton had several more hits and Stigwood established his own publishing, promotion and management company.

Stigwood ran into trouble following a less than successful UK tour by Chuck Berry that his company had promoted. But he quickly rebuilt his empire. He created the Reaction label, distributed by Polydor, and The Robert Stigwood Organisation, which would later set up its own RSO label. Stigwood had great success with Cream and The Bee Gees, but he also developed a role as a theatrical producer, responsible for such stage and movie hits as *Evita* and *Saturday Night Fever*.

Baker realised that the dynamic Stigwood could transform the fledgling band's fortunes, and asked him to take charge. Stigwood's first act was to contact the interested parties, including Mayall's manager John Gunnell, to discuss Clapton's defection. (John was the brother of Rik Gunnell, who ran The Flamingo club in Wardour Street, central London, home of many of the current crop of R&B groups.) Stigwood seemed keen to help the all-star trio, but was heavily involved with promoting The Bee Gees, the vocal group newly arrived in Britain from Australia. As Baker recalls: "In the same *Melody Maker* edition that had a tiny article about Cream getting together, there was a full page advert for the Bee Gees."

"Ginger and I agreed to bury the hatchet, and to have a play with Eric. The magic was there from the word go."

Nevertheless, Stigwood decided to manage the group and, as well as signing the band to management and to his record label, Reaction, he would get them an all-important American deal when he signed them to Ahmet Ertegun's prestigious Atlantic Records, long the home of all the best blues, jazz and soul music.

"It was very much Ginger's idea to ask Robert to be the manager," recalls Bruce, "although in the early days the business decisions were left to Ginger, while the artistic decisions were more Eric's. Eric would decide on album covers and the choice of clothes. I was against the decision to bring in Stigwood because I didn't think we needed a manager. We had a good agent in Robert Masters. We just needed a good accountant, and I felt we could manage ourselves. But Ginger didn't agree with that. He thought we should have Stiggy. I thought that was a most unfortunate decision. If we had had a bit more time and care spent on us, instead of being constantly put on the road, we could have had a month or two off to go and write material together. We never had any real time to do that. A lot of the bitterness that came in later might have been avoided."

Discussions were over. Now the group had to get to work – and fast. After the jam session at Baker's home, the group switched to a school hall near Kensal Rise in north-west London for rehearsals. As the man from *Melody Maker*, I was invited to attend and so witnessed the first ever "public" performance by the group, in front of Robert Stigwood, a troop

“You can imagine what it’s going to sound like with full amplification...”

of Brownies, and a caretaker. The Brownies – a junior version of the Girl Guides – were kicking up a lot of dust with their strenuous group activities. The caretaker scowled and acted like a jobsworth: it was more than his job was worth to put up with the row being made by these strange hirsute hippies wandering around his domain, smoking, drinking and breaking into the occasional choice expletive. The guitar player seemed particularly distracted by a group of girls hanging around outside the hall. They had somehow discovered that a pop group was on the premises, and Clapton and the girls exchanged choice pleasantries.

Bruce remembers that strange day every time he drives through the area. “That’s where we set up our Marshall speakers and started getting it together. We didn’t have any songs but we played a lot of blues. Eric had an amazing knowledge, especially about the more esoteric stuff. You have to remember that Ginger and I were jazzers at heart, passing ourselves off as rockers. We were kind of fugitives from Ornette Coleman. I had played with Alexis Korner and knew the Howlin’ Wolf and Muddy Waters stuff, but I didn’t know very much else about the blues. Fortunately Eric did, and we’d play tunes like ‘Cat’s Squirrel’ and ‘Lawdy Mama’.”

When I arrived on at that hall one sunny afternoon in July 1966, a thunder of drums and guitars echoed out. The band were supposed to be rehearsing for their official debut at the Sixth National Jazz And Blues Festival, due to be held in Windsor, Berkshire, over the weekend of July 29th-31st. The school hall was a far cry from the kind of high-powered “showcase” presentations that any semi-pro band might put on a decade or so later. There were no guitar techs to handle Clapton and Bruce’s equipment, no experts crawling over rigs and plotting computerised lighting effects, no sound engineers setting up PA systems and monitors. Such things did not exist in 1966.

Clapton appeared wearing white bell-bottomed trousers, sideburns and a guitar slung at the hip. How did he feel? “Nervous,” came the terse reply. The group were only using the minimum of equipment, and Baker played on a snare and bass drum – though he was already planning a “monster kit” of seven drums including two bass drums. “We’ve only got about a sixth of the gear here,” explained Clapton, “so you can imagine what it’s going to sound like with full amplification and Ginger’s tom toms as well.” The three musicians stood in a sea of cigarette ends and prepared to run through a few numbers.

Baker, who was sporting a villainous-looking beard, crouched over his drums with the stool set at its lowest possible position and his ride cymbal sloping at an acute angle. Bruce, clutching his six-string bass guitar and wearing a harmonica harness, waited for Clapton to count them in, and the band launched into action. They played just a few choruses of each number, taking a few moments to work out bass drum and bass guitar patterns, and to sort out tempos and various instrumental breaks.

Baker, who was using a pair of enormous sticks which Phil Seamen called Irish navvy poles, suggested doing a comedy number. This turned out to be a traditional jug-band tune called 'Take Your Finger Off It'. At the somewhat confused end of the piece Clapton looked at Bruce and grinned. "You mucked up the end," said Clapton. "Yes, I did, didn't I," replied Bruce coolly. It was at this point that Robert Stigwood decided that what he needed was a second opinion. "Are they any good?" he asked me casually. Stigwood seemed pleased with the affirmative. So the seeds for a mighty empire were sown.

"We want to cancel the idea of three solo musicians clashing and be a group that plays together."

It was at this point that the band decided to take a tea break and the bass player, who had been smoking to calm his nerves, drove Baker, Clapton and me in a van to a nearby transport café. Over egg and chips, the group chatted enthusiastically about their aims, although Clapton already seemed to have a slightly different slant, as if he was already attempting to maintain his detachment and independence.

What kind of music would Cream play? "It's blues Ancient & Modern," said Clapton. "We call it sweet and sour rock'n'roll," said Bruce. Clapton agreed that the phrase would make a good headline and a fine alternative name for the band. Baker said: "At the moment we're trying to get a repertoire up for all the gigs we've got to do. We're digging back as far as we can, even 1927."

Bruce told how they already had a lot of originals they wanted to do – including, he claimed, 'Long Haired, Unsquare Dude Called Jack', a tune which Paul Jones had sung with Manfred Mann, although this failed to materialise. When I asked if there would be any jazz influence to their music, Clapton was adamant. "I'd say jazz is definitely *out*, and sweet and sour rock'n'roll is *in*."

At this point the band had only been rehearsing for three days but already considered that they were "half ready" to make their debut. This makes an ironic contrast to the way contemporary pop outfits take months to choreograph their acts before they set foot on a stage. Clapton, sipping his tea, said: "Most people have formed the impression of us as three solo musicians clashing with each other. We want to cancel that idea and be a group that plays together."

When asked about stage presentation, Clapton said without a moment's hesitation: "We want a turkey on stage while we're playing. We all like turkeys and it's nice to have them around. Another dada thing – I was going to have this hat made from a brim with a cage on top and a live frog inside. It would be very nice to have stuffed bears on stage too. We'd ignore them and not acknowledge their presence at all." His levity suggested that he wasn't taking the project as seriously as the others. Maybe this was because he could already feel his original concept slipping from his grasp. He had hoped that Cream would be a contemporary blues band, one that would play new versions of classics by Robert Johnson and Son House.

For their official debut at the Sixth Jazz & Blues Festival at Windsor in July 1966, Cream shared the bill with Diane & Nicky and The Harry South Orchestra. It poured with rain, but the crowds cheered for more.

"We were quite lost for material," Clapton recalled later. "Luckily Jack had amassed quite a lot of stuff and we worked on those things first. We also tried out some old blues things I brought in." In the event they did play some standard blues material, but they mainly used Bruce's songs, including the first one that he wrote for the band, 'NSU'.

Bruce says 'NSU' was written for the band's first rehearsal. "It was like an early punk song," he explains. "The title meant 'non-specific urethritis'. It didn't mean an NSU Quickly – which was one of those little 1960s mopeds. I used to say it was about a member of the band who had this venereal disease. I can't tell you which one... except he played guitar."

Among those who, with avid interest, read the story about this newly-formed band was Ben Palmer. He was encouraged to get in touch with Clapton again. Palmer recalls being unsurprised that Clapton had made the move. "I think he'd found life with John Mayall's band pretty tedious. John was a very strong-minded bandleader. Little did Eric realise that he was joining a band with *two* very strong-minded bandleaders, who didn't agree on a single thing! But that was all to come." After calling Clapton to see if the new group needed a driver, and a subsequent visit to see Stigwood, Palmer was hired as Cream's first roadie.

It was just ten days after the first rehearsals in London that Cream gave its first public performance, at a secret warm-up gig at The Twisted Wheel club in Manchester on July 29th 1966. It was a trying ordeal, not just for Baker, Bruce and Clapton, but for their new driver, who thought his sole responsibility was to get them to the gig on time. "The first gig was at the Twisted Wheel," he says. "I was still under the misapprehension that once I'd got the car up to the club, the rest of the evening was my own. So I thought I'd pop out for a pint of beer and go back and listen to the band. Of course they were all still in the dressing room when I came back.

"Ginger said, 'Is the stage ready?' Even then I didn't realise. I thought, 'Why doesn't he go and look for himself? Nothing to do with me.' So I wandered out and had a look, came back and said, 'No, it's not ready, everything is still in the car.' Then it suddenly dawned – they were expecting me to set it up. I had never even plugged in a guitar lead. When we were in a band together, I used to give my piano lead to Eric to plug in somewhere. I didn't understand that stuff at all. When I told Ginger, he did help me set up the stage – for the first and last time.

"Ginger pointed out that from then on, everything other than playing the drums was my business. The Twisted Wheel gig was just a warm-up to iron out any problems. I think I was the biggest problem. A few days later was the Windsor Festival, so I thought, 'I'll just get that done and resign. Quickly!' But there never was time. I just had so much work to do with the car and the amplifiers and stuff that I never got around to resigning."

When Cream made their official debut at Windsor, a huge crowd turned out to greet them at the festival. Unfortunately it poured with rain just as Cream came on stage, but the fans ignored the weather and stood and cheered as Baker, Bruce and Clapton launched into 'Spoonful', 'Traintime' and 'Stepping Out'. Cream caused a sensation. It was clear that here was the biggest new band of the year. So it seemed odd that they were now saddled with a string of small club dates that had been booked in advance for little money. Management had not really expected them to be any bigger than the old Graham Bond Organisation.

But the sheer power of the music and the magnetism of the three individual players ensured Cream's success. They would outlive the cosy club scene and usher in a new age of stadium rock. For the moment, however, they had to remain in the back rooms of pubs, earning the same paltry money as gigging jazz players and bluesmen. They had a fight to get their meagre pittance increased, but events soon overtook them. Says Palmer: "In those days nothing was together, really. Nobody had any experience and everything was chaos. It took quite a while to get it working right."

Baker says that at first Cream simply took all the gigs that the Graham Bond band had played, but for £5 more. "Everybody agreed to this," he recalls, "except for the Black Prince in Bexley, south-east London, so we never played there. We were going out for £40 a night with Graham and we started off Cream at £45 a night [about $65]. Robert Masters, our

TUESDAY

ARTWOODS
100 Club, Oxford Street

"GEORGE", MORDEN: KEN COLYER. Bar extension to 11.30.

GOOCH & John Perkins with a load of jazz, blues and folk at the Scots Hoose, Cambridge Circus.

KLOOKS KLEEK
THE CREAM
ERIC CLAPTON
JACK BRUCE
GINGER BAKER

WOOD GREEN. MIKE COTTON SOUND with **LUCAS!** (Fishmongers' Arms, 2 mins. from Underground.)

Cream were stuck with small pub gigs like Klooks Kleek, at the Railway Hotel in north-west London. They played in the cramped upstairs room on August 2nd 1966, a couple of days after their festival debut.

agent, said the venues wouldn't do it. I said, 'Well bloody ask 'em!' And they paid up. I was sitting in the office every week saying, 'Robert, you've got to ask for more money.' He was highly surprised that the promoters agreed to pay.

"Nobody realised just how big the band was going to be," Baker continues, "although Graham's band had been very popular and we were packing places then, playing 320 gigs a year. But when Cream turned up, there were as many people outside the gigs as there were inside. The band was immediately successful. There was a definite buzz around the scene, because all three of us were popular in our own right."

"All of a sudden Robert Stigwood had an extremely successful rock band on his hands."

However, just as Cream seemed to be making headway, there came an extraordinary occurrence. "I got the sack after three months," says Baker. "Oh yeah!" The band were playing in Camberley, to the south-west of London, for promoter Bob Potter, and the place was packed. They were contracted to play for an hour. Cream played the set, then Potter came up to Baker with the £45 fee. The promoter then said that he wanted them to do another set. Baker said, "Well, give us another £45, Bob, and we will." Potter resisted. So Baker said, "Well that's it, I'm out of here." Bruce and Clapton went on stage and did the extra set on their own, and decided to fire their recalcitrant drummer.

Baker recalls that Clapton then changed his mind and decided that in fact the drummer shouldn't be fired. "And that was the end of me leading the band," says Baker. "From then, it became a co-operative. I said, 'Well, that's OK. But everything should be co-operative. The whole shebang: writing and everything.' Really, Stigwood should have been taking care of business, but he was more interested in The Bee Gees. Then all of a sudden he found he'd got an extremely successful rock band on his hands."

Palmer, meanwhile, formed the impression that Robert Stigwood was more interested in and supportive of Cream than Bruce or Baker supposed, certainly in their early days. Stigwood spent money on Cream, says Palmer, and at first encouraged them to wildness. "But Robert could handle The Bee Gees better than he could handle Cream. They were keen and compliant and relatively simple-minded compared to the firebrand Jack Bruce. So we began to see very little of Robert." Palmer says he can only remember seeing the manager on two or three occasions when they went abroad, and can't remember Stigwood coming to a gig. "We would get on a

Cream pictured on August 16th 1966 playing their first gig at the Marquee, by now in Wardour Street in central London. Clapton takes lead vocal, while Baker looks unusually subdued.

plane with a small folder full of contracts and be told that we'd be met at the airport by a travel agent who would direct us to the hotel. There was no pre-planning like now. A rock tour today is a world of specialists, but nobody knew what to do then. You had to improvise the whole time."

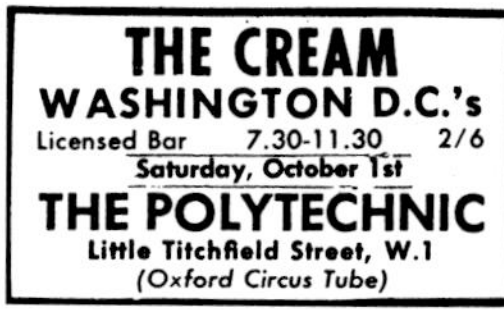
THE CREAM
WASHINGTON D.C.'s
Licensed Bar 7.30-11.30 2/6
Saturday, October 1st
THE POLYTECHNIC
Little Titchfield Street, W.1
(Oxford Circus Tube)

Assuming you could manage the necessary 2/6 (about 13p, or 20¢) you'd have seen Jimi Hendrix, a young American guitarist newly arrived in London, jamming with Cream at the October 1966 gig advertised above.

The first Cream single was 'Wrapping Paper', released on October 7th 1966.

Although a traditional manager could not impose ideas about presentation, attitude or music on a band like Cream, he could still ensure maximum publicity for his charges. To this end Stigwood employed two enthusiastic young press agents to help promote the band. They were Ray Williams and his partner Simon Hayes, who had just launched Mayfair Public Relations. Cream was their first major account. Williams was only 18 when he took on the task of promoting Cream in the press and on TV. He had worked for Cathy McGowan on ITV's *Ready Steady Go* pop show, and got to know Brian Epstein and then Stigwood.

Williams and Hayes soon had to fend off national newspaper inquiries about drugs as much as promoting Cream's new records, although Mayfair PR is commemorated by the assertive sleevenote they supplied for the first Cream album. "It was a very exciting period," says Williams. There was no brief on how to promote Cream, he explains. He was simply told to get column inches in the press. "Ginger Baker in particular really was the wild man of pop and a mass of uncontrollable energy. He was naturally enthusiastic. I remember going to a firework party for his kids at his house – and he was like a kid himself with the fireworks.

"Eric was a nice bloke," Williams continues. "A lot of people were very stuffy in those days – incredible to think of it now – but Eric never was. I remember him bringing his mother along to a Cream gig. He was a very homely sort of guy. Jack Bruce was very solid, and was the one you had to push hardest to the press, because there wasn't so much history attached to him. The press seemed to be more interested in Ginger's old drug habits. He was notorious at that time, although today it wouldn't be so sensational."

Williams notes how enthusiastic Stigwood was about Cream, and reckons the manager invested £250,000 in the band. "But everybody was having a good time in those days," he recalls. "I remember Stiggy, Epstein and Eric coming round to our flat in London once at one o'clock in the morning, banging on the door. They'd been for a night on the town. We got the drinks out and it all got a bit crazy. We started throwing 45rpm singles at each other. Stiggy threw one at me and I threw it back, and everybody joined in. But it all stopped when one hit Stigwood on the forehead and slit him like a knife. There was blood gushing everywhere and this jolly evening suddenly ended. But they were great times, though we were probably all out of our depth, because

Cream perform 'Wrapping Paper' on Ready Steady Go! at a Wembley television studio in November 1966.

the industry was so new. Cream wouldn't have happened if they hadn't had a benefactor like Robert Stigwood. Some people criticised him later on, but there were problems that weren't necessarily of his making. On the positive side, I thought he did a terrific job. He believed in it."

As Cream travelled further afield it wasn't feasible any more to travel with the equipment in one car, and another roadie, Mick Turner, was brought in to drive the second vehicle. It was clear to original roadie Ben Palmer that, from the beginning, there was tension within the band. "They brought all their problems with them. Their suitcases were packed when they joined the band. Jack has a temper. And so does Ginger, by golly. I'd get the sack two or three times a week and be constantly criticised. But he didn't mean it."

Clapton found a way to cope with the problem of inner tension. Certainly the band's success and popularity made perseverance seem worthwhile, even if disagreements could be sparked over details such as the size of the stage or which member got picked up first. It was Palmer's role to act as peacemaker. But he generally acted alone. "Eric stayed out of it

Early at the Ready Steady Go! studio, and Cream work on camera angles. But is that a pressed rat or a warthog on Baker's head?

Ludwig
GINGER

completely. He didn't really need any support from me because he just detached himself entirely from it all. It was the sensible thing to do."

Meanwhile the band found themselves almost too busy to argue, with a series of dates booked during August 1966, including the Cooks Ferry Inn in north London, the Ram Jam Club in Brixton, south London, and The Marquee and Flamingo clubs in Soho in the centre of town. It was great fun for the fans packing these small venues to see their heroes close up and in action. A typical set at this time would include 'Cat's Squirrel,' 'Spoonful,' 'Rollin' And Tumblin', 'I'm So Glad' and 'I Feel Free'.

One of the most exciting gigs at this time came when a young, unknown American guitarist sat in and proceeded to stun the audience... and the band. It occurred on the night of October 1st 1966 at The Polytechnic in Little Titchfield Street, central London. Ben Palmer watched events from the side of the stage with some amazement. "Jimi Hendrix came down to see us after he'd only been in London a week. He showed up with his manager, Chas Chandler. Chas said, 'Jimi's come along to sit in.' He was the first person who ever sat in with Cream, and the last. It was certainly a shock for Eric. Jimi played on a number, I can't remember which, but he played the devil out of it. The band sort of knew that Jimi had previously played with Little Richard and were expecting just a good rock'n'roll guitar player, but you couldn't mistake Hendrix for that."

NEW SEDALIA JAZZ BAND, Botley.

"NOW"! Club White Hart, Southall Broadway. **FREDDY SHAW JAZZBAND.** First Anniversary of Club. Bar open 11.45 pm.

THE CREAM
THE CREAM
East Ham Town Hall Saturday, November 5 6s. 6d. 7.30-11.30 p.m.
THE CREAM

WOOD GREEN GOTHIC JAZZ BAND

Jack Bruce recalls that he invited Jimi to sit in when he came to the gig, and the guitarist was plugged into a spare channel on Bruce's bass gear rather than Clapton's amplifier. However, Clapton welcomed the strange new guitarist to the stand. He listened in some surprise as the young American tore into Howlin' Wolf's 'Killing Floor'. He was impressed by Jimi's clothes and youthful attitude as much as his technique, but the rest of the band felt that Jimi was trying to upstage them. Some time later Jimi would pay tribute to Cream when he broke into a version of 'Sunshine Of Your Love' on BBC TV's *Lulu Show*.

While Hendrix was giving a taste of the Experience to come, Cream performed a strange little song called 'Wrapping Paper'. It caused a wave of disappointment among the band's fans when it was released as their debut single on the Reaction label, some months later than expected, on October 7th 1966. The track was recorded at Rayrik Studios in Chalk Farm, north London, together with a version of the blues standard 'Cat's Squirrel' for the b-side.

The a-side seemed a strange choice to launch such a powerhouse band. 'Wrapping Paper' was a kitsch 1920s-style ditty, complete with pub piano and Bruce humming the chorus. It seemed more suited to the Bonzo Dog Doo Dah Band than a heavy rock trio. It was laudable to come up with something unpredictable, but the song just wasn't very good. The gossip columnist The Raver in *Melody Maker* said: "New Cream single too weird for us." Reviews were even less enthusiastic, with one claiming that "the musical content is nil". Music-lovers were encouraged to listen instead to 'Cat's Squirrel' on the b-side. The single performed poorly in the UK charts, struggling to reach number 34 in November, although Reaction blamed this on their own story that 10,000 copies had to be "withdrawn" due to "pressing faults".

Ginger Baker wasn't thrilled by this first choice for a single. "'Wrapping Paper'? That was the first Bruce-Brown fiasco!" he says today. "We were sat in this rehearsal room in Haverstock Hill and they came up with this silly number that we all had to work on. It wasn't until it was released that I saw it was credited to Bruce-Brown. I said, 'That's a bit strong, guys.' And it continued that way. Some 70 per cent of all Cream writing is credited to Bruce-Brown."

The glories of East Ham Town Hall in east London beckoned on November 5th 1966 (ad, opposite), while to the north of town the Starlite ballroom on December 4th promised a "knock-out atmosphere and modern low lighting".

This division of composer credits would prove to be another source of internal friction for years to come. But the band was hungry for material, and in the beginning there were only two people who could be relied on to deliver the goods. Jack Bruce and lyricist Pete Brown ensured that Cream were supplied with hits, but they also gave the whole band a musical direction and stature that it might not otherwise have achieved. As Baker admits: "In a way there were two bands. There was the studio band and the live band. A lot of the studio stuff we hardly ever played live, like 'Wrapping Paper'."

Before the Bruce-Brown partnership got into its stride the band had recorded their debut album *Fresh Cream*, released in December 1966. The album had a cover depicting the group wearing airmen's flying gear and goggles. It got to number 6 in the UK album charts, and consisted mainly of the traditional blues numbers that Eric Clapton fans expected, including dynamic versions of Willie Dixon's 'Spoonful', Muddy Waters's 'Rollin' And Tumblin', Robert Johnson's 'Four Until Late', Skip James's 'I'm So Glad', and the traditional 'Cat's Squirrel'.

This was solid, satisfying fare, but it was supported by five original numbers. Bruce contributed 'NSU', 'Sleepy Time Time' and 'Dreaming' while Baker came up with 'Sweet Wine' and his drum solo, 'Toad'. A new single 'I Feel Free' coupled with 'NSU' was released in December and eventually climbed to number 11 in the UK charts during January 1967.

The a-side featured Clapton using a distinctive new "woman tone" sound on his Gibson guitar, while Bruce's vocals were accompanied by echoing handclaps and Baker's dancing snare drum. It was a bold, confident and original performance which was much more pleasing to the band and to the fans.

'I Feel Free' was Bruce's first attempt at writing a three-minute pop song. "Eric saw the potential of that song but he was very upset by his playing on it," remembers Bruce. "He wanted to re-record the track, which would have been quite difficult. It had fairly intricate backing vocals, and to try to get that down on a 4-track recording machine was quite hard. We didn't have a George Martin to help us. We were very inexperienced. The first recordings we did for *Fresh Cream* and the early singles were done in such a rush that I was amazed they came out as well as they did."

'Wrapping Paper', Cream's controversial debut single, was released in the UK on Robert Stigwood's Reaction label in October 1966, with 'Cat's Squirrel' on the flip.

There was no great master plan or strategy for either the launch of Cream or the evolution of its musical direction. Says Bruce: "I think there were as many plans as there were people. My idea was to take a blues

The second Cream single was 'I Feel Free' backed with 'NSU'. It first came out in the UK on Reaction in December 1966, but was later reissued on Polydor, including a number of picture-sleeve releases.

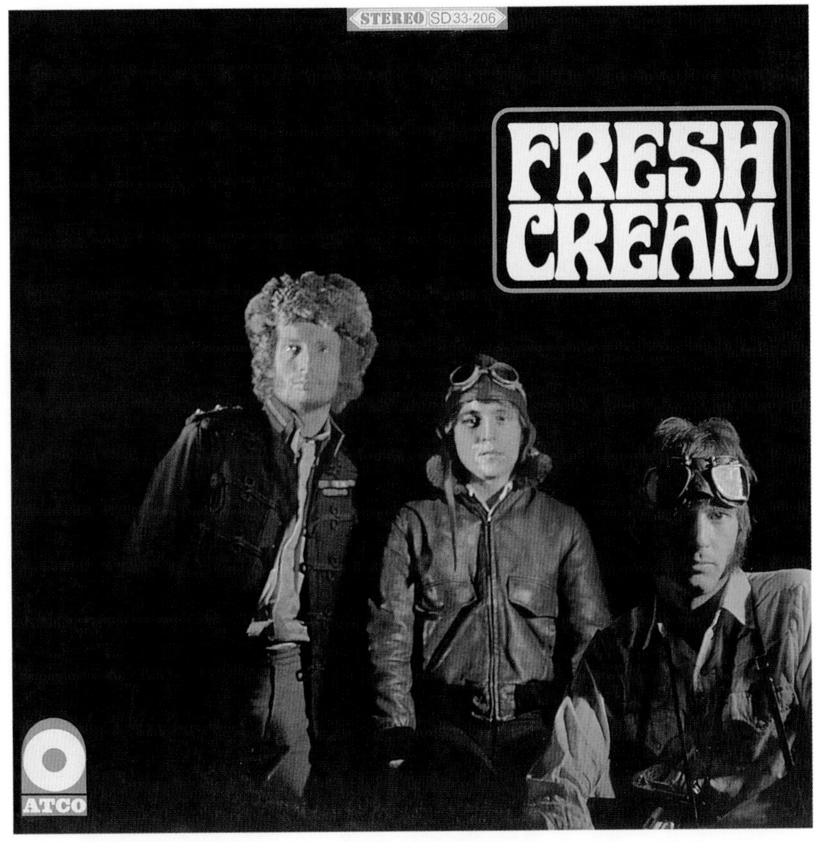

The first album, Fresh Cream, appeared in late 1966 in Britain on Polydor, and in early 1967 in the US on the Atco label. It packed solid performances, but "was all done in a rush".

feeling and apply it to what I had been writing. We didn't want to be like John Mayall and just try to recreate the sound of a Chicago blues band or a particular style. We wanted to be ourselves and take the fabulous language of the blues and apply it to rock music. When we played 'Spoonful' it was a kind of stretched-out version of the original. I think we only had three numbers when we started. We were frantically trying to get material. I had a flat in Hampstead, north London, and I remember us all round there, a bit out of our brains. I've got some really silly tapes that I made of us playing mad Goon-style 'Ying Tong' songs. Those were the good old days when we really had fun!

"Then Pete Brown got rowed in and he was supposed to write with Ginger. We were sitting around at my little pad and nothing was happening," Bruce continues. "My then wife Janet Godfrey turned out to be a very talented lyricist. Janet had previously run the Graham Bond Organisation fan club. She began writing with Ginger and composed the lyrics for 'Sweet Wine' and a couple of other things. So I always say that Ginger got my wife and I got Pete Brown! Pete and myself started writing, and there was a definite rapport." One of the first pieces that Bruce and Brown composed together was 'Wrapping Paper'. Bruce describes it as a brave attempt to put the feeling of the blues into a pop song. "It was actually a 12-bar blues," he says, "but it didn't really work. I have to admit it was a failed experiment. It shocked our potential public, because it was a bit like the Lovin' Spoonful. I'm the first to admit it wasn't a success.

Baker goes into overdrive at a Freak-Out Ball at The Roundhouse in Chalk Farm, north London, on December 30th 1966 (ad opposite). It's all happening, man...

Nobody knew what to make of the song. I remember we did 'Wrapping Paper' on ITV's *Ready Steady Go* TV show, and Manfred Mann were on too. You could see them giving us looks, as if to say, 'They've blown it!' I quickly realised I had goofed, although of course I would never have admitted it at the time.

"Then I came through with 'I Feel Free' which was a synthesis of feelings and influences. That one worked. It could have been better recorded, but none of us had any experience in the studio. In those days musicians were very much the workers. I used to do session work before Cream and the important people were behind the glass panel in the control room. They'd say, 'Do it again,' and when it was finished you might be allowed to listen to the playback, if you were lucky. You couldn't say, 'Oh no, that's wrong. Can we do it again?' So the workings of a studio were a huge mystery, and you were never allowed into the control room. Cream didn't operate like The Beatles, who were very fortunate in having George Martin involved in the whole process."

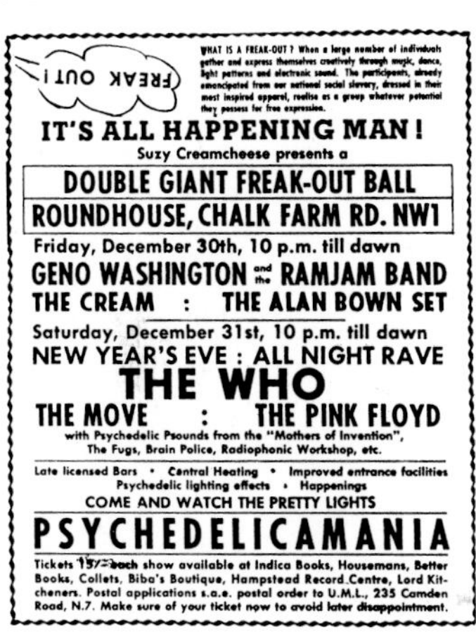

Bruce remembers working with Cream in Spot studio in South Molton Street, central London, where the control room was so far away from the playing area that they had to communicate by monitor speakers. "That's where we recorded the numbers for *Fresh Cream*. John Mayall came in to hear them and he was very encouraging. We worked very hard, although it was difficult to find the time. We weren't allowed six months off to write an album. We'd have to fit it into a day off from gigs. We would work through the night and come up with material, because Eric hadn't started writing at that time."

Bruce now feels that Cream should have written more together, as a team. "It was probably my fault," he admits. "In those days I was so possessive about my music and ideas. I'm not that way now, but then I really wanted to be a writer and was being kind of selfish. I'd get an idea and hug it to myself. I'd write it out in manuscript and arrange the piece, which was very old fashioned. It was because of my classical training."

Despite these disputes, the Jack Bruce-Pete Brown team proved a valuable asset when it came to working on the next Cream album, *Disraeli Gears*. It would seal the band's success in America and ensure their place in rock's hall of fame.

CHAPTER 4

AS YOU SAID

Ginger Baker took several crucial decisions during the formative months of Cream's career. One that would have far-reaching effects was asking Pete Brown to help with the band's creative output. "Pete got involved when I asked him to come down to write some lyrics with us," says Baker. "And by 'us' I meant Eric, myself and Jack. That was the idea."

A poet, singer and bandleader in his own right, Brown helped devise some of Cream's greatest work, including 'I Feel Free', 'White Room', 'Politician' and 'Sunshine Of Your Love'. His skill at blending ringing phrases with dark poetic imagery had much to do with Cream's artistic success. Undoubtedly he was a great asset to the band, although there were some mutterings when it became apparent that he would also enjoy a considerable share in the band's financial success. In a music business driven by royalties and publishing rights, songwriting tends to be better rewarded than musicianship alone. But nobody was more surprised at the way the royalties accrued than the composer himself.

'I Feel Free' was among the earliest collaborations between composer Jack Bruce and lyricist Pete Brown. Here Cream perform the song on BBC's Top Of The Pops in January 1967.

Cream roadie Ben Palmer knew Pete Brown through a mutual friend, kazoo-player and poet Michael Horowitz. "He was a student at Oxford when I was living there, a friend of Paul Jones," says Palmer. "So I knew Horowitz and faintly knew Pete Brown. He was a poet – and there were so few poets about then. You thought, 'A poet? Must be a funny sort of fellow.' But you tolerated them, you know? I thought poets were all dead! But he got on with Jack, and whenever Jack appeared with new songs, they had Pete Brown's lyrics."

Pete Brown was born in London on December 25th 1940. His enthusiasm for music and literature helped to spark off a jazz and poetry movement which impinged on many of London's top musicians during the

1960s. Pete later founded his own experimental rock groups, The Battered Ornaments and then Piblokto!, and remains active as a record producer. He first met Bruce and Baker during his beatnik days. "I was one of Britain's only professional poets, partly because I couldn't do anything else," Brown remembers. "I had been writing since I was 14, and had my first stuff published at 18. It was something that I could do. I was inspired by the American beat poets, and I went out doing poetry readings to earn 20 quid a week."

Pete Brown, lyricist supreme, invests one shilling in half a pound of Ginger Nuts as he contemplates the impending success of Disraeli Gears.

Brown hooked up with Michael Horowitz to appear at arts festivals. As a result of the funding then available they were able to afford a band to take around with them. Dick Heckstall-Smith and Graham Bond were involved, as well as some longer-established British jazz musicians. "All these guys used to play at the Café des Artistes in Fulham," says Brown. "It was actually Dick's band and I remember he got fired from the club for smoking a herbal cigarette – and it really was a herbal cigarette. Ginger Baker used to play there a lot and Graham would sit in. We were always hanging around with Dick, and that's where I heard them all play."

Brown was keen to promote jazz and asked a friend to help him finance a concert at St Pancras Town Hall in central London in 1961. "We booked a big-band with the sax player Bobby Wellins and a quintet with Dick, Graham and Ginger, and John Burch on piano. Ginger was playing in an Elvin Jones groove in those days, although he always sounded like himself. Then Graham, Jack and Ginger joined Alexis Korner's Blues Incorporated, which the jazz establishment rather frowned upon. Jack and Ginger were very different from the average bebop musicians. They once did an audition for Johnny Dankworth's Big Band to be their new rhythm section. The Dankworth band didn't like them, because they were too loud."

Brown's enthusiasm for the idea of mixing jazz and poetry resulted in a regular showcase for his New Departures outfit at The Marquee club in 1963. It was a wild time. Brown admits he became heavily involved in drink and drugs, leading to a self-destructive life style that he finally gave up as a bad job in 1967. "In fact 1966 was a horrible climax to it all," Brown says. "During the early 1960s I was busy being a beatnik and living in a slum with lots of people. I remember one night I went to a party that didn't exist and got stoned on Leapers." Brown went back to the flat that he was sharing with a drummer friend, which had become a regular haunt for wandering bohemians. At 4am there came a knock at the door. Ginger Baker appeared with a posse of musicians, explaining: "We've just come back from a gig with Alexis Korner and we'd like to play." A battered piano was available and the visitors were welcomed. "Great, come in," said Brown. Baker, Graham Bond and 15 others piled into the flat for a booze-up and jam session that went on for hours and hours. "We were all totally out of our minds," recalls Brown. "Ginger and Graham played until 7 the following morning. It was great!"

Brown later met Jack Bruce through Dick Heckstall-Smith and trombonist friend John Mumford, thus creating a kind of musical commune. It was in this atmosphere that Brown says the Graham Bond Organisation was formed, which in turn led to the creation of Cream. It was also thanks to these associations that Pete Brown became much in demand as a lyricist.

Baker remembers enjoying the St Pancras Town Hall "Jazz And Poetry" concert, where Pete Brown read poetry to the audience while the jazz musicians sat on-stage. Says Brown: "Ginger knew me much better than Jack did at that time. As far as my addled memory of the time goes, one day I got a phone call asking me to come down to a recording studio in Chalk Farm. They'd written a song for Cream and needed some lyrics. It was as simple as that. I went down and there was the tune waiting for some words. "It was 'Wrapping Paper'. I had been writing poetry specifically to be done with music, and I had strong awareness of blues lyrics. I was also a big film fan, so my head was full of movie imagery as well. Somehow I wrote a lyric for 'Wrapping Paper'. When I listen to it now, as a piece of music, it's kind of interesting, but I overloaded the whole thing and filled it with too many conflicting images. I suppose there is something in it, but it's not one of my great successes.

Jack Bruce was still with the Graham Bond Organisation when he met songwriting partner Pete Brown.

"Nevertheless, it became apparent what I could do, and I started writing with both Jack and Ginger," Brown continues. "I wasn't really into rock'n'roll at the time; I was more of a blues and jazz fan. That's why I loved the Graham Bond band so much because it had all those elements. But I went to meet Cream and when they played me their songs I understood what they were trying to do."

At the same time as Brown was being offered the biggest break of his career, which would mean some intensive creative effort, he was suffering ill health and mental strain. "I remember an awful time when I was living in *the* white room," he says. "It was a small room around the back of Baker Street, central London, in someone's flat. It was right next to a fire station and the alarms would keep going off, just when I was having a nasty trip. I remember Ginger picking me up from there one day and driving me to Neasden at incredible, frightening speed in his yellow Rover. We did a set of demos in a studio around the back of what is now a Waitrose supermarket on the Finchley Road in Swiss Cottage, north London. That's when Jack and I first wrote several things. One of them went: 'He started off in Canada, selling fridges to the Eskimos.' That never got demo'd. The other one went: 'You make me feel like a hatstand.'"

Pete Brown, with his first post-Cream band The Battered Ornaments, looks suitably ramshackle.

Apart from the blues, another important influence on the group was *The Goon Show*, the popular BBC radio comedy series from the 1950s starring Spike Milligan, Harry Secombe and Peter Sellers. "There was a lot of British humour in Cream," says Brown. "It was one of the stranger components of the band. We didn't get it right to start with. No one quite knew how to build in the humour, but we did it later with things like 'Politician' and 'SWLABR' – actually 'She Walks Like A Bearded Rainbow'. Then we began to get the mix of humour and blues right. We ended up doing things like 'Pressed Rat And Warthog' and 'Mother's Lament'. Ginger was into the music-hall side of things while Eric was really into *The Goon Show*, which was a great inspiration to budding anarchists. That's why he wanted to have stuffed bears on stage with the band."

Brown characterises Jack Bruce as a romantic writer. "He wrote big landscapes with lots of meaning, which I found very inspiring. You could almost touch the atmosphere and imagery. I often thought I was just translating his ideas: Jack had the imagery; I just had to identify and translate it. All three band members were very broad-minded. They were interested in 'world music' long before anybody else. And because they are all so intelligent, I often wondered: why on earth do they need me? Why me? But then I suppose I did have that chemistry with Jack. And there was a huge shortage of material. They were on the road all the time and they had few opportunities to write. It was really down to who could come up with stuff fast. I always wrote on the spot with Jack. Most songs, like 'Sunshine Of Your Love', were written very quickly."

Brown recalls how that particular Cream classic was created. "We had written a few things. We were getting pissed off with each other, for some

"One of the first things we wrote started: 'You make me feel like a hatstand...'"

Pete Brown was a great fan of the Graham Bond Organisation (left to right): Bond, Dick Heckstall-Smith, Ginger Baker, Jack Bruce.

reason, and by now it was five o'clock in the morning. Jack said, 'Well, what about this then?' He picked up a string bass and played the riff. I looked out the window and it was getting near dawn, so that's how I wrote the lyric. It was really quite instant.

"That's how Jack and I produced the bulk of the material – although Ginger was unhappy about the split," says Brown. "He felt he contributed things that should have resulted in him getting pieces of songs. He was always a bit bitter and even thought there was a conspiracy between me and Jack. But that was absolutely untrue."

Baker's grievance began when he saw the credits on the band's first single, 'Wrapping Paper'. He says that it wasn't until the record was released that he realised it was credited to Bruce-Brown, and thought this was unfair. "But I did things like the 5/4 bolero rhythm at the beginning of 'White Room'," says Baker. "The original intro was in 4/4 and I put a

bolero timpani on there. I'm not saying I wrote the whole song – not at all. But if they'd given me five per cent, I'd have been happy. Same as 'Sunshine Of Your Love'. Maybe just a little bit to say thank you for your contribution. It started out very fast: diddle-ee-dit, dit, dit, dit, dee-dah-doo. I said come on, let's slow it down. So we did. And I played the 'backwards' drum-beat on that – which not many drummers can play, although lots have tried."

Clapton saw how the division of writing within the band was leading to problems. He explained later how Baker had felt that the royalties from Cream material should have been split more fairly. "But it would have been difficult to have kept that up," Clapton said. "It meant you would have had to write under pressure. Jack and Pete were prolific writers and they could churn out a lot of stuff. If you were going to keep up with them, you probably were going to have to spend much more time songwriting than you cared to."

Pete Brown expresses his frustration at not being Miles Davis.

Brown understands how Baker's resentment might have arisen, but says that he was happy – and amazed – to be involved in the Bruce-Brown writing team. "We were just the fastest. Later on Ginger virtually accused me of stealing his birthright by writing all those songs and copping a living from them. He felt that perhaps he should have been doing it. On the other hand, with all due respect, I did help the main hits along which did quite a lot for them. I wouldn't have argued about a four-way split. After all, I'd been living on 20 quid a week, so suddenly I was doing an awful lot better. I still get royalties from those songs and they've been licensed a lot for commercials and films. They've been in a long list of movies, and of course the records still sell pretty well."

Brown is proud of his work from the period. "When you look at the songs we wrote for Cream, they're all incredibly different. They are extremely varied, and most of them were performed live. They're not at all repetitive or a matter of resting on laurels."

'Politician' was one of the most striking and memorable of the Bruce-Brown collaborations. "My second demo session was me trying to sing the lyrics," Brown recalls. "I did a version of 'Politician' which was just a 12-bar blues, but with no riff. Then of course in the great rush of getting material for Cream, Jack became aware of it. The song was very long and lasted seven minutes with a whole story attached. I did a demo of it with John McLaughlin which I've still got, played at a completely different tempo. I put it forward and Jack instinctively found that raunchy riff."

Brown says that 'White Room' started life as an eight-page poem. "This was when I was living in that white room. I was starting my life again at the time. I had some money from songwriting, but I was still boozing and

Cream performing at the Record Star Show, an event sponsored by the Daily Express newspaper. It was staged at the Empire Pool, Wembley, on April 16th 1967 – just two weeks after the band's return from their eventful American debut.

drugging. It was in my white-painted room that I had the horrible drug experience that made me want to stop everything. I was pretty strange at the time." Even now Brown finds it hard to comprehend fully his own behaviour during his freak-out years. "I got a few of my things out of storage to put in the white room and started talking to them. I was drunk. But I started talking to these objects. My girlfriend of the time completely freaked out. I was talking to bits of furniture and she was scared stiff. So the song was about going through serious changes and starting life again. I think Jack had the music and I had the idea."

All these songs would become highly successful. The impoverished poet found himself deluged with royalties. He felt overwhelmed by the sudden rush of money and took a flat in Montagu Square in central London. He regularly ordered taxis to go shopping in the nearby Selfridges store. "I'd keep the taxis waiting for hours while I bought everything. I've got money! You see, before that I had been a bum. All I'd ever done before was sell shoes or hitchhike to Liverpool to read poetry for ten shillings."

Brown says he never had a contract with Cream. "That was very wise. I just did the writing on a song-by-song basis. I never had an exclusive contract with them. I believe Cream received a very small percentage of their earnings. The band was among the highest earning acts in the world at that time. By the time they played their last tour they got $68,000 for one gig alone. I never went out on the road with them myself. During the time when I was freaked out, loud music used to frighten me, so I found it hard to go and listen to them. I once went to a May Ball in Oxford that was very funny. There were all sorts of incidents. Jack found a coal scuttle full of puke that he put in one of the don's rooms, and Ginger cycled his bike through the bar causing a commotion."

"It was in my white-painted room that I had the horrible drug experience."

There was a gap between the material that Bruce and Brown wrote for the first Cream releases and the writing sessions that produced the second and third albums. In Brown's recollection, the reason he didn't make any contribution to the first album, *Fresh Cream*, is because he had stopped taking drugs and was getting anxiety attacks. "I kept getting the horrors," he says, "and had to run out of the studio. I was very twitchy, but I was straight and eventually got back into it. We had already written 'I Feel Free' before the album sessions and it was a big hit. It was the only pop song I've ever written and it's got such a great hook. It's very lyrical at the top, and on the bottom it's ferociously driving. Such a contrast, and it worked like a charm. I don't think anyone had ever done that before. It was Jack's brainchild, really. It's as much a complete musical vision as anything Brian Wilson ever did with The Beach Boys."

Brown also remembers how satisfying it was to have a hit record. "It was very exciting. I couldn't believe it. 'Wrapping Paper' got into the Top 30. We heard that it had been bought in to the chart, and I see no reason to disbelieve that. But 'I Feel Free' was a bona fide hit. It also started to move a bit in America, too."

'I Feel Free' was recorded at Spot studio in central London, engineered by John Timperley. Although Robert Stigwood was supposed to be in charge and booked the studio for the band, he left the musicians to their own devices, especially after one hectic episode when he was forced into one of Baker's drum cases that was then rolled down a flight of stairs.

There were quite a few arguments in the studio during these sessions, and some demo tracks recorded later at Spot were lost for many years. They included such songs as 'The Clearout', 'Weird Of Hermiston' and 'Hey Now Princess'. "There were a few numbers which mysteriously vanished," says Brown. "They were recorded as demos by Cream, and Stigwood may have thought they were going in the wrong direction and were not commercial, so he suppressed them. Then they turned up again many years later." Some of these previously unreleased takes were heard legitimately for the first time on the 1997 four-CD Cream box-set *Those Were The Days*.

SUNDAYS at the SAVILLE
A NEMS PRESENTATION
OCTOBER 1st*
PINK FLOYD
TOMORROW
Featuring KEITH WEST
GUEST STAR TIM ROSE
*Presented in association with Brian Morrison Agency
OCTOBER 8th
JIMI HENDRIX EXPERIENCE
OCTOBER 15th*
JR. WALKER ALL STARS
*Presented in association with Rik and John Gunnell
OCTOBER 22nd
THE WHO
OCTOBER 29th
THE CREAM
BOOK: TEM 4011

The Saville Theatre in Shaftesbury Avenue, London, presented superb shows under the aegis of Beatles' manager Brian Epstein. Cream played at their best on those exciting nights during 1967, especially when they shared the bill with their own favourites, The Bonzo Dog Doo/Dah Band (see programme page, opposite).

While Cream's creative department went into overdrive, the hard work of touring continued at such a pace that the musicians suffered from exhaustion. During the last weeks of 1966 and the first couple of months of 1967 the band's popularity was boosted by the success of both *Fresh Cream* and 'I Feel Free'. They enjoyed some TV and a fair amount of radio exposure, as well as sell-out gigs. In December came Cream's first European date when they went to Paris for a warmly received gig at La Locomotive club; back home, their remaining club dates were sold out. Where the Graham Bond Organisation might have felt it was enjoying a good night if there were 800 fans at a gig, Cream were regularly drawing 1,500 a night and packing venues to overflowing.

In November and January Cream recorded shows for BBC Radio's *Saturday Club*, and they also made a short film, probably in February, of 'I Feel Free'. It was a kind of early promo video, and was meant to be shown in the US. But it was banned, allegedly because the group were seen cavorting in a park dressed up as monks and smoking cigarettes. Their management announced: "The Americans felt it might offend people's religious susceptibilities."

During February and March Cream embarked on some dates in Germany, Denmark and Sweden. They also fitted in a show at London's Saville Theatre early in February. The venue was a converted cinema in Shaftesbury Avenue, central London, which had been taken over by Beatle manager Brian Epstein and turned into a showcase for the best in music. During its short reign it hosted some remarkable Sunday-night concerts featuring a variety of The Beatles' favourite artists, including everyone from Fats Domino and Lee Dorsey to Jimi Hendrix, The Bonzo Dog Doo Dah Band, The Bee Gees, and Cream. The Jimi Hendrix Experience were performing at the Saville on the night that Brian Epstein died at his London flat in August 1967.

Cream's performances at The Saville were distinguished by their intimacy and comfort. They were certainly among the best enjoyed by their British fans. Apart from the relatively large Windsor Jazz & Blues festivals, the band never played at the sort of sizeable UK arenas that bands like Led Zeppelin would dominate in the coming decade. Nor did Cream play at the hippie psychedelic clubs like UFO favoured by bands such as Pink Floyd.

The Saville Theatre provided comfortable plush seating, good acoustics and a clearly visible stage. Cream were on top form when they played there in February. By now they had a clearly defined show. Blues numbers from their first album, *Fresh Cream*, including 'Cat's Squirrel' and 'Spoonful', intermingled with the single 'I Feel Free' and the showcase numbers 'Traintime', 'Toad' and 'Stepping Out'.

'Toad' was Baker's spectacular drum solo, always a guaranteed crowd-pleaser and an exciting climax to the show. His drumming style had developed during his years with Graham Bond and was now given a long feature spot. Armed with double bass-drums and a forest of tom toms and cymbals, Baker was able to construct an almost symphonic solo that was both logical in its construction and dynamic in its development. He would start by setting up a ride cymbal rhythm, playing left-hand fills on the snare drum. Gradually he'd incorporate the various tom toms, creating shifting patterns to produce a polyphonic effect, before bringing back the cymbals to unleash a cascading sound, finally submerged into a thunder of triplets from the snare and bass drums. With his feet pumping furiously, hands and arms a blur and red hair flopping over his sweat-drenched face, Baker invariably brought an uproarious response from that night's audience – while the bassist and guitarist paused for a welcome smoke in the wings.

Baker was also called on to provide the locomotive beat on the wire brushes during Bruce's solo number, 'Traintime'. Bruce would sing and wail on harmonica on this blues number first devised in the Bond days. With the need to provide a constant backbeat as well as explosive breaks, fills

Sitting on top of the world, Cream coolly contemplate the conquest of America.

and solos, Baker was constantly busy throughout every Cream show. It wasn't surprising that he often collapsed in the aftermath. Baker described his approach to drumming in a 1967 interview. "The way I play," he said, "as well as being musical, is very athletic. I use all my limbs. I get near to a blackout every night after the solo and sometimes I can't stand up. I play the solo to a pattern so the others know when to come in, but I try to do something new every time. I never play the same solo twice, but if you are playing with a band you've got to play to a pattern."

While young drummers sat and watched Baker's every move at these exciting concerts, so Clapton's fans were agog whenever he kicked into the joyous theme of 'Stepping Out' – which had been so popular when the guitarist was with John Mayall's Bluesbreakers.

But Clapton's guitar work was crucial throughout Cream's performances, carefully deployed to maximise its effectiveness within the confines of a three-piece band. Unlike many guitarists who found themselves in such a setting, Clapton did not simply solo away selfishly with little regard to what was going on musically around him. He always managed to play with taste, and would fit his playing into the structure of the songs. Coupled with this, he instinctively knew when not to play, and similarly would choose the right moment to step forward into the spotlight. However, there came a point later when Clapton became irritated with and frustrated by audiences who were too uncritical and laudatory, and he'd start to fool around.

"When we went to America we were supremely confident – and there's nothing like confidence to get you really playing."

One night he hung his guitar from chains suspended from the ceiling and let it feed back, implying that people would applaud anything in their advanced state of hysteria. But it was the summer of love... and as 1967 proceeded Clapton was happy to sport a mop of curly hair and wear pink satin trousers and a psychedelic satin blouse with the best of the hippies. Even Bruce and Baker wore caftans and beads – although they might have preferred duffel coats and sneakers.

Cream were greeted with adulation that bordered on hysteria. Then came even more exciting news. In March *Fresh Cream* had been released in America on the Atco label, and it had gotten into the lower reaches of the US album chart. The way was open for the band to start its conquest of the West. Baker, Bruce and Clapton were convinced they could make it in America, even if their manager was persuaded it was more likely that The Bee Gees would become the UK's biggest pop export.

"All of a sudden Robert Stigwood found he'd got an extremely successful band on his hands," says Baker. "When the first album got into the American charts, everyone got very excited. It only went in at number 198, but it was *there*. It was on the charts for ages and it eventually got to number 20. Then Stigwood came up with this American tour and we went out there for $3,000 a gig. He said it wasn't big money but the tour would make the band. We went over to the States and we were going to do a record while we were there. When we first went out, we were supremely confident. And there's nothing like confidence to get you really playing. We felt we were going to blow those Yanks away."

CHAPTER 5

SITTING ON TOP OF THE WORLD

Cream arrived in America toward the end of March 1967. Robert Stigwood had been assiduously working to set up a US visit since the previous November. Their first Stateside dates were no ordinary gigs, but in fact turned out to be something of an ordeal.

The band were booked to play for a week on Murray The K's Easter show in New York. Murray was a highly influential DJ whose broadcasts on New York's top stations had helped to introduce the music of The Beatles and The Rolling Stones to America. Although known to some as "the fifth Beatle" and supposedly at the forefront of the contemporary scene, Murray's idea of an all-day stage show with a variety of different acts, each performing a couple of songs, seemed like a throwback to the days of vaudeville. Nevertheless, from Stigwood's point of view this seemed like a good way to have Cream seen by as many people as possible in the shortest time. The band would also be able to use the residency to get acclimatised before embarking later on a full-scale US tour.

Invasion party ahoy! Cream row across the lake in Central Park, New York, during a break in recording.

Murray The K's "Music In The Fifth Dimension" shows, held at the RKO Theatre on 58th Street in Manhattan, have since become the stuff of legends and a source of both amusement and chagrin to the participants. The shows featured as many acts representing "today's music" as it was possible to cram on stage in the space of an hour. Then the theatre would be cleared, a new audience would be brought in, and the show would be started all over again. The impressive line-up was planned to have included Simon & Garfunkel, The Who, Mitch Ryder, Wilson Pickett, Smokey Robinson, Steve Katz & The Blues Project, Phil Ochs, The Young Rascals, The Blues Magoos, and "direct from London, The Cream".

As each act was only to be allowed about five minutes on stage, it meant that Cream could only play two numbers – usually 'I Feel Free' and 'I'm So Glad'. They would have to play these five times a day for ten days, using borrowed equipment. As it turned out, the theatre was practically empty for most of the time. The Who stole the show, and not all of the biggest acts showed up. "We did four or five shows a day at the RKO Theatre," remembers Bruce, "which didn't do us much good. I think we got cut down to half a song toward the end."

Baker recalls the Murray The K event as a complete fiasco. "Murray came up and said we could only do three numbers," says Baker. "He thought it would only take three minutes. Well, three numbers for Cream was 45 minutes to an hour. We were only supposed to be on for 15 minutes. So instead of having four shows on the opening night, it over-ran by 80 minutes and they only had three. There was all sorts of panic going on backstage." Baker chuckles as he describes Murray The K "freaking out". After the second show, the DJ came down to Cream's dressing room and begged the band to cut down their set. He was not reassured when he saw the drummer lying underneath a table, having consumed most of a bottle of Bacardi. "How's he gonna play?" screamed the hapless promoter.

"Direct from England", Cream were thrust among a motley crew of stars for their first US gigs, at Murray The K's ambitious but fated New York shows.

Despite the fact that Cream were bottom of the bill and were soon reduced to playing just 'I'm So Glad' every night, the musicians were thrilled to be in America and enjoyed discovering New York. "That's where I met Buddy Miles," says Baker. "We used to go and jam at a little club on 47th Street after the Murray The K shows. It was very exciting going to the States."

If the musicians found the shows a frustrating routine, so did the roadies. Ben Palmer recalls that the first curtain-call was at ten o'clock in the morning. "That show was for the schoolkids on holiday. There were four more shows, and the last one was for the late-night supper crowd, taking in a late show on their way home after a night in Manhattan. But stars like Simon & Garfunkel and Smokey Robinson & The Miracles, who were supposed to be on the show, never turned up. There was some act called Jim & Jean, who were folk singers, and of course Murray The K's wife and her dancers. Let's not forget them." Jackie & The K Girls performed a "wild fashion show" between each band as the stage was being set up. Much to the fury of the bands, the dancing spot became longer and longer.

"It was so hectic," recalls Palmer, "and awful. You didn't have time to form an opinion about the whole thing. There was hardly time to think about the last disaster before the next one was upon you. It wasn't even a proving ground for the band in America, because they could only play one number and that had to be specified by Murray. He liked the quote from the 1812 Overture in 'I'm So Glad', so that had to be played every time. And of course The Who had to destroy everything five times a day as well. There was no respite."

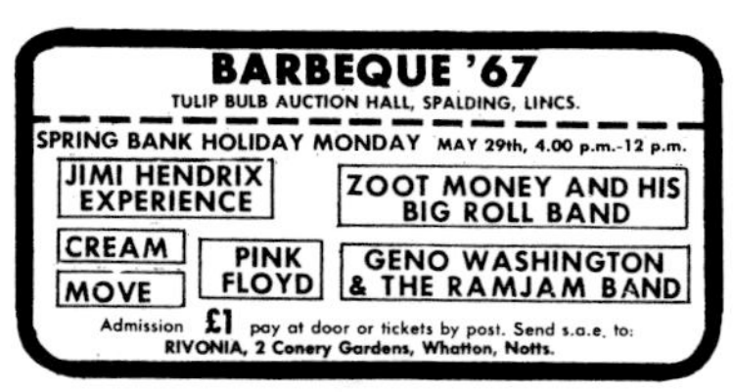

Sounds like a great gig, and all for a 1967 £1-note. But the reality that May was different, the main culprit being the doomed Tulip Bulb Auction Hall itself. Evidently not purpose-built for loud rock bands, this "large shed" provided one of the most unsuitable venues that Cream ever played.

With Keith Moon, Pete Townshend, Eric Clapton and Ginger Baker in town together, you might expect a barrage of mischief. But Palmer reports an iron hand kept them under control. "Murray The K wouldn't put up with any misbehaviour backstage. If he heard that anybody was planning anything for light relief, it was stopped. You weren't even allowed out of the theatre or even the dressing room unless you had a good reason. It seemed strict to us, but when you looked at the way American bands were run, it wasn't anything new to them.

"Wilson Pickett used to stand by the door at the back of the stage, leading to the dressing room. As his band came through he would tell them what their fines were. I heard him fine them for everything, from playing over his singing to borrowing his car. Most of the musicians were in debt to him because of his fines. He fined them continuously. It was pretty strict, so the idea of bands larking about just didn't happen. That was very much a British thing. In America you could be replaced at a moment's notice. There is a 17-year-old postman in the town you are playing who is as good as you, whoever you are. There are musicians everywhere."

Clapton phoned *Melody Maker* in London just after the RKO Theatre season was completed and seemed in high spirits. He told me the show was very funny, all part of an enjoyable introduction to the Big Apple. "The Murray The K show was great – too much!" said Clapton over the transatlantic phone line. "The audience were mostly 13- to 14-year-old teenyboppers. Everybody went down well and as we only had one or two numbers each, everybody pulled the stops out. The Who stole the show. They only had to smash everything up and everybody was on their feet. We did 'I'm So Glad' and 'I Feel Free' but the whole thing had nothing to do with music. We took the actual show as a joke. There was no chance for Ginger to play his solo and we had to use The Who's equipment because we couldn't take any with us, and there was none provided – as usual. Smokey Robinson just refused to do the show, because it wasn't his scene."

Rumours reached London that the British contingent had staged a huge mock battle in the theatre. Explained Clapton: "We had all these 14-pound bags of flour and some eggs we were going to use on stage on the last night, but Murray got to hear about it and said we wouldn't get paid if we did. So we spread them all around the dressing rooms instead. The whole cast joined in and Pete Townshend ended up swimming around in his dressing room, fully clothed, when his shower overflowed. It was rumoured that Murray spent $30,000 on the show and lost $27,000. He was very distraught, wandering about throwing his hands in the air."

"He was not reassured when he saw the drummer under a table and having consumed most of a bottle of Bacardi."

Ben Palmer was deputised to organise these end-of-show celebrations, which it seems involved Jackie & The K Girls getting literally plastered. "I had to go out and buy unfeasible quantities of flour and eggs," remembers Palmer. "But Murray heard about it and said, 'If anything happens, it'll come out of your wages.' So there was just a scuffle in the showers, but it wasn't legendary.

"After the Murray The K show Robert Stigwood rang me up and said, 'How are the boys taking it?' He was nervous that he had let them in for something that was inappropriate, as indeed he had. It was the worst possible exposure they could have had in America. And I said, 'Well, they are pretty pissed off, Robert.' That was when he arranged the first recording sessions at Atlantic. He said, 'Tell them I've got them booked into the studios with Tom Dowd, and Ahmet Ertegun is dead keen. That should cheer them up.' And, of course, it did."

Clapton soon found a way to escape the tensions backstage. Once he'd got past the security guards at the gig he could explore New York's club scene and meet different musicians. He especially enjoyed discovering Greenwich Village, where he'd sit in with members of The Mothers Of Invention or Mitch Ryder at the café where Jimi Hendrix used to play. "I made a lot of friends there, including Al Kooper who used to be Dylan's organist," the guitarist said later. "New York is incredible. Everybody was so much more hip to the music scene. Taxi drivers talking about James Brown. Could you imagine that in London?"

As well as meeting Kooper, then in the throes of rehearsing his new band Blood Sweat & Tears, Clapton also jammed with BB King at the Café Au Go Go for a three-hour set. Clapton's discographer Marc Roberty says this remarkable performance was recorded by the management but never released, not even on a bootleg. In 2000, more than 30 years later, Clapton and King would team up for their splendid hit album *Riding With The King*. Meanwhile, Murray The K's shows were over by April 2nd 1967 and Cream were ready to start recordings for their second album. It turned out to be one of the first examples of a British band recording a complete album in an American studio. Baker, Bruce and Clapton looked forward to using relatively high-tech equipment, including 8-track recorders, and working with engineers who didn't read the racing newspapers or take a tea-break during sessions.

Baker's recollection is that Ahmet Ertegun, boss of Atlantic Records, gave the band two weeks to make *Disraeli Gears*. The relatively brief sessions probably took place on two separate occasions: once in April after the Murray The K concerts, and then again in mid-May. "That's when we met Felix Pappalardi," says Baker. "He turned up at the studio on the first day. We didn't have any material as such for the album. I do believe we did 'Lawdy Mama' and Felix went off and wrote some new words for it as 'Strange Brew'. Jack hated it because he played a wrong note on the bass on 'Strange Brew', but I thought it sounded OK. It kind of makes it."

Eric with fresh perm and Les Paul Custom in Atlantic's recording studio, New York City, 1967.

Ahmet Ertegun had begun a policy of signing up the best of Britain's new rock acts for his US Atlantic label. His roster would later include Led Zeppelin, Yes and ELP. Ertegun's involvement with Cream began when he did a deal to distribute Stigwood's Reaction label in the States. It was Ertegun's decision to send Cream to Atlantic's own 8-track recording studio at West 60th Street and Broadway in New York City. The band would liase with the studio's staff engineer Tom Dowd, a man of high repute who had previously worked with such artists as Ray Charles and John Coltrane.

Dowd received an urgent phone call one afternoon and was told to get over to the studio and get the best out of this English band before their visas expired and they had to leave town. When he arrived at the studio the next morning, on April 3rd 1967, he found the road crew unloading huge speaker stacks and a double bass-drum kit. He wondered what the hell was going on. At this point he knew nothing about the group, except that it

was a three-piece and two of them could sing lead. Clapton was delighted that they should be involved with an experienced engineer like Tom Dowd and technicians who regularly worked with heroes like Otis Redding and Aretha Franklin. When the pressing question of material for the proposed album arose, the "missing" demo tape that the band had put together back in London at Spot studio in March was presented to the producer and record boss. The tape included 'Hey Now Princess', an unusual performance that featured semi-spoken vocals from Bruce, frantic

"Could you play that again, please, Eric? We just ran out of tape..." Cream grapple with production problems during the Disraeli Gears sessions at Atlantic, 1967.

Climbing Ben Nevis during the summer of love seemed like a wild trip.

drumming from Baker and freak-out guitar work from Clapton, quite different from anything he'd done before. (The demo was eventually included on Cream's *Those Were The Days* CD box-set in 1997.) The demo sessions had yielded a number of other new songs, including 'We're Going Wrong', 'SWLABR', 'The Weird Of Hermiston', 'The Clearout', 'Take It Back' and 'Blue Condition'.

Four of the songs – 'We're Going Wrong', 'SWLABR', 'Take It Back' and 'Blue Condition' – ended up on the finished album, although the demos sounded quite different. It was a source of annoyance to Bruce that some of his most innovative songs were dropped during the selection process. 'The Weird Of Hermiston' didn't make it, and 'The Clearout' was dumped in favour of 'Mother's Lament', a cockney music-hall song which Clapton and Baker used to enjoy singing in the local bar during the Atlantic sessions. Both of those dropped songs by Bruce would appear in 1969 on his first post-Cream solo LP, *Songs For A Tailor*, while 'Hey Now Princess' would have to wait until his *Question Of Time* album of 1990.

Under the aegis of producer Felix Pappalardi, Tom Dowd, Ahmet Ertegun and Robert Stigwood, the recordings were completed and *Disraeli Gears* turned out to be a satisfactory album. The band's next big hits 'Strange Brew', 'Sunshine Of Your Love' and 'Tales Of Brave Ulysses' were among the highlights.

Felix Pappalardi was born in the Bronx, New York, in 1939. He was hailed by many critics as the man who helped Cream focus their work in the studio. A musician himself, he had started out playing guitar and

Where are they now? Cream meet some passing children during a photo session in Battersea Park, London, in that same summer of '67.

singing folk and blues with Tom Rush and Tom Paxton in the 1960s. In late 1966 Pappalardi had produced The Youngbloods' debut album for RCA. When Pappalardi heard Cream's debut album, *Fresh Cream*, he was so enthusiastic that he was determined to meet them, and nurtured a desire to produce their next record.

Pappalardi made sure he was in the studio when the band turned up at Atlantic, not quite knowing what they were going to record. It was clear they needed help. He was happy to oblige. The band spent only a few days in the studio in early April, then went back again in May to record 'Sunshine Of Your Love' and complete the sessions. On that first post-Murray The K visit in April they recorded 'Lawdy Mama' and 'Strange Brew', the band's third single that was released in May 1967 in the UK and July in the US. It got to number 17 in Britain, but it would be another year before the band saw any chart action in America. Their biggest hit, 'Sunshine Of Your Love', would get to number 5 in the US *Billboard* chart in 1968, although curiously it only managed to reach number 25 at home.

In retrospect, it's surprising to learn of the reaction of record company bosses when they first heard some of Bruce and Brown's latest compositions for Cream. These tunes are now hailed as classics of 20th-century rock, constantly revived and most readily identifiable as Cream anthems. Yet that was not how they were perceived at the time. "Trying to record songs like 'White Room' and 'Sunshine Of

Your Love' for Atlantic was a struggle," reveals Bruce. "Ahmet Ertegun decided that the band was all wrong. Eric should be the front man and me and Ginger should just be his backing group. That's why they brought in Felix Pappalardi, who just happened to be at Atlantic when we were there.

"Ahmet said to Felix, 'Go in and see if you can get anything out of these guys.' I played 'Sunshine Of Your Love' and 'White Room' to them and they said it was rubbish. I think 'psychedelic hogwash' was one of the

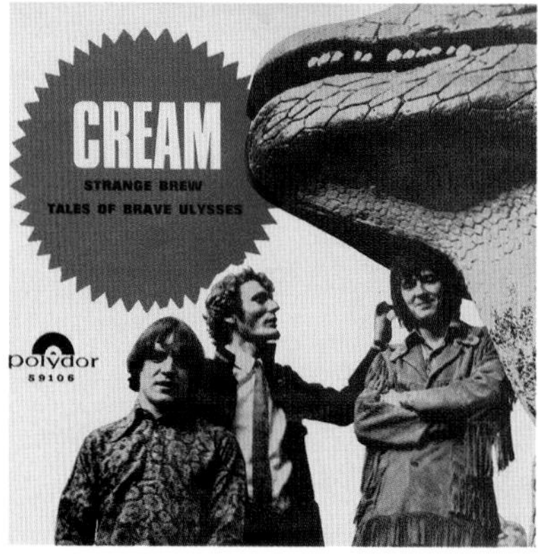

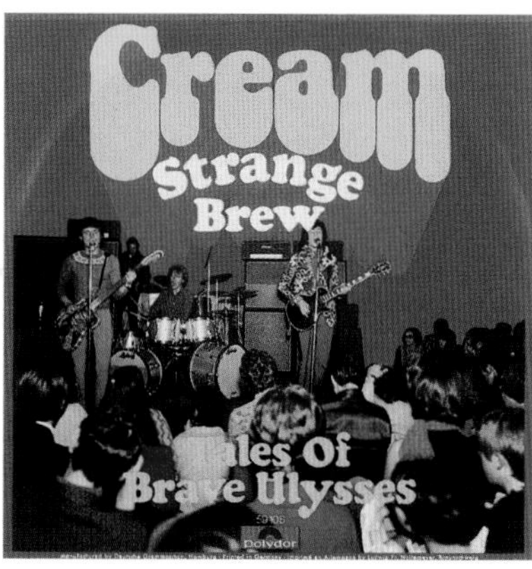

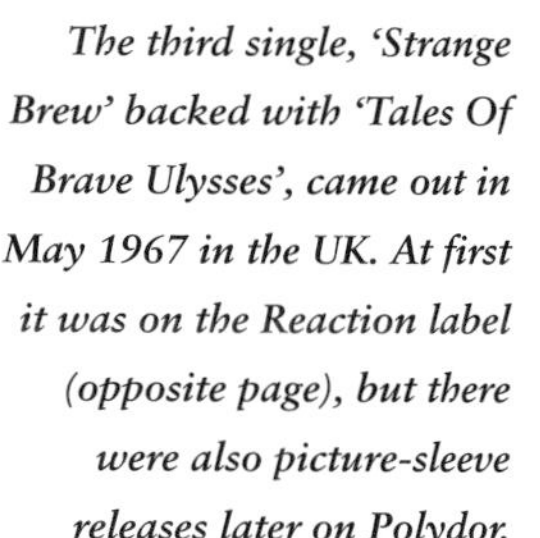
The third single, 'Strange Brew' backed with 'Tales Of Brave Ulysses', came out in May 1967 in the UK. At first it was on the Reaction label (opposite page), but there were also picture-sleeve releases later on Polydor.

phrases they used. They also said, 'You're not the lead singer. Eric is going to be the lead singer and you guys are just the backing group.' So they got Felix to go home, take the backing track of 'Lawdy Mama', and graft on this song which became 'Strange Brew' with Eric singing lead. It really annoyed me because the bassline is not from that tune. There is a bass note at the beginning which goes up to the sub-dominant and shouldn't: 'Lawdy Mama' does; 'Strange Brew' doesn't."

Cream had played 'Lawdy Mama' live for some time. Clapton seems to have modelled the band's arrangement quite closely on a 1960s version recorded by bluesman Junior Wells (and featuring guitarist Buddy Guy), although the song itself is considerably older. Cream recorded this, their "normal" version of 'Lawdy Mama', at the Atlantic sessions, though it remained unreleased until the *Those Were The Days* set.

But the version of 'Lawdy Mama' on to which Pappalardi grafted the new lyrics and tune to create 'Strange Brew' was an entirely new arrangement that Cream seem to have concocted while at Atlantic. The pre-'Brew' recording would turn up later as a US 45's b-side and as the only studio track on 1970's *Live Cream* LP. This new and different version was strongly influenced by blues guitarist Albert King in its style and feel, and the overall bass/guitar/drums arrangement effectively provided the basis for 'Strange Brew', with a new tune by Pappalardi, new lyrics by his wife, Gail Collins, and some extra guitar overdubs.

"Fortunately for me," says Bruce, "and unfortunately for their plans, Eric couldn't handle being the lead singer at a gig, and he couldn't write, so they had to use my *terrible* material, such as 'White Room', later, and 'Sunshine Of Your Love'. So it really was quite a struggle for me to get the songs accepted. Then the attitude changed very quickly. Since then 'Sunshine' has had over a million plays on the radio and it became the biggest-selling single that Atlantic had ever had up to that time."

It seems odd that Ertegun should misunderstand the way the group was structured and miss the point of a creative three-piece – which was only called Cream because each member had equal musical status. It turned out he had only seen Clapton with John Mayall's Bluesbreakers, during a previous visit to London, and had rightly perceived him then as a star in the making. He was expecting a similar band to the Bluesbreakers, in which Clapton would be the lead singer and guitarist. One day Clapton would achieve that role with his own groups. But for the moment he was part of a unique group that required special treatment. Or at least a bit of understanding.

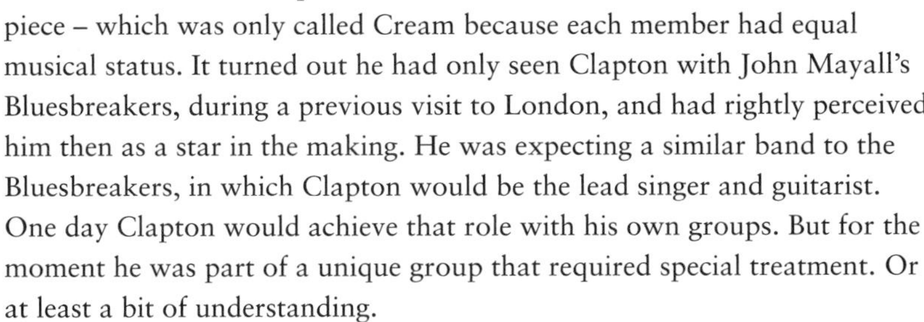

Disraeli Gears was released in November 1967 complete with hippie-era Day-Glo fluorescent psychedelic cover. The sleeve was a montage designed by Clapton's flatmate, the Australian artist Martin Sharp, who worked for *Oz* magazine. Pictures of the band were interspersed with cut-up images taken from magazines. The bizarre title came from a conversation that Baker had with roadie Mick Turner about racing bicycles. Turner mentioned "Disraeli gears" when he actually meant "Derailleur gears". It gave Baker a laugh and was considered a much better title for the album than plain *Cream.*

The powerful opening cut, 'Strange Brew', was sung in haunting fashion by Clapton. It was co-written by him along with Felix Pappalardi and his wife Gail Collins. (Pappalardi was shot dead in 1983 by Collins after an argument.) 'Sunshine Of Your Love' was powered by Baker's distinctive on-beat tom tom rhythm, sounding like so many American Indian war drums, along with those grinding guitar and bass riffs. It was easily the most popular track on the album. But the lesser-known songs made an impact too, notably Pappalardi's 'World Of Pain', a piece inspired by a tree in his garden, apparently a rare sight in Greenwich Village.

'Tales Of Brave Ulysses' was a Clapton tune with lyrics written by Martin Sharp, inspired by a holiday visit to Spain and the Balearic island of Formentera, where legend has it the sirens sang to Ulysses (the Roman name for Odysseus, of Homer's epic poem). 'SWLABR' was properly titled 'She Walks Like A Bearded Rainbow', a rather surreal Bruce-Brown collaboration. Clapton played at his funky best on 'Outside Woman Blues' and 'Take It Back'. The former piece was the only straightforward blues track on *Disraeli Gears*, in strong contrast to the band's first album. It was written by an obscure blues artist, Blind Joe Reynolds, and had been recorded by him in the late 1920s. 'Take It Back', on the other hand, was a Bruce-Brown protest at the Vietnam war.

"I played White Room to them. I think 'psychedelic hogwash' was one of the phrases they used."

Pete Brown could only hear about these developments from afar. He was stuck back in London with no chance of coming over to New York to hear how his lyrics were being used in the studio. "I was quite pissed off about that," he says. "Stigwood didn't like me very much. I think he regarded me as a necessary evil. Nevertheless, I thought the second album was a giant leap forward. Felix was certainly the right producer for Cream. He made them a success for the American public. The stuff he produced was faultless and still sounds great, because he knew what to do with them and, apart from being a superb producer, he was an excellent musician. Nobody knew how to produce Cream until Felix came along."

Disraeli Gears came rather late in the psychedelic era. The Beatles' *Sgt Pepper's Lonely Hearts Club Band* and Pink Floyd's *The Piper At The Gates Of Dawn* had been released during the "summer of love" in 1967. When Cream came back from America they found the hippie community and music business astonished by the Jimi Hendrix Experience and their albums *Are You Experienced?* and *Axis: Bold As Love*. An LP that featured Clapton and Baker singing a cockney pub song was not seen as a mind-expanding experience. Blues fans were also disappointed that the band seemed more wrapped up in three-minute songs than the kind of freewheeling improvisation they had come to expect. It was a shock to Cream that the Hendrix trio was threatening to outdo them.

Nevertheless *Disraeli Gears*, while not quite a classic, had sufficient power and professionalism to establish Cream as a major band in America. And it certainly yielded some great hit songs and diverse material. Given the way a modern pop album is produced under laboratory conditions with vast sums spent on marketing and hairstyling – let alone the production – this 1967 set of rapidly-conceived and highly-original performances remains a remarkable achievement.

Cream returned to England from New York and the Murray The K shows to play more concerts, and they found themselves often revisiting the small venues they had known before their hits. They might even have played at the historic hippie event, the Monterey Festival in San Francisco, held in June 1967 and which featured Janis Joplin, Jimi Hendrix and others. The group didn't know it at the time, but their manager apparently turned down an invitation for them to appear. Instead, they were booked to share bills with bands like Geno Washington's Ram Jam Band, and instead of jamming with the hippies, they were bussed into Barbeque '67, at the Tulip Bulb Auction Hall,in Spalding, Lincolnshire.

"Although the band was tremendously successful," says Bruce, "even Eric has said it was successful despite Stigwood, not because of him. Stigwood might take the credit, but he made terrible decisions. I expect we were asked to play all kinds of other big events that we never got to hear about, and we should have been at them. Instead, we were doing some terrible little gig somewhere. I think he was very unimaginative."

"Nobody knew how to produce Cream until Felix Pappalardi came along."

Bruce says that while it's generally reported that Atlantic Records didn't want to know about Cream, some even repeat a story about how Ahmet Ertegun saw "this beautiful young man playing the guitar" and just wanted to sign him. "It was all about Eric," says Bruce. "But it wasn't like that. Cream was very much Ginger's idea and it was a three-piece band, with three equal members. Eric might have had more of a reputation and was better looking than us, but it certainly wasn't his band. But that is how it's perceived. There was a terrible thing on TV in America in the late 1990s, I was watching this programme called *60 Minutes* with a special on Eric, and it said there was this band called Cream, which had Eric Clapton, Ginger Baker and Jeff Beck! It's a shame how the band's history is being rewritten... and wrongly."

Bruce stresses that the band was a success, but that things appeared to happen by accident. "The way we were handled was kind of unhip," he says, "old-fashioned and unimaginative. There was no marketing at all, and apparently we only got a record deal with Atlantic as a kind of rider on the Bee Gees contract. The incredible success was really because of the times and the strength of the band. Our reputation only began to grow after we played at The Fillmore in San Francisco in 1967."

Bruce reiterates that there was no master plan for Cream. He says that the people in control were shortsighted: they should have seen the potential

of the band. "The Beatles all became individuals," he points out. "It wasn't just Paul McCartney and John Lennon with a backing band. Cream was the same in that it contained strong personalities with different interests. There was Ginger with his African drumming, me with my classical side, and Eric's future role as a singer/songwriter, as well as being one of the world's greatest guitarists. If they had been bright enough, they could have seen the potential in developing a great band. Instead they tried to squeeze as much out of it as quickly as possible. They wanted to keep us out on the road earning bucks."

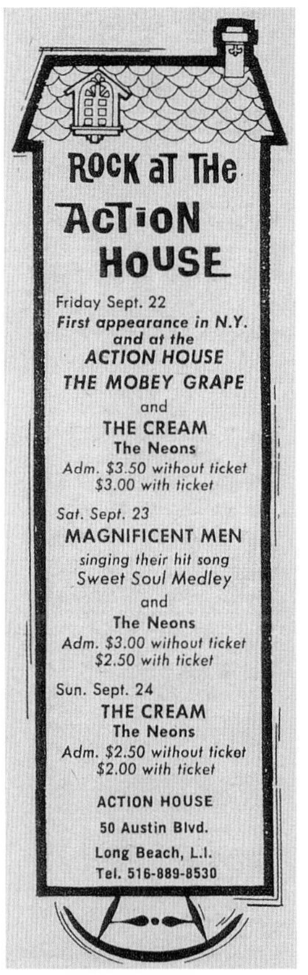

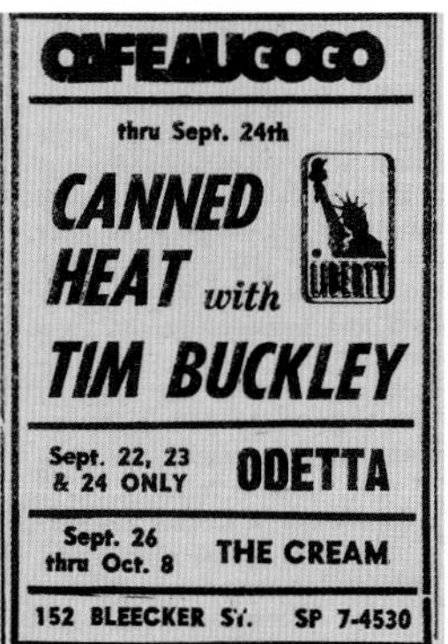

The band returned to America for their first full tour in summer 1967. The first engagement was eleven dates at the Fillmore Auditorium in San Francisco, between August 22nd and September 2nd. During September and October they appeared in a number of other cities and venues, including the Whisky A Go Go in Los Angeles, the Psychedelic Supermarket in Boston, and The Action House on Long Island, New York, with their last dates for this tour in Detroit in mid October. Clapton was relieved that during their first visit to New York both Bruce and Baker had stayed relatively cool. He remarked later: "Ginger had never been to a foreign country before where they spoke English and they could understand him, so he kept very quiet, placid and kind."

Cream had been welcomed like heroes when they arrived in California in the summer of 1967. The Bay Area of San Francisco was home to the hippies, who had established a virtual commune in the Haight Ashbury district. It was here that the alternative culture first took hold, sweeping away old, established values, as students and drop-outs, musicians and artists called for greater freedom and an end to war and materialism. Love and peace was the cry from a generation that was openly receptive to new and revolutionary ideas.

It was in this heady atmosphere that rock music flourished – and one of the focal points of the Bay Area's music scene was Bill Graham's Fillmore Auditorium. A former dancehall, the venue could accommodate around 2,000 people. There was a permanent lightshow and an excellent sound system. It cost concert-goers around $3 to see the best of the hippest local bands, including Jefferson Airplane, Country Joe & The Fish, Big Brother & The Holding Company, and The Byrds. Graham was also keen to present the new wave of British bands, and Cream were among the most popular of all the visitors. Cream made an impression, not only on the fans but on Bay Area bands, some of which began to veer away from acoustic sounds and folk-rock toward a heavier style.

Ads from '67 and Cream's first US tour (opposite): the Fillmore in San Francisco, plus New York's Cafe Au Go Go and Action House.

With wildly responsive audiences and the freedom to play full sets of their own choosing, Baker, Bruce and Clapton could solo and improvise at length. As the band began to stretch out on numbers like 'Spoonful', 'NSU' and 'I'm So Glad', the audience would shout: "Just play!" Cream responded by increasing their regular 45-minute set. If there was less emphasis on shorter songs and the more experimental numbers that graced *Disraeli Gears* it didn't seem to matter. The band knew that the fans were loving everything they played, even if many of them were so stoned they just let the music wash over them in a wave of psychedelia.

At first the band welcomed the adulation. Jack Bruce recalls that they were met in San Francisco by a posse of Hells Angels, who "adopted" the band and gave them a motorcycle escort into town. But quite early in their career Cream and even their helpers began to wonder about the unquestioning nature of the fans' reactions.

Ben Palmer says that he doubts the audience even understood most of what was going on. "After a 20-minute drum solo," the roadie says, "I bet very few of them knew when the band was going to come in again. If you ever encountered the hippies of San Francisco, you'd realise they were non-judgemental. So, everything was good. They had undertaken to accept life in a blissful state of mind – and that's what they did. Throughout the 1960s I was amazed at the lack of analytical criticism that anybody brought to bear on anything at all. If you started to have reservations about how good somebody or some endeavour might be, it would stop a conversation. Evaluation of what was being listened to was almost entirely absent at that time. It was regarded as heresy. But I think at The Fillmore the band

Poster (above) from Detroit's Grande Ballroom promoting the three gigs in October 1967 that closed Cream's first full American tour.

It's Saturday night, November 18th 1967, and as part of an eight-day stint in Scandinavia Cream open their set at the Idrottshuset at Örebro, Sweden.

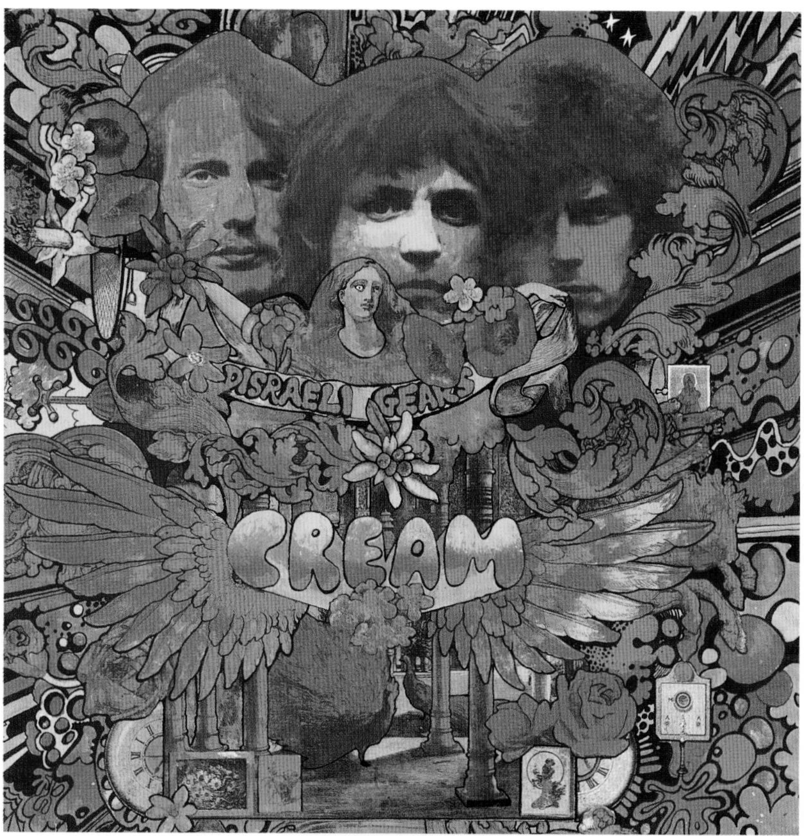

Cream's classic second album, Disraeli Gears, came out in November 1967 in a psychedelic sleeve designed by Martin Sharp. The UK edition (front, above, and rear, centre) was on Reaction, while the US version (front, opposite, and rear below) was on Atco. Sharp's artwork was adapted for the 1997 CD-set Those Were The Days; a rare promo-only selected edition is pictured here.

realised its full potential – and when you consider who they were and how they played, that was a very big potential indeed."

Clapton too began to have reservations about the hippies. "The 'love philosophy' is a fad in many ways," he observed at the time. "It involves a new way of dressing and thousands of people are drawn to that. I don't see much harm in this as long as the people don't prostitute it." In California,

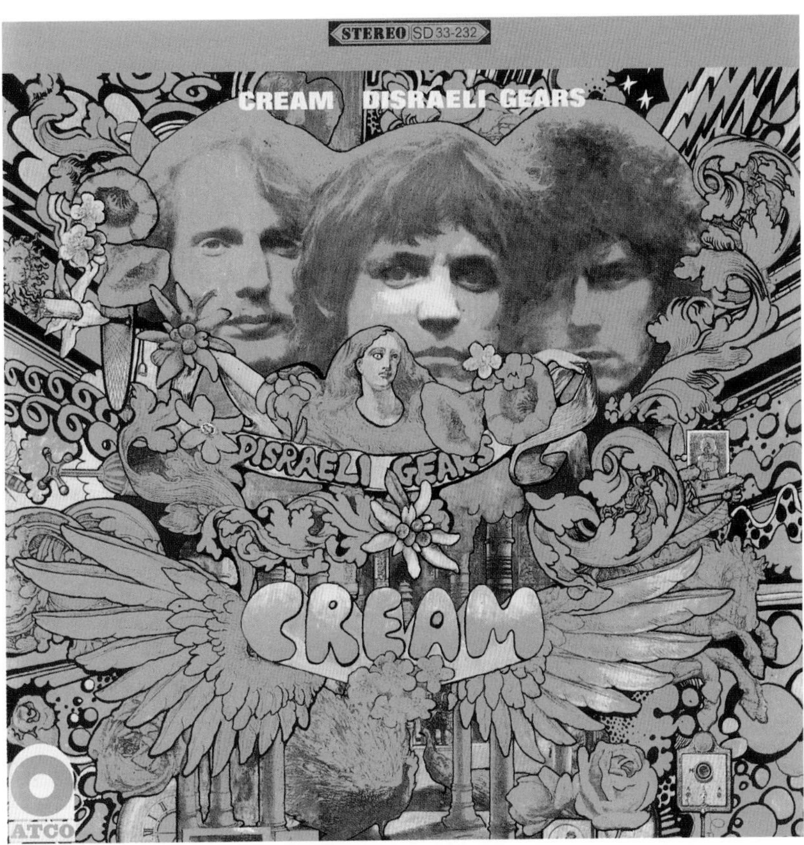

tempers began to flare again as the pressure of life on the road began to build up. "Eric kept away from all the flash points and stayed in his hotel room a great deal," recalls Ben Palmer. "He has quite a strong self-protective streak and he realised that if he ever got involved in one side of an argument, there would never be an end to it. So, wisely, he didn't participate in any of the difficult business. He kept his head below the parapet, and anyway was not interested in it. You couldn't go to him and say, 'I've just had this big set-to with Jack and Ginger.' He wouldn't listen. He'd just say, 'Well, it's nothing to do with me.' It was the sensible thing to do, and nobody picked on him. He was completely safe," says Palmer. "It was only people who didn't know the band who would get involved."

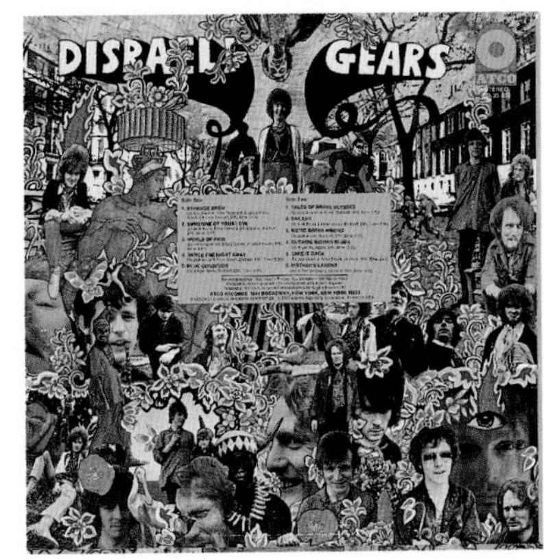

Promoter Bill Graham was one of those who unwisely decided to step into the middle of a Cream row. It took place backstage at his Fillmore Auditorium venue in San Francisco, the home of hippie rock. "He prided himself on being able to play a part in anything anyone was doing, anywhere in the world," says Palmer, with a touch of irony. "He would enter the fray and come out worst. He would in fact make the whole thing worse. The thing to do was to ride it all out. When we first went to the Fillmore there was something wrong with the running order and the band didn't want to go on until it was sorted out. My practice was to get them all in the dressing room, sit them down, get someone to keep them in there, and go off and sort out the problem. I went to Bill and said, 'I'm not putting the band on until things are right.'"

November 1967 British press ad for the release of Disraeli Gears.

On hearing that there was trouble with Cream, the mercurial American promoter went straight to the British band's dressing room and started an argument with Baker and Bruce. Palmer agrees he was perfectly entitled to do this, as he was paying the money. "He didn't *have* to deal with me. But it would have been better if he had. Now it turned into a three-sided row – and he ended up having to buy them antique gold watches to put it right. He never forgot it. When we had lunch at The Savoy in London to celebrate Eric's 25 years in showbiz, Bill Graham was there and he made a speech. He referred to that incident, and it was clearly still with him all those years later. Once you had got into a row with those two, you certainly didn't forget it."

Bruce has fond memories of Cream's conquest of America, but he could see the pitfalls. "There were great gigs all down the line. The Fillmore was a big event, but then every gig was a big event, really, especially during the first year-and-a-half. Then it started getting silly. We'd walk on stage to a standing ovation, before we'd even played a note. And that wasn't fantastic, because we'd be doing gigs we weren't happy with, and yet we'd get this enormous wave of adulation. We'd think, 'Come on, that wasn't the best stuff.' It got silly – and it got unbelievably loud. I think it was in Texas when Eric turned round to me and said, 'I've had enough of this.' So I said, 'Tell you what, so have I.'"

Cream played New York's Village Theater, at Second Avenue and Sixth Street. The venue would be turned into the Fillmore East in March 1968, again run by Bill Graham. But in September 1967 it was the site for

Cream's first appearance in Manhattan since the Murray The K shows. This time they could play what they wanted, and they went down very well. But even at this stage in their career the group's out-of-town performances were not always a guaranteed success. "We played to very few people at the Psychedelic Supermarket in Boston," Baker recalls of another September gig. And when they played at The Action House at Long Beach on Long Island on the 22nd and 24th only around 50 people turned out to see them. The Café Au Go Go on Bleecker Street, in Greenwich Village, was a very small venue where the patrons were deafened by the band's volume in a confined space. Nevertheless Cream received some very positive reviews for these dates and the New York fans were very receptive.

After their New York gigs, Cream finished this first full US tour with three nights at the Grande Ballroom in Detroit, from October 13th to the 15th. Although Detroit was the home of Motown and soul music, the city also had a hardcore blues following, and bands like the MC5 were very popular. As a result Cream – the British blues band – was very successful with the Detroit fans.

> "We'd walk on stage to a standing ovation – before we'd even played a note."

One reviewer said: "The shows were magnificently performed and rapturously received." Many critics felt that the breakthrough in Detroit was even more significant than the group's Fillmore triumph, because it indicated that the group could appeal to a majority of blue-collar workers and not just the West Coast hippies. It certainly encouraged the band to want to tour America again, as quickly as possible.

When the band returned to Britain, after a few dates in Ireland and some in Scotland they played at the Saville Theatre in London, on October 29th, as part of a string of exciting Sunday-night shows there that included Pink Floyd, Jimi Hendrix and The Who. After a short tour of Scandinavia in November, Cream rounded out 1967's punultimate month with more one-nighters in the UK, including a booking for one of their last club gigs, at The Marquee in London, on November 28th.

Disraeli Gears had finally been released in November and was given excellent reviews, notably in *Melody Maker* which proclaimed it as "a quality heavy package of incredible Cream super power". Another review, in the American *Cheetah* magazine, suggested that the band "lacked rhythmic drive, their rhythms are accurate and square". This seemed odd, given that this was the most jazz-influenced and creative rhythm section in rock. Despite such criticism, the album shot to number 5 in the UK and peaked at number 4 in the US charts.

CHAPTER 6

WE'RE GOING WRONG

Some fans and critics were disappointed at the lack of heavy lead-guitar playing on *Disraeli Gears*, but matters were being addressed back in the studio where work had been going on to produce a batch of new recordings. The result would be one half of the impressive double-LP set *Wheels Of Fire*. Produced by Felix Pappalardi "by arrangement with Robert Stigwood", it featured two sides of material from the studio. Work had begun at IBC in London in July and August 1967, and then later at Atlantic in New York during September, October and December 1967. More sessions took place at Atlantic in February and then June 1968.

Highlights were Bruce-Brown's 'White Room' and 'Politician', as well as keen versions of Howlin' Wolf's 'Sitting On Top Of The World' and Albert King's 'Born Under A Bad Sign'. Further studio tracks included some interesting songs written by Baker in collaboration with jazz pianist and composer Mike Taylor – 'Passing The Time', 'Pressed Rat And Warthog' and 'Those Were The Days' – together with two more Bruce-Brown songs, 'As You Said' and 'Deserted Cities Of The Heart'.

Baker and Clapton on-stage at Hunter College, New York, in March 1968 during the band's marathon second American tour.

The two sides of the second LP of *Wheels Of Fire* featured live performances from San Francisco. Cream had returned to North America for their second major tour, beginning on February 23rd 1968 at the Civic Auditorium in Santa Monica, California. They moved on to Santa Barbara and San Fernando, and then on the 29th started a series of dates at the Winterland in San Francisco, playing 16 shows in total there, as well as dates at the Fillmore Auditorium. From concerts at those two venues between March 7th and March 10th came epic live recordings of 'Crossroads', 'Spoonful', 'Traintime' and 'Toad' which appeared on *Wheels Of Fire* (as well as other pieces that turned up later on *Live Cream* and *Live Cream Volume II*). Although the *Wheels* sleeve proclaimed that its four live tracks were recorded "live at the Fillmore" in fact only 'Toad' was from there, with the rest recorded at Winterland. The

The Cream at Carnival 1968

Reactions by Pete Flowers. Photos by Simon Newton.

Report of an appearance by Cream at University College in London in February 1968 (left), just weeks before the long American tour began.

album was released in August 1968 in a distinctive silvery psychedelic cover, again designed by Martin Sharp. It was an immediate hit, topping the US chart and consolidating the band's success. The live tracks gave Cream fans much intensive jamming to absorb, but these extended versions also revealed some inherent weaknesses that critics were quick to exploit. Taken out of the context of a complete show with all its atmosphere and tension, a 20-minute drum solo or long harmonica solo might seem self-indulgent. And while Clapton's own playing and singing was exemplary – the solo on 'Crossroads' soon became a big talking point among guitarists – on 'Spoonful' he appeared to be entangled in layers of repetitive riffs at the expense of cohesive playing.

Although *Wheels Of Fire* is regarded by aficionados as one of the highspots of Cream's recording career, Jack Bruce says now that the intention was different at the time. "It was never done as a live album," he says. "We just did some gigs at the Fillmore and at Winterland which got recorded." The Winterland was an ice-rink converted to a concert hall simply by covering the ice with sheets of plywood. Bill Graham had begun using this as his main venue, because it could hold over 5,000 people, compared to a capacity of some 2,000 at the Fillmore Auditorium.

'Sunshine Of Your Love' came out in February '68 in the US, on Atco, and in the UK on Polydor in September.

"Those were primitive days for live recording," Bruce says. "Some of that stuff is very good, and I'm not knocking it. I used to do the harmonica soloing on 'Traintime' for minutes on end. I had a lot of puff in those days. When I did 'Traintime' and 'Rollin' And Tumblin'' I used to get *so* high, from the circular-breathing technique. I would just leave the planet – without any drugs. It

Intense concentration prevails as Cream work hard at Atlantic studios in 1968 during sessions that would produce the "studio half" of Wheels Of Fire.

U.S.A. 60 cents

music
FEBRUARY 1968
maker

CREAM AT FILLMORE/
MONKEE MIKE MEETS
JAZZ/BALDRY/DENNY
ZEITLIN/DRUM SPECIAL/
THREE SHILLINGS

was an amazing feeling, singing and playing the harmonica. I used to get well out of it. I didn't even have a pint. Ginger used to play great brushes behind me on that piece. Since those days I've played with some great drummers – like Tony Williams, Billy Cobham, and Simon Phillips – but going back to Ginger, you realise just how good he is. He is a unique player, and other drummers have a lot of respect for him. He's not just a good rock'n'roll player, he's somewhere else. He has a feel and a melodic way of playing."

When Baker switched from sticks to brushes on 'Traintime' he showed how quietly the group could play when necessary. But problems would often surface once the amplifiers were turned up. "It was the volume that really got to me in Cream," the drummer recalls. "When the band started, it was really cool. But then all of a sudden they found these Marshall amps and speaker cabinets. First they went to a double stack, and then they had four each. I can remember one gig where Eric had about eight of them.

"I couldn't hear myself play it was all so loud. The drums then had to be miked up to compete. I would get back to the hotel after a gig and my ears would be ringing. My hearing is damaged now, from that period. The last year of the band the volume got so awfully loud that it just ruined it for me. As for monitors, what would have been the point? There were speakers everywhere. It was when the whole sound thing went crazy. To this day I can't handle that volume. It hurts my ears, it's physically painful."

Poster for the famous Fillmore and Winterland concerts in March 1968 that provided the "live half" of the Wheels Of Fire album.

Baker claims that during one show it got so loud that both he and Clapton stopped playing for two choruses – and Bruce carried on, regardless, because he could not actually hear that the other two weren't playing. In common with several musicians who worked during the first age of heavily amplified rock, Bruce has suffered with tinnitus and hearing damage since 1977. "It's something that I've learned to control, so it doesn't get worse," he says. "I have special ear plugs that I wear on-stage. There is no cure, but one of the treatments is to ignore it. It sounds very obvious, but you can try. Otherwise it drives you bananas. At least you don't need any wake-up calls in the morning," laughs Bruce. "I've learned to live with it, although there are times when it becomes unbearable. It's like the ringing in your ears you normally get after a gig – except it doesn't go away."

Bruce panicked when it first happened. He went to many doctors, one of whom advised him that the only course of action was to give up music. In fact he did stop playing for a while because he thought he was going to go completely deaf. He has since managed to control the tinnitus and, mercifully, it hasn't got any worse. "I'm very careful, and never play amplified music without ear plugs," he explains.

"I don't play as loudly as I used to, either. It's not necessary these days because the equipment is so much better. In the Cream days the excitement came from the amps on stage, but nowadays you can play as quietly as you like and it will still be loud out front. I go to watch very few live gigs nowadays because of my ears."

Despite the increasing volume level at the gigs, studio recording remained a productive experience for Cream. Baker is very happy with the recordings that the band made, particularly *Disraeli Gears* and *Wheels Of Fire*. "We had some great people with us in the studio, like Tom Dowd and Felix Pappalardi," says Baker. "Their contribution was enormous and set us on a whole new plane. They were using recording techniques that we had not thought of before, although we were still only on 8-track recorders. The drums had two tracks of their own, while Eric and Jack were on the other six. Then we did overdubs and started using the studio. Despite that, a lot of the drumming was lost. That was the problem with 8-track. The drum mix was done there and then, and that was it. With only eight tracks, you couldn't have the drums on several tracks."

When Tom Dowd with engineer Bill Halverson recorded Cream live they used two 8-track recorders in a mobile studio. To capture the power of the band's extended numbers like 'Stepping Out' they used close-miking on the speaker stacks, and overhead miking on the drums. Dowd had found it hard enough to record Cream's cranked-up Marshall speakers in the studio; recording them in concert at full volume presented more challenges, especially as the sound of the guitar and bass had a tendency to "leak" into other microphones. Clapton had to alter his guitar tone and settings in order to accommodate the engineers and this sometimes resulted in a thin sound.

April 1968, and with Cream unexpectedly back in Britain to take a week's "holiday" from their US tour, Melody Maker is already seeking answers from their manager on rumours of a break-up.

Cream back in Britain for holiday

CLAPTON

THE Cream flew back to London unexpectedly last week for a 10-day holiday.

Manager Robert Stigwood cancelled dates on their US tour so that Jack Bruce, Eric Clapton and Ginger Baker could have a few days at home. "The schedule I arranged was too intensive. I had to cancel 10 days dates and they will be re-playing these at the end of the tour in June," he told MM.

Rumours at the weekend that the Cream was to break up were categorically denied by Stigwood "Nothing could be further from the truth," he said.

A moustachioed Eric Clapton, still brandishing his psychedelic Gibson, at Cream's Hunter College gig in New York, March 1968.

The new studio recordings showed once again how well the Jack Bruce-Pete Brown writing partnership worked. When Clapton and Baker tried their hand at composition it didn't seem to work. In May 1968 'Anyone For Tennis', written by Eric Clapton and artist Martin Sharp, was released as Cream's follow-up single to 'Sunshine Of Your Love'. It was charming, but seemed a bizarre choice for Cream. Clapton admitted later: "I was a stumbling songwriter. I really didn't have a knowledge of theory or how to go about it. To me, writing a song was a miracle. At that stage I was good for about a song a year."

A performance of 'Anyone For Tennis' was filmed in colour that May for the American TV programme *The Summer Brothers Smother Show*. A

ACME

MAY 11, 1968, THIRTY-FIVE CENTS

ROLLING STONE

The Rolling Stone Interview: Eric Clapton

CREAM

BY JON LANDAU

I recently had an opportunity to see the Cream do an hour and a half concert; after what I had found to be a disappointing second album, it was a refreshing experience and for the most part an entertaining one. Yet I found myself leaving the concert with a sense of frustration not unlike the one I receive from listening to them on record.

With the opening wall of sound announcing their arrival, the group established their absolute virtuosity. I understand that they usually begin their sets with "Tales of Brave Universe," (as they did here) and it is certainly one of their best original compositions. By taking the pace of the song down just a bit from the recorded version, they gave their performance a more biting quality. They also extended the soloing at the end of the piece, but other than that their performance of this number corresponded more closely to the recorded version than anything else they did.

With "Sunshine of Your Love," their second number, they got into their extended improvisation work and gave the audience a chance to see what they are really into. After going through the entire song as they recorded it, they loosened the rhythm and then just played for well over ten minutes. And it was at this point that my own disappointment with the group began to stare me in the face.

Cream has been called a jazz group. They are not. They are a blues band and a rock band. Clapton is a master of the blues cliches of all of the post-World War II blues guitarists, particularly B. B. King and Albert King. And he didn't play a note that wasn't blues during the course of the concert. Ginger Baker's sources are more from the rock side of the picture and like Clapton he can run through the licks and cliches with his eyes blindfolded. And during the improvisation that was added on to "Sunshine" that is precisely what the two men did—run through their licks, albeit absolutely flawlessly.

Yet melodically, the improvisation was indistinguishable from the one that took place on their next number, "N.S.U.," and rhythmically they never did anything more advanced than a 4/4. By abandoning the chord progression of the song they started out with and improvising solely around the root chord, (which, by the way, is a far cry from having abandoned a chord structure, which Clapton says he is prone to do) they insure the incompatibility of the solo compared with the song. And ultimately what I wound up hearing was three virtuosos romping through their bag, occasionally building it into something, occasionally missing the mark altogether, but always in a one-dimensional style that made no use of dynamics, structure, or any of the other elements of rock besides drum licks and guitar riffs.

The specific reason why I discount Cream as jazz is this: In jazz the focus is always on improvisation. Improvisation means the creation of new musical ideas spontaneously. It does not mean stringing together pieces and phrases of already learned musical ideas. It means using these phrases as a basis for exploration and extension. A rock guitarist who improvises in the manner of a jazzman is Larry Coryell. Clapton's problem is that while he has vast creative potential, at this time he hasn't begun to fulfill it. He is a virtuoso at performing other people's ideas. In the particular solo of which I am speaking there were flashes of both Kings (as James Payne pointed out recently [*Correspondence*, ROLLING STONE, *Feb. 24*], *Disraeli Gears* is pervaded by the influence of Albert King and Chuck Berry).

One got the nagging feeling that the whole solo could be charted out to show the source of every phrase.

As strong as this reservation sounds I do not mean it as a condemnation of the group. I don't believe there are more than a handful of American bands that come within miles of Cream. Despite the derivative styling of Clapton, I think any comparison between Cream and people like the Doors or Big Brother would be in the nature of a joke. Compared to Cream, such groups don't even have the technical equipment, the understanding of their instruments, with which to play rock. Clapton himself seems to feel that way about white American groups in general and he has labelled San Francisco a "fashion" and stated that "black records" are still the best thing coming out of this country.

The shortcomings of "Sunshine" were again present when the group performed "N.S.U." This is another of their originals and I think it a terrible song, both melodically and lyrically. Yet I enjoyed it most when they were actually singing and playing the tune. Here they were recognizing the nature of rock and roll, the fact that it really is a heavily structured music—and they worked with that structure, using their understanding to draw the song out.

In general interpreting a song is the most difficult task confronting a rock instrumentalist, for in that situation he is in a position where he has to respond to a vocalist, a melody line, and a pattern not present in freer musical forms. Once the improvisation began, wholly unrelated to the context that the song had set for it, indistinguishable from the improvisation on the song that preceded it, the whole concept of interaction, the whole concept of a band was destroyed. It was every man for himself and back to the clichès. What was particularly disconcerting was that the entire improvisation centered again around a single chord, thereby severely limiting Clapton in terms of the range that he could explore.

"N.S.U." was followed by what Cream chose to do as their slow blues for the evening, "I'm Sitting On Top of the World." This tune is a white country blues originally done by Bill Monroe, and recorded a few years ago by Doc Watson. The Grateful Dead did a version of it on their album at a super hyped-up tempo. Cream did just the opposite and slowed it down to a slow crawl, with a heavy, heavy beat. They performed the number as a straight blues with little improvising and it was probably the shortest number they did all night.

Clapton's guitar playing, which was here given the full melodic range of a blues progression to play itself off against, (instead of the simple root chord improvisations he used on the previous numbers) was among the best blues playing I've ever heard, even though it was again largely derivative. Clapton was able to transcend his own limits because he was truly playing the song. It was only here that he was the mast licks, only here that he tra his limitations, by knowing are. (Bruce's singing, by which seems to me to be sig better live than it is on re at its best and helped to p ton admirably.)

Following these four nun group moved into a series featuring one member of t each time. For Clapton's f did "Stepping Out." Regrett version he recorded with M years ago was far superior I saw him do live. Bruce st the middle of this piece anc and Baker got into some ir teraction with each other. C the entire thing, which wer nearly twenty minutes, was long. Clapton was repeatin from earlier solos and even the end, earlier parts of Baker's drumming was n busy, as it often is, and sho again that it is often more for the virtuoso mentality to thing easy than to do someth

"Stepping Out" was follov extended harp show piece which was easily the low their performance. Bruce is not very good on that instrument and 15 minutes of him working out on it is simply ludicrous. It amazes me that such brilliant musicians can be oblivious to their own shortcomings.

They closed with Baker's show piece, "Toad." Baker is a solid drummer who gets a fantastic sound out of his drums. However, he is extremely repetitious, not particularly creative, and highly over-active. He took two or three extended solos during this particular concert and by the time he got to the end of "Toad" I found it all to be terribly boring.

Cream live, as on record, are clearly in a transitional stage. Having mastered the rudiments of their instruments they are rapidly approaching the point where they have to ask themselves where they want to go with it. Currently, their live style and their record style reveals both their talent and also their aimlessness. The whole is not equal to its parts. And the greatest pitfall that stands before them is that an over-accepting audience in the United States will lull them into a complacency in which they increase their virtuosity at the expense of their own involvement. It would not be difficult for a group of this caliber to start making it all sound like scales.

Yet the Cream, even now, are so much more than simple masters of their instruments. When they get over their virtuosity hang-up—which is what I think their kind of virtuosity is—we may really see something. At the moment they're just warming up.

The Cream as they looked in the beginning

Cream has been called a jazz group. They are not. They are a blues band and a rock band. Clapton is a master of the blues cliches of all of the post-World War II blues guitarists, particularly B. B. King and Albert King. And he didn't play a note that wasn't blues during the course of the concert. Ginger Baker's sources are more from the rock side of the picture and like Clapton he can run through the licks and cliches with his eyes blindfolded. And during the improvisation that was added on to "Sunshine" that is precisely what the two men did—run through their licks, albeit absolutely flawlessly.

The caustic Rolling Stone article that upset Clapton and, according to members of the band, was among the pressures that led to the break-up of Cream.

Jack Bruce lost in the blues, somewhere in America, summer 1968.

clip surfaced many years later in a Cream video documentary and revealed the band sheepishly swatting tennis rackets at a butterfly on a wire to the sound of canned laughter. A moustachioed Clapton sang, looking very unhappy, while Baker had a cigarette casually pasted to his lip. In retrospect the piece looks like a forerunner of MTV's celebrated *Unplugged* series, with Clapton playing an acoustic guitar and Baker on conga drums.

Given a more serious treatment, 'Anyone For Tennis' could have been salvaged and turned into something more meaningful. Such low-key performances could even have opened up a new direction that might have removed some of the pressure on Clapton. But at the time of the American TV show, it clearly wasn't working. Clapton confessed later that he felt

completely out of his depth and had reached the point where he no longer knew who or where he was. The only freedom he experienced was at the nightly gig, where he could lose himself in his playing – but even then he felt there was only about one night in four where the band really came together. Clapton had planned to write 'Anyone For Tennis' with Pete Brown, but it didn't happen. Brown wasn't around enough to form a working relationship with Clapton. "I never went on the road with the band, and that was a big mistake," Brown says. "I feel now that we could have got so much more done if Stigwood had had the foresight to send me out to the States with them. We could have written a lot more. Maybe I would have written more with Ginger and Eric? I once lived in a room in the same place as Eric. I was homeless and he got me a place when he was living in The Pheasantry in the King's Road in London with Martin Sharp. Eric was very nice and got me this tiny room.

By the time of this June 1968 New York gig (ad, left) Cream had played 62 dates of their ultra-long US tour – with just two more to go.

"Unfortunately, it was Martin's flat and he hated my guts," Brown continues. "I blew it, really, because I insisted on rehearsing in this room with John McLaughlin and a whole band. We weren't that loud, but we must have bugged the hell out of poor old Martin. He was an artist and a friend of Richard Neville: they did the *Oz* magazine together. It was a very salubrious pad behind The Pheasantry, a beautiful place. I eventually got thrown out of there. Eric and I were never close, but we got on well enough and we had lots of mutual friends."

"Tom Dowd and Felix Pappalardi were using recording techniques that we had never thought of before."

The second US tour stretched from February through to June 1968. That summer the band managed to fit in a return visit to the Atlantic studio in New York to complete the studio tracks for *Wheels Of Fire*. It was during this time that the first real cracks had begun to appear within the band. Their engineer at Atlantic, Tom Dowd, noted that when they listened to playbacks in the studio control room there was a danger that all three might starting fighting. Dowd has said: "There were times when I thought they were going to kill each other."

Baker tried to play down growing rumours of their demise. He reported to *Melody Maker*: "It's all right most of the time. They put up with me – and I tend to be bad tempered. I think it's a load of crap when people say we aren't working out as a group. We have had some plays that have been absolutely tremendous. We draw big crowds and they thoroughly enjoy themselves. We are three totally different personalities, and none of us thinks alike, but we get more and more together musically. It's a world-class band and I don't think there are three others musicians to touch us."

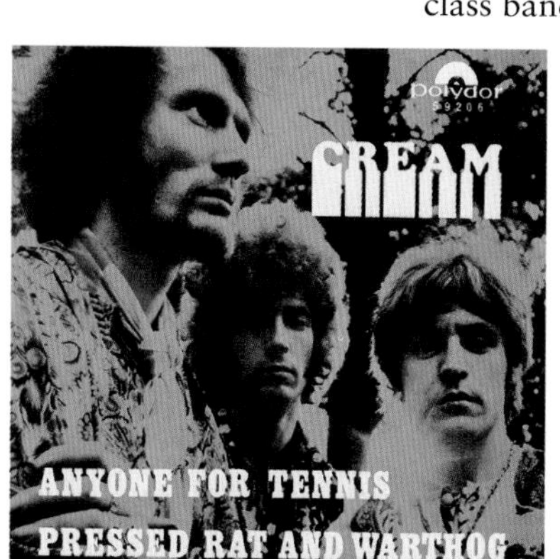

The pairing on 45 of 'Anyone For Tennis' and 'Pressed Rat And Warthog' first appeared in May 1968.

It was a tragic situation. Cream had now achieved all that they had dreamed of, and more. When Baker had hoped to launch "a pop group", even he could not have predicted just how successful they would become. With albums and singles dominating the charts and fans clamouring for more concerts, the demand for their services seemed likely to continue forever. And here they were now, on the verge of breaking up.

A combination of factors contributed to the band's demise. There was the simmering resentment over royalties and composer credits. There was the problem of increasing volume, and the kind of ego-clashing on stage that Clapton had hoped would not be a problem when he agreed to collaborate with the group. Yet Clapton was expected to act the guitar hero for the audience, delivering high-speed bluesy solos while competing against a barrage of bass and drums. It certainly resulted in some exciting music, but it rapidly became too much to cope with. While fans and even their most supportive critics among the music press loved hearing the band in action, they might only experience Cream in concert a few times a year. The musicians, however, had to turn it on night after night, following a day of travelling by plane or car, and no doubt many nights of revelry designed to obliterate the strain. It was understandable that Clapton would begin to find it a burden and an imposition. He had been able to walk away with relative ease from untenable situations with The Yardbirds or John Mayall, because there wasn't quite so much riding on his decisions.

Cream was now like a treadmill, made worse by some personal blows that undermined Clapton's confidence in the project. He began to doubt the very nature of the band's music, and yearned to play something quite different in a less pressured setting. Yet he was not alone in feeling that by the summer of 1968 Cream had reached its peak and should break up.

It was in the British press that Cream's break-up was made public, largely through my interviews and pieces in *Melody Maker*. The band had made an unscheduled return to Britain for a week in April 1968, taking a much-needed break from the apparently endless second US tour that had started in February. The Eric Clapton I met at his flat in London's King's Road was tired and frustrated. "We've been doing two-and-a-half months

Cream on film? 1968's Savage Seven – with its mad bikers speeding through Indian reservations for fun – featured Cream's wholly inappropriate Anyone for Tennis. For the 1968 Danish film Det Var En Lørdag Aften, Cream mimed in a Copenhagen hall (below) that was overrun by dope-smokers. Very cold, too.

of one-nighters," he told me, "and that is the hardest I have ever worked in my life. Financially and popularity-wise we're doing unbelievably well in America. But it's strange... I've changed a lot through living in America. I've tended to withdraw from making contact with people. I'm harder to get to know than I was a few years ago. I don't trust people so readily."

"We all know where it's at in the group. Each one of us has got to be free to move."

Officially, Clapton told me that the rumours of Cream breaking up were "all denied". He admitted that the group couldn't last forever, and for publication said: "It's not going to break up in the foreseeable future. If we hadn't had this holiday, we might have broken up anyway. We all know where it's at in the group. Each one of us has got to be free to move." In fact, off the record, Clapton told me then that the group were going to break up. But I had to wait for the official announcement. My front-page story headed "Cream Split Up" in *Melody Maker* of July 13th 1968 would be the first to break the news.

At that interview in April, Clapton's thoughts were on the blues, and he raved about jamming with BB King in New York. "In a pop group, the first things you suffer from are jealousy and terrible insecurity. So many groups are making it on the pop chart scene, you keep wondering if what you are playing is out of date. You get really hung up and try to write pop songs or create a pop image. I went through that, and it was a shame, because I was not being true to myself. I am and always will be a blues guitarist."

Clapton talked too about how much he was looking forward to playing on the same bill as Frank Zappa at a gig at Chicago's Coliseum on the band's return to the US tour. And he played me some of Bob Dylan and The Band's recordings – what we now know as *The Basement Tapes* – which had clearly made an impression. "I think this music will influence a lot of people," Clapton said. "Everybody I have played it to has flipped. The Band is releasing an album called *Music From Big Pink*, and since I heard all this stuff all my values have changed. I think it has probably influenced me."

Certainly this new music was more melodic and more laidback, far less frantic and competitive than Cream. Heading to the bus stop in the King's Road in a daze I realised that I had witnessed the conversion of Clapton. I had a glimpse of his musical future that would be revealed in Blind Faith, in Derek & The Dominos, and in the many versions of Clapton's own band over the years. He had found a faith that would last a lifetime, and discovered that the blues could be a friend and not an enemy.

Lyricist Pete Brown's view is that Cream got bored with the three-piece format. "They were thinking of having Graham Bond in the band," he

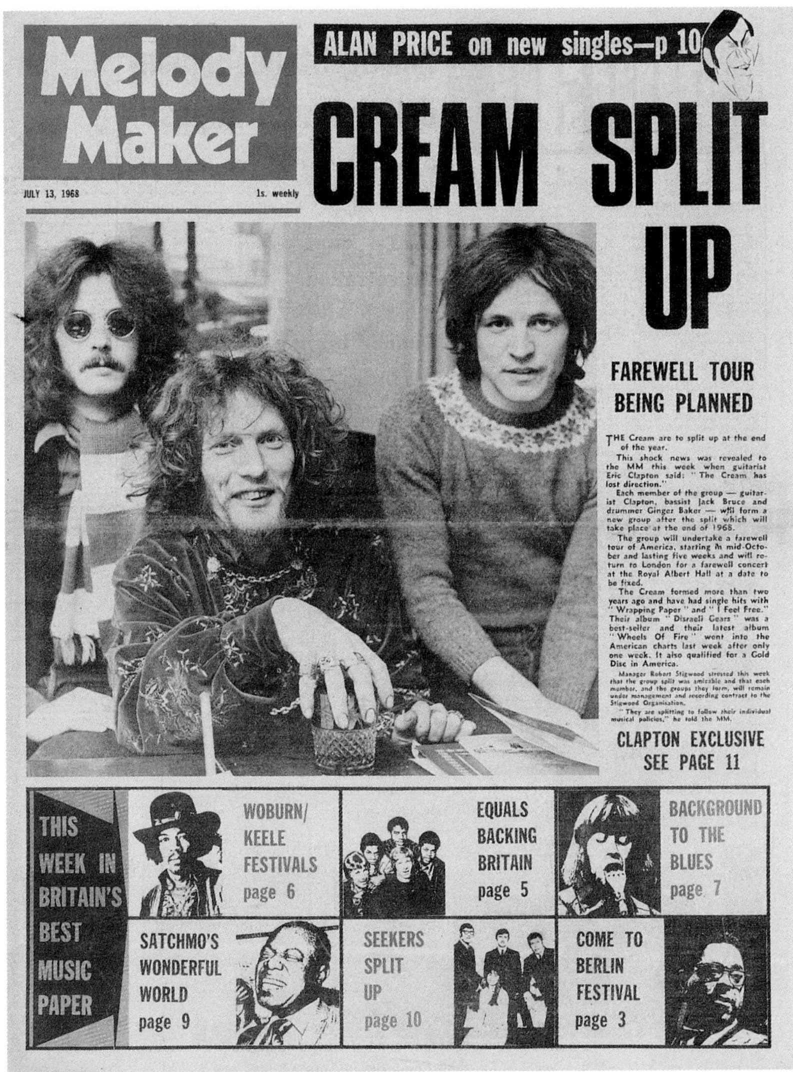

Melody Maker

ALAN PRICE on new singles—p 10

JULY 13, 1968 1s. weekly

CREAM SPLIT UP

FAREWELL TOUR BEING PLANNED

THE Cream are to split up at the end of the year.

This shock news was revealed to the MM this week when guitarist Eric Clapton said: "The Cream has lost direction."

Each member of the group — guitarist Clapton, bassist Jack Bruce and drummer Ginger Baker — will form a new group after the split which will take place at the end of 1968.

The group will undertake a farewell tour of America, starting in mid-October and lasting five weeks and will return to London for a farewell concert at the Royal Albert Hall at a date to be fixed.

The Cream formed more than two years ago and have had single hits with "Wrapping Paper" and "I Feel Free." Their album "Disraeli Gears" was a best-seller and their latest album "Wheels Of Fire" went into the American charts last week after only one week. It also qualified for a Gold Disc in America.

Manager Robert Stigwood stressed this week that the group split was amicable and that each member, and the groups they form, will remain under management and recording contract to the Stigwood Organisation.

"They are splitting to follow their individual musical policies," he told the MM.

CLAPTON EXCLUSIVE SEE PAGE 11

THIS WEEK IN BRITAIN'S BEST MUSIC PAPER

WOBURN/ KEELE FESTIVALS page 6

EQUALS BACKING BRITAIN page 5

BACKGROUND TO THE BLUES page 7

SATCHMO'S WONDERFUL WORLD page 9

SEEKERS SPLIT UP page 10

COME TO BERLIN FESTIVAL page 3

Front page news as Cream's break-up is made official.

remembers, "but Stigwood didn't like Graham, so they talked about having Stevie Winwood – who eventually surfaced in Blind Faith. Years later, The Police, which was sort of Cream-derived, had a big horn-section, three keyboard players, whatever they needed, and it sounded great. Cream could have done the same sort of thing."

Ben Palmer thought the break-up could have happened at any time during the preceding year. "The reason was the differences between the members," he says, "which had reached and remained at boiling point for quite a while. I don't think anybody will find any difficulty with that opinion, and there wasn't any other real reason for them to split. The band

Wheels Of Fire was a double-LP, its sleeve another psychedelic onslaught from Martin Sharp. Seen on this page are the front and inner designs of the US Atco version. In Britain too the album was available in double-LP form, but also as two individual single-LPs: In The Studio and (opposite) Live At The Fillmore.

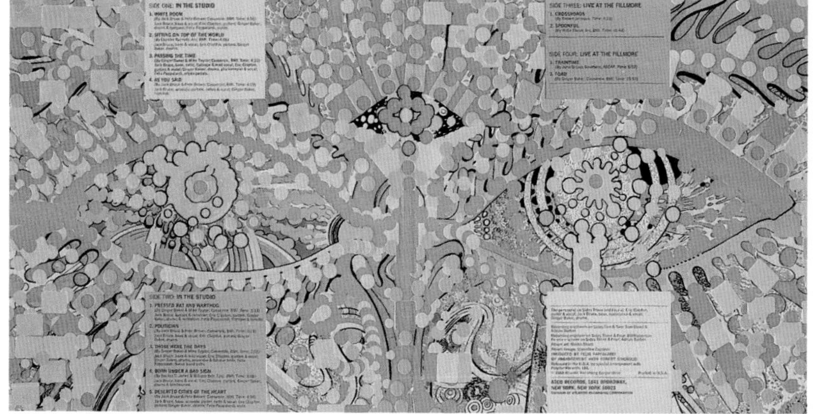

was certainly still viable and could have gone on to do other things, but not under those conditions. It happened when it happened. There wasn't any one incident that sparked it off. But it was mainly due to the problems between Ginger and Jack." Palmer is of the opinion that Cream were not

especially happy with their management. "Some years later we made a film about Eric Clapton's band with George Terry and Marcia Levy," he recalls. "It was a full-length documentary. We hired a German state train and went all around Europe with Muddy Waters. We just lived on the train, and didn't use hotels. We ran into Robert Stigwood in Paris and he came to the concert.

"The crew were doing some fly-on-the-wall filming, and I think Eric realised his chance had come, so he attacked Robert. He got him round the neck and said, 'Where's all the money! You gave it all to the Bee Gees!' He put on this great show. He was only acting, but there was a sting in the tail – and Robert didn't want that scene to appear in the film."

Added to the rows about money was Clapton's need for new musical experiences. "He didn't want to work in that kind of atmosphere any more," says Palmer. "By then, Eric sought the company of other people who he could get along with better and without all that tension, which led along very quickly to Blind Faith. We were thick with Stevie Winwood who was a much easier person to get along with than Jack or Ginger. Stevie's a

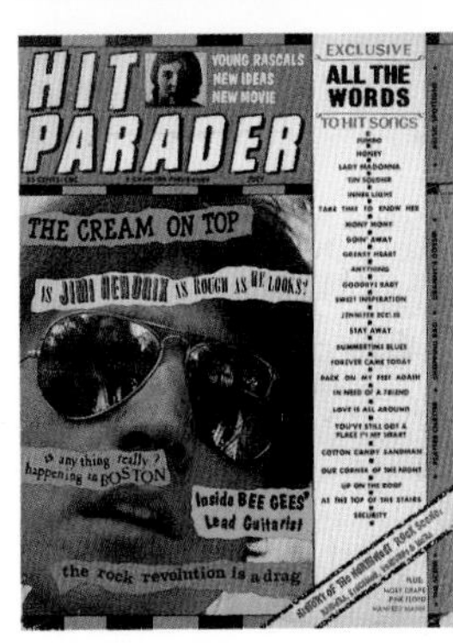

Cover star Jack Bruce. But does he know all the words?

loveable chap. Eric will put up with things for a long time until a way out presents itself. It's never of his own making. When it comes along, as it inevitably does, he's out. It happens overnight. The whole of his life before that point is just left behind.

"And so it was quite easy for him to drop Cream," says Palmer, "although funnily enough he ended up with Ginger again in Blind Faith. Ginger was very keen to get another band going as quickly as possible, and the potential of having Stevie and Eric in the same band together was amazing. They all had their own followings, and to have Stevie and Eric in one band together meant you had at least two audiences."

"We went from getting a couple of pounds for playing the Flamingo to getting massive royalties from platinum-selling albums."

Although Palmer could see the split building up, Jack Bruce thought it came quite suddenly. "There was a distinct moment when Cream went sour," says Bruce. "There was a very, very bad feature on the band that was featured in *Rolling Stone* magazine. It was the old story: when a band is underground it can do no wrong; and then when it crosses over and becomes a success, it's a case of let's knock it down. It was a very bad piece of writing and it kind of destroyed the band. Journalists don't realise the power they have.

"Some people can shrug those things off. Other people get very hurt by them. Eric certainly was hurt. I got used to being slagged off, but Eric was hurt by this piece. Funnily enough, later with BBM [Jack Bruce, Ginger Baker and Gary Moore] the same thing happened. The reason that band didn't go on was because of the very bad things people were saying about Gary, like, 'He's not Eric Clapton.' Well, clearly he isn't Eric Clapton. He's Gary Moore, and he's brilliant. But the critics wouldn't accept him in that line-up."

Bruce is adamant that Cream started to go wrong following the bad review in *Rolling Stone* in May 1968. "It just soured things for Eric. It was also around this time that The Band's first record came out, *Music From Big Pink*, and that was very influential. Eric wondered what he was doing in this power-rock band, when he could be doing something more subtle. He felt he was in the wrong musical situation – and he probably was. I certainly wasn't happy with the trio format any more. I was beginning to write things where I could use horns and could be slightly more adventurous. That was the beginning of the end of the band. The irony is that it came

Soundchecking in a giant arena during Cream's "farewell" US tour of 1968.

Out in October 1968, 'White Room' was the last US single issued before Cream's split.

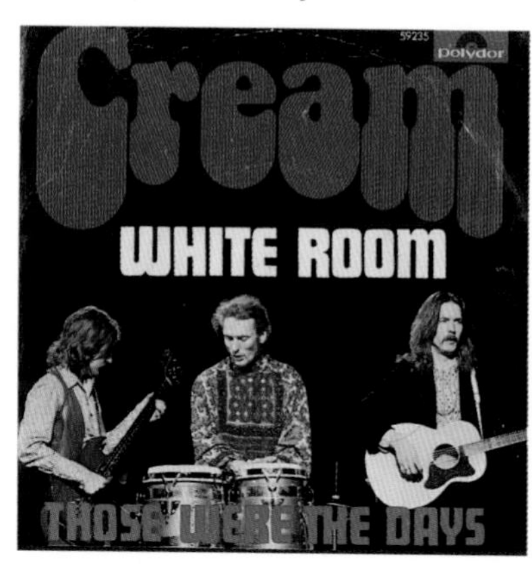

when we were being really successful. It was honest, at least." The *Rolling Stone* review (see pages 130/131) bitterly described Clapton as "a master of the blues clichés..." and belittled the young British musician, who seemed to be getting so much attention at the expense of local talent. If it was meant to hurt, it certainly succeeded. Clapton revealed latter that he actually fainted when he read the piece. It was based on an interview he'd done some months earlier when the group had first played at the Fillmore Auditorium. He was feeling pleased with himself at the time for out-playing groups like Big Brother And The Holding Company and pleased with Cream for holding their own against the Grateful Dead. The interview depicted him as showing off, and an accompanying review was scathing. *Rolling Stone* was not so widely read in Britain at the time, and few of the fans back home ever knew about this blow to the group's confidence. Yet they would have to suffer the consequences – and the band's premature demise.

While rumours about discontent continued to surface in the press, the band carried on with their touring commitments. They were earning up to $60,000 a night where once they had only been paid £45 (about $65) for a gig. The formerly starving musicians certainly enjoyed the influx of riches. "We had done very well," says Bruce, "and suddenly we could buy a couple of houses and a Ferrari. It was very hard to take in. We went from getting a couple of pounds for playing the Flamingo club to getting massive royalties from platinum-selling albums. It was a wonderful time." Despite their good fortune and their huge and growing popularity, the joint decision to break up was finally made in May 1968, over half-way through their marathon second US tour. The news was made public with an official statement from their management in July, when it was announced they would undertake a farewell tour of America.

There would be only two concerts in Britain, in November in London at the Royal Albert Hall, where the shows would be filmed by documentary-maker Tony Palmer for BBC TV's *Omnibus* arts programme, as well as for cinema release. Clapton tried to explain that, although the band had been a thrill, Cream had just run out of steam. "You can't be that inspired for that long," he said. There was an outpouring of criticism from disappointed British fans, but it was too late for the band to change their minds.

Jack Bruce told *Melody Maker* of some of his feelings about the break-up and his plans for the future in an interview published in August 1968. He said that Cream had got to the point where they weren't able to progress. "The only thing we could have done was to play to more and more people in more places," explained Bruce. "We formed expecting to have months and months grinding away, but it happened that we were

Madison Square Garden, Saturday November 2nd 1968. Cream have just two more US dates, and a little over three weeks, before their final split.

successful overnight. When we went to the States we found we could just wail and the audiences would dig it. It was a nice feeling.

"I'm getting into so many things that are new for me, like electronic music," Bruce said in the course of that 1968 interview. "I've written a thing for a fairly large jazz orchestra and voice. I'm not going to deliberately write or record things that are commercial, but things that I like. I've never made a decision in my life. Things just happen to me and I go along with them. That's the way it seems to be."

British fans had to wait until September 1968 to buy 'Sunshine Of Your Love' as a single – seven months after its release in the States.

Clapton has described the final days of Cream as a painful period which he tried to blot out. "I went under and blamed everybody."

Bruce now feels Cream should have played more countries, and more dates in Britain. "We should have played in Japan and Australia, but we only really did the States. It was quite a tragedy." For the farewell tour of October and November 1968, Cream played major US cities including Detroit, Chicago, Los Angeles, Dallas and Boston, and earned an average of $25,000 a night. On November 1st the group played at The Spectrum in Philadelphia, while on the following night came an especially notable show at Madison Square Garden, New York, in front of an audience of 22,000 Cream fans.

"*Wheels Of Fire* had been a huge hit," says Bruce, "and it was the first double-album to sell a million, so it earned a platinum disc. That was presented to us by Ahmet Ertegun and Robert Stigwood at Madison Square Garden. It was a very strange gig, on a revolving stage, which must have been horrible for the audience. They'd get a glimpse of the drums, guitar and bass and then they'd all go away again." Bruce puts the Garden show right there near the top of his list of bizarre gigs. It also includes a performance at Streatham Ice Rink in London – where the crowd was still skating – and at the Locarno in Glasgow, where the band stepped out from another revolving stage to what he describes with a smile as "a very small audience".

That Glasgow gig had happened on a trip to Scotland back in summer 1967, when they'd also visited Inverness. During an afternoon off, Bruce had suggested they all try to climb Ben Nevis, the highest mountain in

Freshly shaved, Clapton dreams of freedom during the last days of Cream.

Britain. They met a Scottish piper on their hike through the glens. Rarely had there been a more fascinating photo opportunity, as the piper engaged Baker, Bruce and Clapton – clad in their finest Chelsea attire – in animated conversation. They capped a pleasantly surreal afternoon by running down the slopes of the mountain while tripping on acid. Bruce remembers that it was very easy to start running, but impossible to stop. These were the fun times, when Cream were still enjoying being a band together and enjoying each other's company. Clapton too has described that same period as the peak time for the group. "That was the high point for me," he said some years later. "We were so together, and loved one another so much."

Meanwhile, back on the farewell tour of the US in 1968, Cream played

Cream name last home date

THE Cream, whose decision to split up at the end of the year shocked the music business and fans a few weeks ago, play their last British date together on November 26 at London's Royal Albert Hall.

There will be only one concert on this date and it will be the group's only appearance in Britain when they return from their farewell American tour.

GINGER

This tour, which will last five weeks and visit major American cities all over the United States, kicks off on October 4.

While in the States, they will record tracks for a last album in studios on the West Coast.

A new British single for the Cream is rush-released tomorrow (Friday). It is " Sunshine Of Your Love," which is already in the American Top Ten. Their latest album release — the double LP set " Wheels Of Fire — is named this month's Pop Album Of The Month in the Melody Maker's LP Supplement (see page 16).

"I was amazed that we played to such full houses at the Albert Hall. I didn't think anyone would remember us."

British fans greet Cream with wild enthusiasm as the band play for the last time, at London's Royal Albert Hall on November 26th 1968.

their final show in the US in Providence, Rhode Island, on November 4th. Then on November 26th the band played the two shows at London's Royal Albert Hall. Cream were supported by Yes and Taste. Baker, Bruce and Clapton seemed surprised at the emotional send-off they received from some 5,000 fans at each show.

Pete Brown went to see one of their farewell concerts, but didn't enjoy it

Taking a bow: Bruce, Baker and Clapton say goodbye.

very much. "I went to the last gig but it was a strain," he remembers, "because I was very over-sensitive, having had this horrible drug experience. When I used to hear Cream live I just used to get frightened at how loud it was. It used to scare me and I would cower in a corner and go white. It was all too much. I occasionally went to the smaller gigs – and got absolutely terrified because it was in such a small place." Bruce recalls the overwhelmingly warm reaction from the crowd at the final Albert Hall concerts in London. "We looked at each other and thought, 'Are we doing the right thing?' There was a feeling of regret, but nobody was able to step forward and say, 'Oh, let's not do this.'"

I attended the farewell shows at the Albert Hall for *Melody Maker*. It was a highly charged occasion, and the three musicians were clearly moved. Baker, Bruce and Clapton were on top form for the two sell-out shows, and the audience gave them a standing ovation, refusing to leave until the band played three encores.

"We looked at each other and thought: 'Are we doing the right thing?'"

After the show, Clapton told me about his plans. "We haven't played in England for… well, I don't know how long, over a year," he said, "and I had no idea we were so popular. I was amazed we played to such full houses. I didn't think anybody would remember us. Of course, it gave us second thoughts about breaking up, but it would be unfair to change everybody's plans now. I've enjoyed playing very much."

Clapton talked about the work the group was doing to complete the forthcoming *Goodbye* album, confirming that some of it would be live, and some recorded in the studio. He also mentioned that he might produce a film in Hollywood, though nothing came of that scheme. But he did say he was working on his own songs for a solo project. "I want to work with American musicians, because most of the good English musicians I know are already in groups and seem settled. I saw John Mayall in America, and we jammed together. His guitarist, Mick Taylor, is very good – frightening. But it's a strange thing, John seems to be going back. He's playing exactly the same as in the old days."

The same issue of *Melody Maker* with my review of the Cream farewell concert had a stark headline on the front page: "Traffic Split Shock". Suddenly, Stevie Winwood was not "settled" in his group, and the possibility of Blind Faith moved closer. For the time being, however, Clapton was about to leave the Albert Hall. "First I want to get into my house in the country," he said, "and get some solitude."

Clapton felt free to express more of his feelings about Cream some years later. "There was a constant battle between Ginger and Jack," he said. "They loved each other's playing, but they couldn't stand the sight of each other. I was the mediator and I was getting tired of that. Then when *Rolling Stone* called me the 'master of the blues cliché' that just about

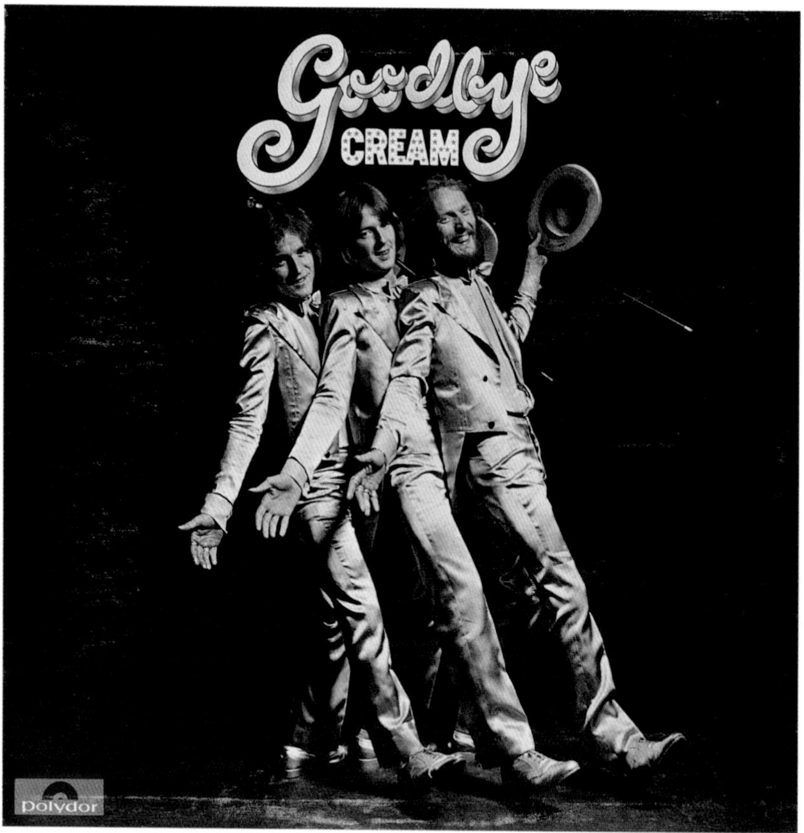

knocked me cold. That's when I decided to leave Cream." However, Clapton acknowledged that Cream had encouraged him to explore his guitar-playing in a way that wouldn't have happened if he had just formed another band like John Mayall's Bluesbreakers.

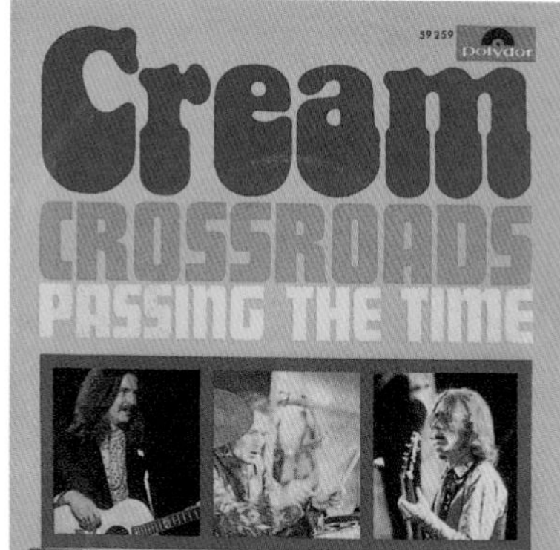

The end of Cream was a blow for the group's founder member. "When we decided to finish the band," recalls Baker, "and I told Stigwood, I don't think he believed us. Then we did the *Goodbye* album and the farewell tour. I don't think our last gig at the Royal Albert Hall in London was very good. And Tony Palmer's film of the show for the BBC was appalling. Eric would never speak to Tony Palmer again after that. We'd be playing a number and all of a sudden we were wearing different clothes. He'd cut scenes from one show and slot them into another one completely. It was unbelievable. And all those zoom shots were very silly. It's sad that it's what most people today see as Cream live. We really were much better than that," Baker observes. "I'm not sure if we were still on good terms when

Cream broke up. I discovered later that my behaviour at the time used to scare Eric to death. I was always getting into scrapes. We parted on fairly good terms. I still have problems with Jack," says Baker, "even today, over the things that went on with Cream. But I miss it, there's no doubt about that."

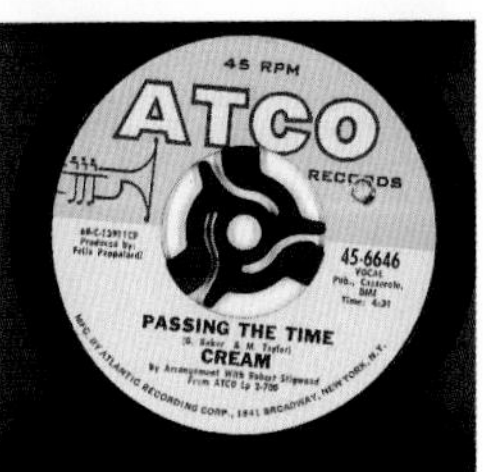

The Goodbye LP appeared in March 1969, featuring three studio tracks and three live pieces. It was preceded a month earlier in the US by a single of 'Crossroads' and 'Passing The Time'.

Their trusty roadie Ben Palmer enjoyed employment with Blind Faith and Clapton's own later bands. By the time Cream split, Palmer had grown used to the shenanigans of the rock'n'roll world. He was proud of Cream. But he wasn't too impressed by the debasement of the blues that he felt such commercially successful rock bands represented. "I've always felt that a great opportunity was lost. I don't want to sound high-minded about this, but I do think that at the centre of the blues there is something which is nourishing and real. Along with jazz, it's the greatest gift that America has given the world. When I consider what the rock'n'roll movement has made of that material… well, I never thought much of it, frankly." Palmer feels that rock has always been inclined to pick up the trivial and the entertaining rather than life's more important matters. He believes that the best popular music should try to deal with people's lives as well as be entertaining.

"I don't think rock'n'roll has done that. The only group that came out of the whole thing that I have any lasting and deep respect for is The Band. They dealt very well with serious matters and a range of influences. They played wonderfully. How they managed to remain that pure in the middle of all the rest of it, I don't know.

"As for Cream," says Palmer, "I think Eric found a style of playing that the band demanded. There was something about that band which almost dictated the way it was going to be. It grew organically. Nobody talked about what it was going to do or really planned its musical future at all. It just developed very quickly and powerfully. Eric was the kind of musician who could survive and triumph under that sort of pressure."

Director Tony Palmer shot not only a black-and-white documentary for the BBC at Cream's final Royal Albert Hall performance, but also a colour film for cinema release, as trailed in this New York ad of June 1969.

Although Ginger Baker wasn't happy with the group's last shows, the fans reacted with tremendous enthusiasm. Some even leapt on stage to hurl confetti during the last number – although they may have been planted to provide some action for the BBC cameras. British audiences still tended to sit dutifully and listen attentively in the days before it became fashionable to whoop, American-style, and leap from their seats.

As the last fans drifted away from the Albert Hall with the sound of 'White Room', 'Sunshine Of Your Love' and 'Crossroads' ringing in their ears, they would soon have only their memories and a brace of farewell albums to savour. The *Goodbye* LP was released in March 1969. It had a showbiz-style cover shot of the band posing in satin suits with top hats and canes – and was the first time they had all been seen smiling since the formation of the band.

The new album was not just a throwaway. It included some tantalisingly good new material, including the classic 'Badge'. This was a sultry,

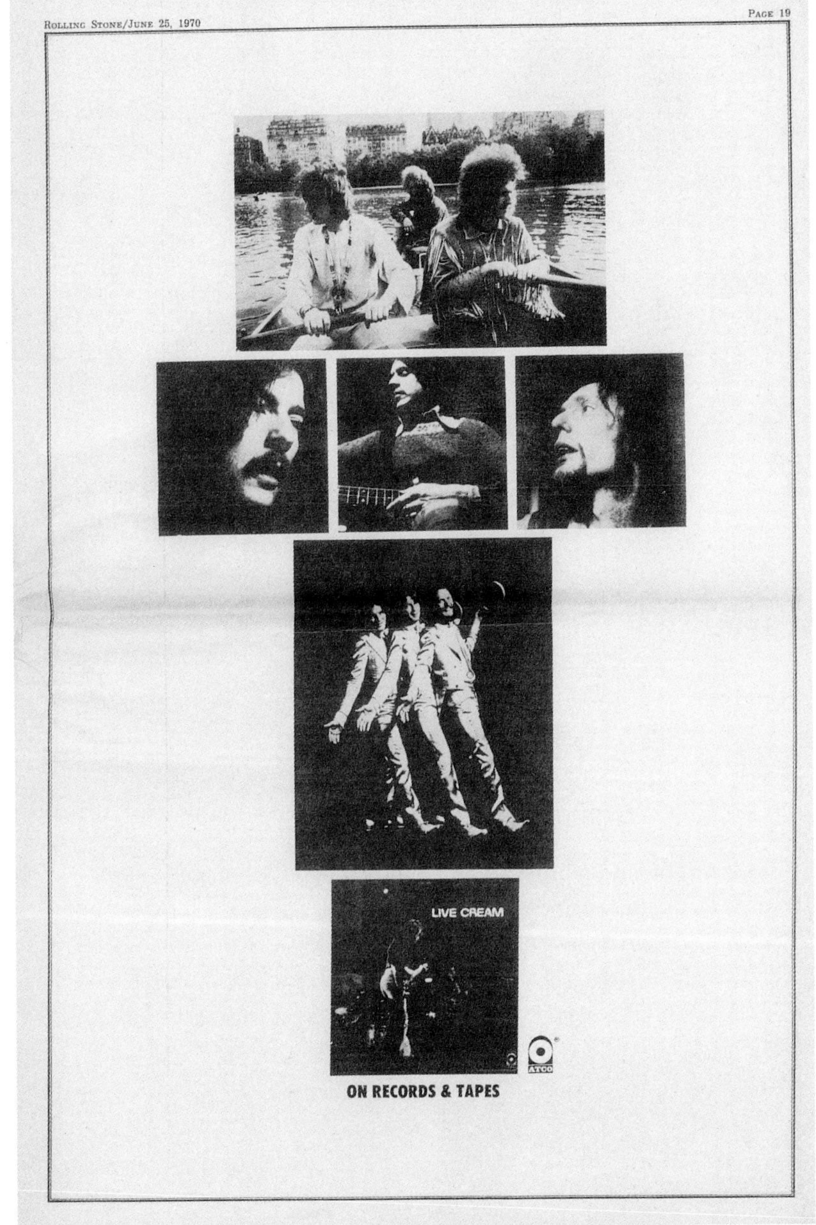
ROLLING STONE/JUNE 25, 1970

PAGE 19

Two official live albums were released after Cream's break-up. This Rolling Stone ad is for 1970's Live Cream LP. Two years later came Live Cream Volume II.

insidious song co-written by Clapton and his Beatle pal George Harrison – and might have been called 'Bridge' if Clapton had been able to read Harrison's handwritten arrangement. It would be regularly featured by Clapton with his bands for years to come. *Goodbye* came with live versions of 'I'm So Glad', 'Politician' and 'Sitting On Top Of The World'

Best Of Cream, released in the second half of 1969, was the first of a stream of compilation albums. 'Badge' backed with 'What A Bringdown' first appeared in April of the same year.

recorded at The Forum in Los Angeles on the farewell tour in October 1968, as well as three studio tracks: 'Doing That Scrapyard Thing' and 'What A Bringdown', alongside 'Badge'. Such was the strength of Cream's reputation that the record topped the album charts in both the US and the UK. Pete Brown was responsible for the lyrics on at least one of the tracks

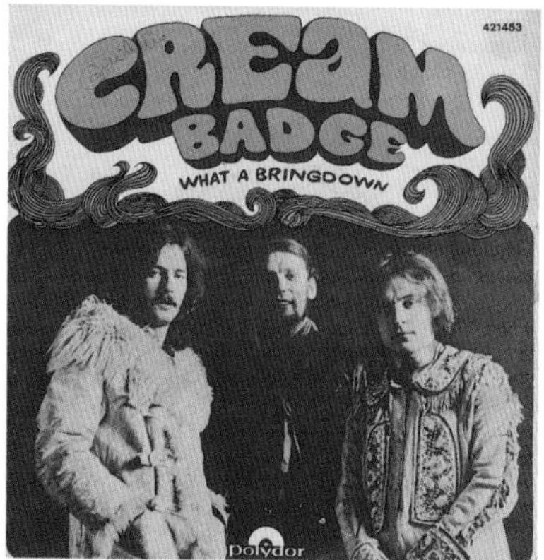

Cream's two official live albums, Live Cream (1970) and Live Cream Volume II (1972), further mined the concert-tape library.

on the final album. "A funny thing happened with *Goodbye*," he says. "Dick Heckstall-Smith was living with me at the time as his marriage had just broken up. Jack was staying in Los Angeles and called me from there at 3am. He said: 'I want you to write the words to this song.' And he played me a theme over the phone, which I recorded on a terrible old Grundig tape-recorder. I wrote the lyrics and then phoned him back. The song was 'Doing That Scrapyard Thing'." Apart from its Beatle-style lyrics, 'Scrapyard' had some very unusual guitar work from Clapton, while Felix Pappalardi played Mellotron and Bruce added piano. Together with 'What A Bringdown' it had indications of how Cream might have found a new direction, if they'd managed to survive.

Bruce remains proud of all their albums. "Considering the way the records were made," he says, "which was very quickly, they're still very good. Perhaps there's something to be said for not spending two years in

the studio making an album. There is something about the spontaneity of going in the studio and having to do it quickly. People still like those records because they were more or less live. There was a certain amount of overdubbing even then, but most of those 1960s records were live. That's why they still sound alive and breathing. Today's electronic sounds are like a photograph of music rather than the real thing. For all their faults, the Cream records work and, despite our limited output, it was all good."

"There was a vacuum at the end of the 1960s when The Beatles and Cream broke up."

Cream were also fortunate that they were filmed in action. So many bands of the period broke up before the video age. "There's a version I've seen on video of us playing 'Crossroads' that was astounding," says Bruce. "There was also some filming done in colour at the Revolution club in London for a French director. I'm wearing a funny Russian hat. It's really good stuff, and it was all done with one hand-held camera. Obviously we could have done more, if we'd had more time to write – and if we'd had the luxury of having a life. There's nothing left in the vaults now from Cream. It's all been used up."

The *Live Cream* album was released in 1970, and then two years later came *Live Cream Volume II*. Both were put together by Felix Pappalardi from the remaining material in the Atlantic vaults, with more live recordings, this time including pieces such as 'NSU', 'White Room' and 'Sunshine Of Your Love'.

"We did Cream in a very idealistic way," says Bruce. "It was just a question of doing what we believed in. I have no regrets that the band didn't carry on – and I've no regrets that I didn't join Led Zeppelin when they asked me. In fact, to be honest, I've no regrets about anything. Led Zeppelin was a much more commercially successful band and lasted longer, but it came after Cream and Hendrix had created this vast audience for rock music. There was a kind of vacuum at the end of the 1960s when bands like The Beatles and Cream broke up. But the whole heavy-rock thing started with Cream."

When the group split up, the members became more friendly to one another than they had been for months. Clapton visited Bruce at his home and hung out for a while as they made plans for the future. Bruce went to see Baker's new band Airforce, which the drummer formed in the wake of the shortlived Blind Faith. "After Cream it felt like a great weight had lifted off us," recalls Bruce. "It had been such an intense period of activity. I suppose we should have split up for a while and then come back together again for the occasional record or concert. But that didn't happen. Eric set out on the road to become a solo star. We all became involved in our own things and grew apart. Then came the reunion for the Rock & Roll Hall of Fame in 1993." The reunion took place at the awards ceremony held at the Century Plaza Hotel in Los Angeles on January 12th 1993. Members of the audience had paid up to $1,000 a ticket to see a band that had sold some 35 million albums worldwide since their last public appearance in 1968.

"It was a funny thing," says Bruce. "When I first went along I didn't even want to be a part of it. Let's face it, it's all lies. It's about an industry that exploited musicians and especially black musicians for years. So I went along being really against the whole concept. But in fact you tend to get sucked in. As the evening goes on and people come up with congratulations, you feel proud to be part of it. And in the end you're weeping. It's like the Oscars or something.

"But the music was nice. We had a rehearsal the day before that was great, but the gig itself was not quite so good. The magic was still right there, and I'm sure we could pick up even now, right from where we left off. I had to say a few words, Eric made a nice speech, and Ginger said, 'I agree with what they said.'"

"I'm sure we could pick up even now, right from where we left off..."

Baker confirms that the run-throughs were better than the performance at the ceremony. "When we played at the rehearsal it was wonderful," he remembers, "but the gig wasn't quite as good, mainly because we had to sit down at a table for eight hours and listen to a load of bozos making these extraordinary speeches. 'I wanna thank my mum and my aunt who lent me 50 bucks 20 years ago, and my cat and my dog.' They *all* made these enormous speeches. To tell you the truth it didn't mean much to me. I'd much rather be in the Jazz Hall Of Fame. But when Cream played again, it was as if we had just been away on holiday. The magic was still there."

It took many years for Clapton to recover from the traumatic Cream experience. It had been so challenging musically, yet so physically and emotionally draining. "The success of Cream left a huge scar," Clapton said, "but I'm better at accepting compliments about it now. When we played at the reunion and I had to make an acceptance speech, I started to cry and had to take a deep breath. I was reunited with two people I loved very dearly. It was very moving."

Whether Cream will ever unite again remains to be seen. Clapton contemplated recording and writing new material with his old partners in the wake of the reunion, but nothing came of these ideas. He may have been mindful of Bob Dylan's words – "Don't look back." If Cream do ever get together again, it would have to be for the right reason: the music. And that's something they've all got plenty left to give.

CREAM DIARY

THOSE WERE THE DAYS

When Cream started out in summer 1966, rock bands in Britain made regular income by gigging. Record contracts were growing in importance, but steady work and immediate cash came from playing live. There were all manner of types and sizes of gigs: clubs in backstreet halls, rooms over pubs, stages in town halls and other municipal buildings, even the occasional cinema or proper theatre. A circuit had grown up since the early 1960s, and Cream joined that circuit.

At first Baker, Bruce and Clapton naturally expected that this is how they would continue to work – just as they had in previous groups like the Graham Bond Organisation, The Yardbirds and John Mayall's Bluesbreakers. Why should Cream be any different?

They also knew that the BBC was important. The corporation then had a monopoly on radio

broadcasting in Britain, even though crackly Radio Luxembourg offered an alternative and the pirate stations were growing steadily more popular. Luxembourg and the pirates played records, records and more records. The Beeb, however, had a "needletime" agreement that limited disc broadcasts, so live or recorded sessions with bands were a necessity. Acts queued up at BBC studios to make their contribution to massively influential programmes such as *Saturday Club* and, later, *Top Gear*.

The making and breaking of Cream proved to be the United States. UK rock bands had been to North America before Cream, of course – most

famously The Beatles in 1964 and the subsequent "British invasion". But Cream's second full American tour, which began in February 1968, was the longest ever undertaken by any British band. It completely changed the traditional pattern of work – and added to the group's growing frustration.

Recording seems to have been fitted in around Cream's gigs. Perhaps the greatest contrast to the way in which a band today might operate comes when one considers Cream's balance of gigs and recording. The diary that follows indicates that Cream played around 275 live dates in a 28-month career, compared to some 50 days in the studio. Who knows what they might have produced if – just like The Beatles – Cream had been given the time to write together and to develop their music in the studio?

This is a guide to the abbreviations used in the **recording** *items in the diary that follows. They identify the relevant stages in the recording process, as well as the records and videos where the items have appeared. The "tape lost" entries often refer to session recordings destroyed in Atlantic's devastating tape-archive fire of 1976.*

UK counties in live gig locations in the Diary use the reorganised post-1974 designations.

RECORDING ABBREVIATIONS KEY:

(B) BACKING TRACK
(D) DEMO
(M) MASTER: READY FOR RELEASE
(R) REHEARSAL/EARLY TAKE
(T) TRACKING: OVERDUBS, FURTHER WORK, ETC
1, **2** etc = VERSION 1, VERSION 2 etc

RECORDS/VIDEOS ABBREVIATIONS KEY:

BL BOOTLEG
CD ON CD RELEASE ONLY
CEV *Cream Of Eric Clapton* VIDEO
DG *Disraeli Gears* ALBUM
ECA ERIC CLAPTON *After Midnight* SINGLE CD 1988
ECC ERIC CLAPTON *Crossroads* BOX-SET
FC *Fresh Cream* ALBUM
FCV *Farewell Cream* VIDEO
FLV *Fresh Live Cream* VIDEO
GB *Goodbye* ALBUM
-I INCOMPLETE
LC1 *Live Cream* ALBUM
LC2 *Live Cream Volume II* ALBUM
LP ON LP RELEASE ONLY
SBV *Strange Brew* VIDEO
TL TAPE LOST
TSU TAPE STATUS UNKNOWN
TWD *Those Were The Days* BOX-SET
UR UNRELEASED
UT UNRELEASED TRANSCRIPTION
WOF *WHEELS OF FIRE* ALBUM
45A SINGLE RELEASE A-SIDE
45B SINGLE RELEASE B-SIDE

JULY 1966

Cream's first gig was at Manchester's Twisted Wheel. Joe Tex & His American Showband were due to play on the 29th, but cancelled at short notice, so there were no local ads for Cream's gig.

fri 29 **TWISTED WHEEL** MANCHESTER, ENGLAND.

sat 30

sun 31 **SIXTH NATIONAL JAZZ & BLUES FESTIVAL** ROYAL WINDSOR RACECOURSE, WINDSOR, BERKSHIRE, ENGLAND.

* For key to recording abbreviations see page 160

AUGUST 1966

mon	1	
tue	2	**KLOOKS KLEEK** RAILWAY HOTEL, WEST HAMPSTEAD, LONDON, ENGLAND.
wed	3	
thu	4	
fri	5	**COOKS FERRY INN** EDMONTON, LONDON, ENGLAND.
sat	6	**TOWN HALL** TORQUAY, DEVON, ENGLAND.
sun	7	
mon	8	
tue	9	**FISHMONGERS ARMS** WOOD GREEN, LONDON, ENGLAND.
wed	10	
thu	11	
fri	12	
sat	13	
sun	14	
mon	15	
tue	16	**THE MARQUEE** CENTRAL LONDON, ENGLAND. *PLUS THE CLAYTON SQUARES*
wed	17	
thu	18	
fri	19	**THE CELLAR CLUB** KINGSTON-UPON-THAMES, LONDON, ENGLAND.
sat	20	
sun	21	
mon	22	
tue	23	
wed	24	
thu	25	
fri	26	
sat	27	**RAM JAM** BRIXTON, LONDON, ENGLAND. **THE FLAMINGO** CENTRAL LONDON, ENGLAND. *ALL-NIGHTER MIDNIGHT-6AM.*
sun	28	
mon	29	
tue	30	
wed	31	

“Cream did their first London club date at Klooks, and when I booked them I noticed at once this new attitude of more seriousness on the part of the listeners and more devotion to a band.” **Klooks kleek owner dick jordan, 1976.**

● **RECORDING** RAYRIK STUDIO (CHALK FARM, LONDON, ENGLAND). WED 3rd. ENGINEER: JOHN TIMPERLY, PRODUCER: ROBERT STIGWOOD. 'THE COFFEE SONG' (R) *UR; BL.* 'THE COFFEE SONG' (M) *FC CD; TWD.* 'BEAUTY QUEEN' (R) *UR; BL.* 'YOU MAKE ME FEEL' INSTRUMENTAL (R) *TL.* 'YOU MAKE ME FEEL' (R) *TWD.*

“I played the Flamingo all-nighters before Cream, mainly with pick-up bands, usually Ginger on drums, Dick Heckstall-Smith on tenor sax, and Johnny Burch on piano. The band-room of the Flamingo in the early 1960s was the centre of the universe. It had a pet rat that used to run in the rafters above. Just a fabulous place to hang out. It would get busted regularly, but they would never come into the band room in those days. A guy called Ronnie Chambers used to look after the Flamingo. He'd get excited sometimes and rush on stage waving his gun about if the music was particularly good.” **JACK BRUCE, 2000**

● **RECORDING** RAYRIK STUDIO (CHALK FARM, LONDON, ENGLAND). LATE AUGUST. ENGINEER: JOHN TIMPERLY, PRODUCER: ROBERT STIGWOOD. 'WRAPPING PAPER' (R) *BL.* 'WRAPPING PAPER' (M) *45A; FC CD; TWD*

* For key to recording abbreviations see page 160

SEPTEMBER 1966

thu 1

fri 2 **BLUESVILLE 66** THE MANOR HOUSE, MANOR HOUSE, LONDON, ENGLAND.

sat 3

sun 4 **RICKY TICK** WINDSOR, BERKSHIRE, ENGLAND.

mon 5

tue 6

wed 7

thu 8

fri 9

sat 10

sun 11 **SKYLINE BALLROOM** KINGSTON-UPON-HULL, HUMBERSIDE, ENGLAND.

mon 12

tue 13

wed 14

thu 15 **GAUMONT CINEMA** HANLEY, STAFFORDSHIRE, ENGLAND. *PLUS THE WHO & THE MERSEYS*

fri 16 **HERMITAGE HALLS** HITCHIN, HERTFORDSHIRE, ENGLAND. *PLUS THE FARINAS, ADMISSION 6/-*

sat 17 **TOWN HALL** GRANTHAM, LINCOLNSHIRE, ENGLAND.

sun 18 **BLUE MOON** HAYES, LONDON, ENGLAND.

mon 19 **UNKNOWN CINEMA** WOKING, SURREY, ENGLAND.

tue 20

wed 21

thu 22

fri 23 **RICKY TICK** CORN EXCHANGE, NEWBURY, BERKSHIRE, ENGLAND.

sat 24

sun 25

mon 26 **STAR CLUB** STAR HOTEL, CROYDON, LONDON, ENGLAND.

tue 27 **THE MARQUEE** CENTRAL LONDON, ENGLAND. *PLUS THE HERD*

wed 28

thu 29

fri 30 **RICKY TICK** HOUNSLOW, LONDON, ENGLAND.

● **RECORDING** SPOT STUDIO (CENTRAL LONDON, ENGLAND). EARLY SEPTEMBER. ENGINEER/CO-PRODUCER: JOHN TIMPERLY, CO-PRODUCERS: CREAM. 'CAT'S SQUIRREL' (R) *UR; BL.* 'CAT'S SQUIRREL' (M) *45A; FC; TWD.* 'CAT'S SQUIRREL' (M: DIFFERENT LEAD GUITAR) *FRENCH EP; BL.* 'I FEEL FREE' (R) *UR; BL.* 'I FEEL FREE' (B) *UR; BL.* 'I FEEL FREE' (M) *45A; FC LP (US) & CD; TWD.* 'NSU' (M) *45B; FC; TWD.*

❝Cream recorded 'I Feel Free' above a chemist's shop. The band recorded at Spot studio in South Molton Street. It was just around the corner from Robert Stigwood's management offices in Brook Street, so most of his artists recorded there: it was one of the first small, friendly studios. The company name was Ryemuse Ltd, from a Mr Rye who owned it, and the studio's name changed from Spot to Mayfair around 1973 (we moved in 1980). Spot was above a chemist's shop, and there was no lift, with the studio and control room on the second floor, so all the equipment had to go up two flights of stairs. There was no window between the studio and control room, because there was a corridor between, so there was no visual communication between the two. That room sounded fantastic, though I think it was a fluke. The Who recorded 'Pictures Of Lily' there, and later T.Rex did some stuff too.❞ **JOHN HUDSON, PRESENT OWNER OF MAYFAIR STUDIO, 2000**

* For key to recording abbreviations see page 160

OCTOBER 1966

sat 1 — **POLYTECHNIC** CENTRAL LONDON, ENGLAND. *ADMISSION 2/6, PLUS WASHINGTON DCs. JIMI HENDRIX JAMS WITH CREAM.*

sun 2 — **COUNTRY CLUB** KIRKLEVINGTON, CLEVELAND, ENGLAND. *CANCELLED. BAND'S FEE WAS CONTRACTED AT £75*

mon 3

tue 4 — **FISHMONGERS ARMS** WOOD GREEN, LONDON, ENGLAND.

wed 5

thu 6

fri 7

sat 8 — **KINGS COLLEGE** BRIGHTON, EAST SUSSEX, ENGLAND.

sun 9 — **BIRDCAGE** KIMBELLS BALLROOM, PORTSMOUTH, HAMPSHIRE, ENGLAND.

mon 10

tue 11 — **FLAMINGO CLUB** CENTRAL LONDON, ENGLAND. *PLUS REYNORS SECRETS, BO-WEEVILS*

wed 12 — **CENTRAL POLYTECHNIC** CENTRAL LONDON, ENGLAND.

thu 13 — **NEW YORKER DISCOTHEQUE** SWINDON, WILTSHIRE, ENGLAND.

fri 14

sat 15

sun 16

mon 17

tue 18

wed 19

thu 20

fri 21 — **BLUESVILLE 66** THE MANOR HOUSE, MANOR HOUSE, LONDON, ENGLAND.

sat 22

sun 23

mon 24

tue 25

wed 26

thu 27

fri 28

sat 29

sun 30

mon 31

● **RECORD RELEASE UK** FRI 7th 'WRAPPING PAPER'/'CAT'S SQUIRREL' REACTION 45.

● **RECORDING** SPOT STUDIO (CENTRAL LONDON, ENGLAND). MID OCTOBER. ENGINEER/CO-PRODUCER: JOHN TIMPERLY, CO-PRODUCERS: CREAM. 'DREAMING' (M) *FC; TWD.* 'SLEEPY TIME TIME' (M) *FC; TWD.* 'SLEEPY TIME TIME' (M: DIFFERENT LEAD GUITAR) *FRENCH EP; BL.* 'SWEET WINE' (R) *UR; BL.* 'SWEET WINE' (R: FEEDBACK) *UR; BL.* 'SWEET WINE' (M) *45A; FC; TWD.*

● **RADIO** BBC MAIDA VALE STUDIOS (LONDON, ENGLAND) RECORDING FRI 21st FOR *BANDBEAT*, BROADCAST ON BBC WORLD SERVICE NOVEMBER 21st. PRESENTER: ALEXIS KORNER, PRODUCER: JEFF GRIFFIN, ENGINEER: JOE YOUNG. 'SPOONFUL' *TL.* 'SLEEPY TIME TIME' *TL.* 'ROLLIN' AND TUMBLIN'' *TL.*

“I was resident DJ at the mod hang-out the New Yorker Discotheque in Swindon. One of Cream's roadies – a big geezer – made off with my trendy leather overcoat after the gig. Once I'd discovered the theft, I called the local police and demanded they apprehend the equipment van at their earliest convenience as it headed off up the A4. Incredibly, the van was sighted and brought to a halt near Reading, where the coat was discovered and returned to me. I am anxious to underline that none of the group was involved in any way with this: they were chauffeured to and from the gig by car.” **BARON VON MULLER, 2000**

“Alexis Korner was known and respected by all the musicians, so he would often tip me off about bands to book before I even knew they were going to happen. One of those was Cream. We booked them for their first BBC session. Studio manager Joe Young had never in his life heard anything as loud as Cream were in that studio. I remember Joe going into the studio to adjust something, and he came back in practically falling over himself.” **JEFF GRIFFIN, 1997**

* For key to recording abbreviations see page 160

NOVEMBER 1966

Cream first appeared on BBC radio's *Saturday Club* this month. The programme had become tremendously important, at times getting a remarkable 25-30 million listeners. A "needletime" agreement between the BBC and a copyright organisation meant plenty of live music on radio, giving many bands their first taste of recording and an early, important connection with their audience. Disc copies, or "transcriptions", of *Saturday Club*'s recordings were often made for use in custom programmes prepared by the BBC for broadcast elsewhere.

❝[For the Redcar gig] Cream's fee of £75 made the 250-mile journey from London worthwhile. The ticket price was about 10 shillings (50p), quite hefty in those days when a local steel-worker earned about £12 a week, but you could get lucky. Really lucky. Not many chances in the North-East to see a band the calibre of Cream before they'd even released their first album… only the b-side *Cat's Squirrel* gave any indication to ticket buyers what lay in store… After one and a half hours they released us, leaving us limp, ears ringing, when they pulled out the jack-plugs and abandoned the stage with a shared smile. It was the biggest surprise of my life.❞

CHRIS SCOTT WILSON, 1996

tue	1	
wed	2	
thu	3	**RAM JAM** BRIXTON, LONDON ENGLAND.
fri	4	
sat	5	**TOWN HALL** EAST HAM, LONDON, ENGLAND. *6/6 ADMISSION*
sun	6	
mon	7	**UKNOWN VENUE** GOSPORT, HANTS, ENGLAND.
tue	8	**THE MARQUEE** CENTRAL LONDON, ENGLAND. *PLUS THE RACE*
wed	9	
thu	10	
fri	11	**PUBLIC BATHS** SUTTON, LONDON, ENGLAND.
sat	12	**LIVERPOOL UNIVERSITY** LIVERPOOL, ENGLAND.
sun	13	**REDCAR JAZZ CLUB** COATHAM'S HOTEL, REDCAR, CLEVELAND, ENGLAND.
mon	14	
tue	15	**KLOOKS KLEEK** RAILWAY HOTEL, WEST HAMPSTEAD, LONDON, ENGLAND.
wed	16	
thu	17	**BURKES** CENTRAL LONDON, ENGLAND.
fri	18	**VILLAGE HALL** HOVETON, NORFOLK, ENGLAND.
sat	19	**BLUE MOON** CHELTENHAM, GLOUCESTERSHIRE, ENGLAND.
sun	20	
mon	21	**PAVILION** BATH, AVON, ENGLAND. *ALSO ADVERTISED TODAY AT COOKS FERRY INN, EDMONTON, LONDON: CANCELLED*
tue	22	**CHINESE R&B JAZZ CLUB** CORN EXCHANGE, BRISTOL, AVON, ENGLAND.
wed	23	
thu	24	
fri	25	**CALIFORNIA BALLROOM** DUNSTABLE, BEDFORDSHIRE, ENGLAND.
sat	26	
sun	27	
mon	28	
tue	29	
wed	30	

● **TV** STUDIO 1, TV STUDIOS (WEMBLEY, LONDON, ENGLAND) MIMING/RECORDING TUE 1st FOR *READY STEADY GO!*, BROADCAST ON ITV FRI 4th. 'WRAPPING PAPER' *TL*. 'NSU' *TL*.

● **RECORDING** SPOT STUDIO (CENTRAL LONDON, ENGLAND). EARLY NOVEMBER. ENGINEER/CO-PRODUCER: JOHN TIMPERLY, CO-PRODUCERS: CREAM. 'FOUR UNTIL LATE' (M) *FC; TWD*. 'ROLLIN' AND TUMBLIN'' (R) *UR; BL*. 'ROLLIN' AND TUMBLIN'' (M) *FC; TWD*. 'TOAD' (R) *UR; BL*. 'TOAD' (M) *FC; TWD*. 'I'M SO GLAD' (M) *FC; TWD*. 'SPOONFUL' (M) *FC; TWD*. ['I'M SO GLAD' AND 'SPOONFUL' POSSIBLY RECORDED LATER THAN THIS SESSION.]

● **RADIO** BBC PLAYHOUSE THEATRE (CENTRAL LONDON, ENGLAND). RECORDING TUE 8th FOR *SATURDAY CLUB*, BROADCAST ON BBC LIGHT PROGRAMME NOVEMBER 12th. PRESENTER: BRIAN MATTHEW, PRODUCER: BILL BEBB. 'SWEET WINE' *UT; BL*. 'WRAPPING PAPER' *UT; BL*. 'STEPPING OUT' *UT; BL*. 'ROLLIN' AND TUMBLIN'' *TL; BL*. 'I'M SO GLAD' *TL; BL*. 'SLEEPY TIME TIME' *TL; BL*.

● **RADIO** BBC PLAYHOUSE THEATRE (CENTRAL LONDON, ENGLAND) LIVE MON 21st FOR *MONDAY MONDAY* BBC LIGHT PROGRAMME. PRODUCER: KEITH BATESON. NO SONG INFORMATION.

● **RADIO** BBC AEOLIAN HALL (CENTRAL LONDON, ENGLAND) RECORDING MON 28th FOR *GUITAR CLUB*, BROADCAST ON BBC HOME SERVICE DECEMBER 30th. PRESENTER: KEN SYKORA, PRODUCER: BERNIE ANDREWS. 'CROSSROADS' *TL*. 'SITTING ON TOP OF THE WORLD' *TL*. 'STEPPING OUT' *TL*.

* For key to recording abbreviations see page 160

DECEMBER 1966

thu	1	
fri	2	**HORNSEY COLLEGE OF ART** HORNSEY, LONDON, ENGLAND.
sat	3	**BIRDCAGE** KIMBELLS BALLROOM, PORTSMOUTH, ENGLAND.
sun	4	**STARLITE BALLROOM** GREENFORD, LONDON, ENGLAND. *PLUS ESSEX FIVE*
mon	5	**BLUESVILLE 66** THE BATHS HALL, IPSWICH, SUFOLK, ENGLAND.
tue	6	
wed	7	**HULL UNIVERSITY** KINGSTON-UPON-HULL, HUMBERSIDE, ENGLAND.
thu	8	
fri	9	**BLUESVILLE 66** THE MANOR HOUSE, MANOR HOUSE, LONDON, ENGLAND.
sat	10	**ISELWORTH POLYTECHNIC** ISELWORTH, LONDON, ENGLAND.
sun	11	
mon	12	**COOKS FERRY INN** EDMONTON, LONDON, ENGLAND.
tue	13	**EXETER UNIVERSITY** EXETER, DEVON, ENGLAND.
wed	14	**BROMEL CLUB** BROMLEY COURT HOTEL, BROMLEY, LONDON, ENGLAND.
thu	15	**UNIVERSITY OF SUSSEX** BRIGHTON, EAST SUSSEX, ENGLAND.
fri	16	
sat	17	**LA LOCOMOTIVE CLUB** CENTRAL PARIS, FRANCE.
sun	18	
mon	19	**AGINCOURT BALLROOM** CAMBERLEY, SURREY, ENGLAND.
tue	20	
wed	21	
thu	22	**PIER PAVILION** WORTHING, WEST SUSSEX, ENGLAND.
fri	23	**ODEON CINEMA** BIRMINGHAM, ENGLAND.
sat	24	**MIDNIGHT CITY** BIRMINGHAM, ENGLAND. *PLUS FAMILY*
sun	25	
mon	26	
tue	27	
wed	28	
thu	29	
fri	30	**THE ROUNDHOUSE** CHALK FARM, LONDON, ENGLAND.
sat	31	

● **RECORDS RELEASE UK** FRI 9th 'I FEEL FREE'/'NSU' REACTION 45, AND *FRESH CREAM* REACTION LP.

● **RADIO** BBC MAIDA VALE STUDIOS (MAIDA VALE, LONDON, ENGLAND) RECORDING FRI 9th FOR *RHYTHM & BLUES*, BROADCAST ON BBC WORLD SERVICE JANUARY 9th 1967. PRESENTER: ALEXIS KORNER, PRODUCER: JEFF GRIFFIN, ENGINEER: JOE YOUNG. 'CAT'S SQUIRREL' *UT; BL.* 'TRAINTIME' *UT; BL.* 'LAWDY MAMA' *ECC.* 'I'M SO GLAD' *UT; BL.*

● **TV/RADIO** UNKNOWN TV AND RADIO APPEARANCES FRI 16th-SUN 18th (FRANCE). NO SONG INFORMATION.

“I remember the Exeter gig for nothing else than the horrendous drive in those days, a real schlep. Everywhere was! We used to dread these gigs, because it was like a whole day. I remember eating a 'chicken fowl' after the gig, I think it was a cat. It had quite a lot of legs for a chicken. Very odd. Definitely on the bone.” **JACK BRUCE, 2000**

* For key to recording abbreviations see page 160

JANUARY 1967

sun	1		● **RECORD RELEASE US** JANUARY 'I FEEL FREE'/'NSU' ATCO 45.
mon	2		
tue	3		
wed	4		
thu	5		
fri	6		
sat	7	**RICKY TICK** THAMES HOTEL, WINDSOR, BERKSHIRE, ENGLAND. *ADMISSION 8/6*	
sun	8		
mon	9		
tue	10	**THE MARQUEE** CENTRAL LONDON, ENGLAND. *PLUS CATCH 22*	● **RADIO** BBC PLAYHOUSE THEATRE (CENTRAL LONDON, ENGLAND) RECORDING TUE 10th FOR *SATURDAY CLUB*, BROADCAST ON BBC LIGHT PROGRAMME JANUARY 14th. PRESENTER: BRIAN MATTHEW, PRODUCER: BILL BEBB. 'FOUR UNTIL LATE' *UT; BL.* 'I FEEL FREE' *UT; BL.* 'NSU' *UT; BL.* 'TRAINTIME' *TL; BL.* 'TOAD' *TL; BL.*
wed	11		
thu	12		
fri	13	**GUILDHALL** SOUTHAMPTON, HAMPSHIRE, ENGLAND. *ADMISSION 8/-*	
sat	14	**COVENTRY THEATRE** COVENTRY, WEST MIDLANDS, ENGLAND.	
sun	15	**RICKY TICK** HOUNSLOW, LONDON, ENGLAND.	
mon	16		● **RADIO** BBC PLAYHOUSE THEATRE (CENTRAL LONDON, ENGLAND) LIVE MON 16th FOR *MONDAY MONDAY* BBC LIGHT PROGRAMME. PRODUCER: KEITH BATESON. SESSION POSSIBLY REPEATED ON *MONDAY MONDAY* MARCH 27th. NO SONG INFORMATION.
tue	17		
wed	18	**TOWN HALL** STOURBRIDGE, WEST MIDLANDS, ENGLAND.	
thu	19	**GRANBY HALL** LEICESTER, LEICESTERSHIRE, ENGLAND.	
fri	20	**CLUB A GO GO** NEWCASTLE-UPON-TYNE, TYNE & WEAR, ENGLAND.	
sat	21	**FLORAL HALL** SOUTHPORT, MERSEYSIDE, ENGLAND.	
sun	22		
mon	23		
tue	24	**CHINESE R&B JAZZ CLUB** CORN EXCHANGE, BRISTOL, AVON, ENGLAND.	
wed	25		● **RADIO** BBC PLAYHOUSE THEATRE (CENTRAL LONDON, ENGLAND) LIVE WED 25th FOR *PARADE OF THE POPS*, ON BBC LIGHT PROGRAMME. PRODUCER: IAN SCOTT. NO SONG INFORMATION.
thu	26		● **TV** STUDIO G, BBC LIME GROVE TV STUDIOS (SHEPHERD'S BUSH, LONDON, ENGLAND) LIVE THU 26th FOR *TOP OF THE POPS* ON BBC1 'I FEEL FREE' *TL.*
fri	27		
sat	28	**RAM JAM** BRIXTON, LONDON, ENGLAND.	
sun	29		
mon	30		
tue	31		

“The Ricky Tick venues were good gigs. They were run by what we called hoorays, from out Windsor way, a couple of very pretty sisters, and two brothers.” **JACK BRUCE, 2000**

* For key to recording abbreviations see page 160

FEBRUARY 1967

wed 1

thu 2

fri 3 **ALL NIGHT RAVE** QUEENS HALL, LEEDS, WEST YORKSHIRE, ENGLAND. *8.30PM-6.30AM, PLUS PINK FLOYD*

sat 4 **EWELL TECHNICAL COLLEGE** EWELL, SURREY, ENGLAND.

sun 5 **SAVILLE THEATRE** CENTRAL LONDON, ENGLAND. *PLUS SANDS, EDWIN STARR*

mon 6

tue 7

wed 8

thu 9 **CITY HALL** SALISBURY, WILTSHIRE, ENGLAND.

fri 10 **BLUESVILLE 67** THE MANOR HOUSE, MANOR HOUSE, LONDON, ENGLAND.

sat 11 **BATH PAVILION** MATLOCK, DERBYSHIRE, ENGLAND.

sun 12

mon 13

tue 14

wed 15 **RICKY TICK** ASSEMBLY HALL, AYLESBURY, BUCKINGHAMSHIRE, ENGLAND. ADMISSION 8/-

thu 16

fri 17

sat 18 **TOFTS** FOLKESTONE, KENT, ENGLAND.

sun 19 **STARLITE BALLROOM** GREENFORD, LONDON, ENGLAND.

mon 20

tue 21

wed 22 **BROMEL CLUB** BROMLEY COURT HOTEL, BROMLEY, LONDON, ENGLAND.

thu 23

fri 24

sat 25 **STAR CLUB** HAMBURG, GERMANY.

sun 26 **STAR CLUB** KIEL, GERMANY.

mon 27

tue 28

"The Saville was a fantastic venue. I went and saw a few people there, too, including Jimi – who nearly got in tune, it was amazing. Our gig was rather good, there were some nice little ideas. They had this amazing hanging-out room, sort of behind the royal box or something, and I remember all if not most of The Beatles were there, Jimi too." **JACK BRUCE, 2000**

"When Cream played at Salisbury City Hall they ate in the Yorkshire Fisheries opposite. I spotted Ginger walking up the side alley to the Hall, and asked if I could accompany him. He said yes. I asked how the gigs were going so far. 'All right.' Me: 'Do you enjoy these provincial gigs?' Ginger: 'They're all right.' Me: 'How do they compare with the big London shows?' Ginger, clenching fist: 'Don't be so fucking nosy!' End of five-star conversation. I remember vividly that Eric broke a string in 'Rollin' And Tumblin'' during the riff. We nascent guitar hawks down the front gazed in wonder as he simply switched strings and frets in mid-stride." **TOM THATCHER, 2000**

● **FILM** PROMO FILM MADE AROUND EARLY FEBRUARY, BROADCAST ON *POPSIDE* TV PROGRAMME (SWEDEN) IN MARCH, AND PRESUMABLY ELSEWHERE. 'I FEEL FREE' *SBV*.

● **TV** RADIO-BREMEN TV STUDIOS (BREMEN, GERMANY) RECORDING FRI 24th FOR *BEAT CLUB*, BROADCAST ON SHOW 17, FEBRUARY 25th. 'I FEEL FREE' *CEV*.

* For key to recording abbreviations see page 160

MARCH 1967

wed 1 — **ULSTER HALL** BELFAST, NORTHERN IRELAND.

thu 2 — **QUEENS UNIVERSITY** BELFAST, NORTHERN IRELAND.

fri 3

sat 4

sun 5

mon 6 — **FALKONERTEATRET** COPENHAGEN, DENMARK. *POP POOL PACKAGE SHOW, PLUS DEFENDERS, HITMAKERS ETC*

tue 7 — **KONSERTHUSET** STOCKHOLM, SWEDEN.

wed 8 — **KONSERTHALLEN** LISEBERG AMUSEMENT PARK, GOTHENBURG, SWEDEN.

thu 9

fri 10

sat 11

sun 12 — **TAVERN CLUB** EAST DEREHAM, NORFOLK, ENGLAND.

mon 13

tue 14

wed 15

thu 16

fri 17

sat 18

sun 19

mon 20

tue 21 — **THE MARQUEE** CENTRAL LONDON, ENGLAND. *PLUS FAMILY*

wed 22

thu 23

fri 24

sat 25 — **MURRAY THE K'S MUSIC IN THE FIFTH DIMENSION** RKO THEATER, CENTRAL NEW YORK, NY, US.

sun 26 — **MURRAY THE K'S MUSIC IN THE FIFTH DIMENSION** RKO THEATER, CENTRAL NEW YORK, NY, US.

mon 27 — **MURRAY THE K'S MUSIC IN THE FIFTH DIMENSION** RKO THEATER, CENTRAL NEW YORK, NY, US.

tue 28 — **MURRAY THE K'S MUSIC IN THE FIFTH DIMENSION** RKO THEATER, CENTRAL NEW YORK, NY, US.

wed 29 — **MURRAY THE K'S MUSIC IN THE FIFTH DIMENSION** RKO THEATER, CENTRAL NEW YORK, NY, US.

thu 30 — **MURRAY THE K'S MUSIC IN THE FIFTH DIMENSION** RKO THEATER, CENTRAL NEW YORK, NY, US.

fri 31 — **MURRAY THE K'S MUSIC IN THE FIFTH DIMENSION** RKO THEATER, CENTRAL NEW YORK, NY, US.

● **RECORD RELEASE US** MARCH *FRESH CREAM* ATCO LP.

● **RADIO** SWEDISH RADIO BROADCAST OF MARCH 7th KONSERTHUSET GIG, BROADCAST DATE UNKNOWN. 'NSU' *UR.* 'STEPPING OUT' *UR.* 'TRAINTIME' *UR.* 'TOAD' *UR.* 'I'M SO GLAD' *UR.*

● **RECORDING** SPOT STUDIO (CENTRAL LONDON, ENGLAND). WED 15th. DEMO SESSION, UNKNOWN STUDIO PERSONNEL. 'BLUE CONDITION' INSTRUMENTAL (D) *UR.* 'HEY NOW PRINCESS' (D) *TWD.* 'SWLABR' INSTRUMENTAL (D) *UR.* 'SWLABR' (D) *TWD.* 'TAKE IT BACK' INSTRUMENTAL (D) *UR.* 'TAKE IT BACK' (D) *UR.* 'THE CLEAROUT' INSTRUMENTAL (D) *TWD.* 'WEIRD OF HERMISTON' INSTRUMENTAL (D) *UR.* 'WEIRD OF HERMISTON' (D) *TWD.* 'WE'RE GOING WRONG' (D) *TWD.*

"On Sunday 5th the group were refused entry into Denmark when they arrived at Copenhagen for concerts. After a three-hour delay at the airport, the permits were sorted out and they were allowed in. On Monday they travelled on to Sweden." ***MELODY MAKER*, 1967**

"We supported Cream at the Marquee, before our first record was out. Eric wanted to buy my Gibson double-neck guitar. We'd already played with them at Birmingham's Midnight City, and he'd wanted to buy it then. When we supported them at the Marquee he played it, during Cream's set. He said do you mind if I play it? Carry on. Sounded sweet when he did, too. But I wasn't selling, though it was tempting. And the double-neck guitars became a trademark for Family. If it had been a few years before, I might have sold it. But things were going well, so I thought not." **EX-FAMILY GUITARIST CHARLIE WHITNEY, 1998**

"The Murray The K gigs are worth a book on their own! It was nice to see Wilson Pickett, that was the first time I'd seen an actual live, working soul band. They were very tight and professional – certainly the opposite of what we were." **JACK BRUCE, 2000**

* For key to recording abbreviations see page 160

APRIL 1967

sat 1 **MURRAY THE K'S MUSIC IN THE FIFTH DIMENSION** RKO THEATER, CENTRAL NEW YORK, NY, US.

sun 2 **MURRAY THE K'S MUSIC IN THE FIFTH DIMENSION** RKO THEATER, CENTRAL NEW YORK, NY, US.

mon 3

tue 4

wed 5

thu 6

fri 7

sat 8

sun 9 **REDCAR JAZZ CLUB** COATHAMS HOTEL, REDCAR, CLEVELAND, ENGLAND. *cancelled*

mon 10

tue 11

wed 12

thu 13

fri 14 **RICKY TICK** PLAZA, NEWBURY, BERKSHIRE, ENGLAND.

sat 15

sun 16 **RECORD STAR SHOW** EMPIRE POOL, WEMBLEY, LONDON, ENGLAND.

mon 17

tue 18 **CHINESE R&B JAZZ CLUB** CORN EXCHANGE, BRISTOL, AVON, ENGLAND.

wed 19

thu 20

fri 21 **THE DOME** BRIGHTON, EAST SUSSEX, ENGLAND.

sat 22 **RICKY TICK** HOUSLOW, LONDON, ENGLAND.

sun 23

mon 24

tue 25

wed 26

thu 27

fri 28

sat 29

sun 30

● **RECORDING** ATLANTIC STUDIOS (NEW YORK, NY, US). MON 3rd-TUE 4th. ENGINEERS: TOM DOWD AND/OR ARIF MARDIN, CO-PRODUCERS: FELIX PAPPALARDI, AHMET ERTEGUN, ROBERT STIGWOOD. 'LAWDY MAMA' (1 B) *BL*. 'LAWDY MAMA' (1 T) *TWD*. 'LAWDY MAMA' (2) *45B; LC1; TWD*. 'STRANGE BREW' (M) *45A; DG; TWD*.

"[There is a superior audience tape of the Ricky Tick gig of the 22nd.] It was recorded by a blues enthusiast and sometime independent record label owner, the late Ian Sippen. He knew Cream, and they apparently gave him permission to record, which he did, using a reel-to-reel machine, with two mikes set up in front of the stage. Although the results are not perfect, the tape really captures the atmosphere of the gig, which took place at a vital time in the band's evolution – between the two sets of *Disraeli Gears* recording sessions. There is a remarkable clarity to the instruments and vocals, and the recording is not swamped by crowd noise – the norm for most audience tapes of this era." **JOHN PLATT, 1998**

* For key to recording abbreviations see page 160

MAY 1967

mon 1

tue 2

wed 3

thu 4

fri 5

sat 6 **CHARITY APPEAL** ROYAL AGRICULTURAL COLLEGE, CHIPPENHAM, WILTSHIRE, ENGLAND.

sun 7 **NME POLL WINNERS CONCERT** EMPIRE POOL, WEMBLEY, LONDON, ENGLAND. *PLUS JEFF BECK, BEACH BOYS ETC*

mon 8

tue 9

wed 10

thu 11

fri 12

sat 13

sun 14

mon 15

tue 16

wed 17

thu 18

fri 19

sat 20 **STADION** WEST-BERLIN, GERMANY.

sun 21 **JAGUAR CLUB/SCALA** HERFORD, GERMANY.

mon 22

tue 23 **THE MARQUEE** CENTRAL LONDON, ENGLAND. *PLUS FAMILY*

wed 24

thu 25

fri 26

sat 27 **PEMBROKE COLLEGE MAY BALL** OXFORD, OXFORDSHIRE, ENGLAND.

sun 28

mon 29 **BARBEQUE '67** TULIP BULB AUCTION HALL, SPALDING, LINCOLNSHIRE, ENGLAND. *PLUS JIMI HENDRIX, PINK FLOYD ETC*

tue 30

wed 31

● **RECORDING** ATLANTIC STUDIOS (NEW YORK, NY, US). THU 11th-SUN 14th. ENGINEER: TOM DOWD, PRODUCER: FELIX PAPPALARDI. 'TALES OF BRAVE ULYSSES' (M) *45B; DG; TWD*. 'OUTSIDE WOMAN BLUES' (M) *DG; TWD*. 'WORLD OF PAIN' (M) *DG; TWD*. 'SUNSHINE OF YOUR LOVE' (M) *45A; DG; TWD*. 'SWLABR' (M) *45B; DG; TWD*. 'WE'RE GOING WRONG' (M) *DG; TWD*. 'TAKE IT BACK' (M) *DG; TWD*. 'DANCE THE NIGHT AWAY' (M) *DG; TWD*. 'BLUE CONDITION' (M) *DG; TWD*. 'MOTHER'S LAMENT' (M) *DG; TWD*.

● **TV** RADIO BREMEN TV STUDIOS (BREMEN, GERMANY) RECORDING FRI 19th FOR *BEAT CLUB*, BROADCAST ON SHOW 20, MAY 20th. 'STRANGE BREW' *CEV; SBV*.

● **TV** BBC TV STUDIOS (MANCHESTER, ENGLAND) MIMING/PRE-RECORDED, MON 22nd, FOR *DEE TIME* ON BBC1. 'STRANGE BREW' *TL*.

● **RECORD RELEASE UK** FRI 26th 'STRANGE BREW'/'TALES OF BRAVE ULYSSES' REACTION 45.

● **RADIO** BBC PLAYHOUSE THEATRE (CENTRAL LONDON, ENGLAND) RECORDING TUE 30th FOR *SATURDAY CLUB*, BROADCAST ON BBC LIGHT PROGRAMME JUNE 3rd. PRESENTER: BRIAN MATTHEW, PRODUCER: BILL BEBB. 'STRANGE BREW' *UT; BL*.'TALES OF BRAVE ULYSSES' *UT; BL*. 'WE'RE GOING WRONG' *UT; BL*.

“That mad gig! We did the Barbeque 67 in Spalding with Jimi, I remember we hung with him. It was a huge shed, and totally mad.”
JACK BRUCE, 2000

* For key to recording abbreviations see page 160

JUNE 1967

“The Gunnell brothers who promoted the Flamingo also promoted the Ram Jam in Brixton, and it was very much a ska, bluebeat place. So when we arrived it was: ‘Where's your organ?’ We didn't go down too well there.” **JACK BRUCE, 2000**

“Ron Leslie was the promoter at the Manor House, and I played there quite a lot with Graham Bond and with John Mayall. Ron was a big Sinatra fan, and he played the records. I'm a Sinatra fan too, but I didn't think it was quite the place for it. He was playing a Sinatra record at a Graham gig, and we came on to do our second set. I started playing a little piano half jokingly, but not completely jokingly, and he got the pin about that. He said, ‘You'll never darken my door again,’ that kind of thing. But when Cream was hot he had to let me in. I felt quite good about that.” **JACK BRUCE, 2000**

thu 1 **PALAIS DES SPORTS** PARIS, FRANCE. *TWO SHOWS*

fri 2

sat 3 **RAM JAM** BRIXTON, LONDON ENGLAND.

sun 4

mon 5

tue 6

wed 7

thu 8

fri 9

sat 10

sun 11 **STARLITE BALLROOM** GREENFORD, LONDON, ENGLAND. *PLUS THE TRIADS*

mon 12

tue 13

wed 14

thu 15

fri 16

sat 17

sun 18

mon 19

tue 20

wed 21

thu 22

fri 23

sat 24

sun 25

mon 26

tue 27

wed 28

thu 29

fri 30 **BLUESVILLE '67** THE MANOR HOUSE, MANORHOUSE, LONDON, ENGLAND.

● **RADIO** FRENCH TV *FIRST FESTIVAL OF POP MUSIC* LIVE PERFORMANCE FROM PALAIS DES SPORTS GIG, THU 1st, BROADCAST DATE UNKNOWN. 'I FEEL FREE' *FLV*. 'WE'RE GOING WRONG' *UR*. NO OTHER SONG INFORMATION.

* For key to recording abbreviations see page 160

JULY 1967

sat	1	**UPPER CUT** FOREST GATE, LONDON, ENGLAND. *PLUS THE MOTIVATION, ADMISSION 8/6*	**● RECORD RELEASE US** JULY 'STRANGE BREW'/'TALES OF BRAVE ULYSSES' ATCO 45.
sun	2	**SAVILLE THEATRE** CENTRAL LONDON, ENGLAND. *TWO SHOWS 6PM, 8.30PM, ADMISSION 20/-, 15/-, 10/-, 6/-*	
mon	3		
tue	4		
wed	5		
thu	6		**● RECORDING** IBC STUDIOS (CENTRAL LONDON, ENGLAND). EARLY JULY. ENGINEER: ADRIAN BARBER, PRODUCER: FELIX PAPPALARDI. 'WHITE ROOM' (B). 'SITTING ON TOP OF THE WORLD' (B). 'BORN UNDER A BAD SIGN' (R).
fri	7		
sat	8		
sun	9		
mon	10		
tue	11		
wed	12	**FLORAL HALL** SOUTHPORT, MERSEYSIDE, ENGLAND.	
thu	13		
fri	14		**● RADIO** BBC PLAYHOUSE THEATRE (CENTRAL LONDON, ENGLAND) LIVE FRI 14th FOR *JOE LOSS SHOW* ON BBC LIGHT PROGRAMME. PRODUCER: IAN GRANT. SOME TRACKS USED IN VARIOUS LATER PROGRAMMES. 'TALES OF BRAVE ULYSSES' *TL; BL*. 'TAKE IT BACK' *TL; BL*. NO OTHER SONG INFORMATION.
sat	15		
sun	16		
mon	17		
tue	18	**UNKNOWN DATE** LOCARNO BALLROOM, GLASGOW, STRATHCLYDE, SCOTLAND.	
wed	19	**UNKNOWN DATE** TWO RED SHOES, ELGIN, GRAMPIAN, SCOTLAND.	
thu	20	**UNKNOWN DATE** BEACH BALLROOM, ABERDEEN, GRAMPIAN, SCOTLAND.	
fri	21		
sat	22		
sun	23		
mon	24		
tue	25		
wed	26		
thu	27		
fri	28		
sat	29		
sun	30		
mon	31		

"From the first quiver of 'NSU' the Cream [at the Saville Theatre] obliterated what had gone before – John Mayall's Bluesbreakers playing the blues like they've always played the blues... and the Jeff Beck Group also playing yesterday's blues only a bit louder and with even less finesse than the grand Mayall... Ginger's hunched figure throwing flicking, deformed images onto the backdrop, Jack Bruce working with the expertise of a clumsy clown, and Clapton a sequinned Sherwood loon standing with all the majesty of a Sherwood oak and playing the guitar with his mind." ***MELODY MAKER*, 1967**

"Ginger tore into his marathon 'Toad' solo, the kit shaking drunkenly under the barrage and the house lights creating weird patterns on the abstract drum skins. Touching down with a final flourish on every drum in sight, Ginger hurled away his third pair of sticks, swung off his stool, and staggered off to lean against Jack's bass amp, glaring at his kit as if considering murdering a dear friend. He postponed the execution to return for the last number, 'I'm So Glad', which Eric turned into an up-tempo 1812 Overture. Before the audience had fully regained their minds the group slipped out into the night and were back at their hotel." **UNNAMED SCOTTISH GIG, *Beat Instrumental*, 1967**

* For key to recording abbreviations see page 160

AUGUST 1967

"I think [the comparison of me with Jimi Hendrix] started because Jimi is more in the public eye than I am. I haven't changed at all. Also, the British scene is so small. Everybody knows what everyone else is doing and the whole thing thrives on competition. Some nights after a good gig I think, well, after that no one could possibly compare me with Jimi Hendrix – but I always get someone coming up and saying I sound like him."
ERIC CLAPTON, *BEAT INSTRUMENTAL*, 1967.

"Frank Zappa introduced 'this dandy little combo', otherwise known as the Cream, to [the Speakeasy audience]. Digging the Cream at such close quarters in such a good atmosphere makes all the difference and, of course, they rose to the occasion. Ginger… gave one of his most exciting yet gently sensitive performances. Eric Clapton just flew. His rapport, too, with Jack the Bruce on bass was a beautiful, spontaneous and lovely affair… Bruce as usual was hitting the most incredibly blue, or were they gold, or even purple notes, and the total feeling of unity in the group sparked off the most splendid vibrations. 'We're Going Wrong' stuck out a mile as the most exploratory, progressive and sensationally creative number that the Cream have got together at the moment. But they've got everything together anyway."
***MELODY MAKER*, 1967**

tue 1
wed 2
thu 3
fri 4
sat 5
sun 6
mon 7
tue 8
wed 9
thu 10
fri 11
sat 12
sun 13 **SEVENTH NATIONAL JAZZ POP BALLADS FESTIVAL** ROYAL WINDSOR RACECOURSE, WINDSOR, BERKSHIRE, ENGLAND.
mon 14
tue 15
wed 16
thu 17 **SPEAKEASY** CENTRAL LONDON, ENGLAND.
fri 18
sat 19
sun 20 **REDCAR JAZZ CLUB** COATHAMS HOTEL, REDCAR, CLEVELAND, ENGLAND. *BAND'S FEE £285*
mon 21
tue 22 **FILLMORE AUDITORIUM** SAN FRANCISCO, CA, US. *FIRST DATE OF CREAM'S FIRST FULL NORTH AMERICAN TOUR*
wed 23 **FILLMORE AUDITORIUM** SAN FRANCISCO, CA, US. *PLUS BUTTERFIELD BLUES BAND, ELECTRIC FLAG*
thu 24 **FILLMORE AUDITORIUM** SAN FRANCISCO, CA, US. *PLUS BUTTERFIELD BLUES BAND, ELECTRIC FLAG*
fri 25 **FILLMORE AUDITORIUM** SAN FRANCISCO, CA, US. *PLUS BUTTERFIELD BLUES BAND, ELECTRIC FLAG*
sat 26
sun 27 **FILLMORE AUDITORIUM** SAN FRANCISCO, CA, US. *PLUS BUTTERFIELD BLUES BAND, ELECTRIC FLAG*
mon 28
tue 29 **FILLMORE AUDITORIUM** SAN FRANCISCO, CA, US. *PLUS BUTTERFIELD BLUES BAND, ELECTRIC FLAG*
wed 30 **FILLMORE AUDITORIUM** SAN FRANCISCO, CA, US. *PLUS BUTTERFIELD BLUES BAND, ELECTRIC FLAG*
thu 31 **FILLMORE AUDITORIUM** SAN FRANCISCO, CA, US. *PLUS BUTTERFIELD BLUES BAND, ELECTRIC FLAG*

● **RECORDING** IBC STUDIOS (CENTRAL LONDON, ENGLAND). EARLY AUGUST. ENGINEER: ADRIAN BARBER, PRODUCER: FELIX PAPPALARDI. 'WHITE ROOM' NO WAH-WAH (T) *UR; BL.* 'BORN UNDER A BAD SIGN' (B). 'FALSTAFF BEER COMMERCIAL' (B) *BL.* 'FALSTAFF BEER COMMERCIAL' (M) *TWD.*

* For key to recording abbreviations see page 160

SEPTEMBER 1967

"The Fillmore had a great PA, and a really good guy doing it called Charlie Button who did the sound for the Grateful Dead. It was great to hear the wonderful sound. This was when we first started doing the extended improvisations, which was new to the band. We usually played very short three-, four-, five-minute versions of the songs. Quite simply, we were fed up with doing that, and the audience was so great at the Fillmore. They were all so out of it, so laidback, and would shout: 'Just play!' They wouldn't let us go. So we just started jamming, and that turned into what we became known for. We didn't sit down and have a big discussion, oh, let's do this. The Who became known for smashing up their equipment, and that became their albatross. Our albatross was having to do very long solos when you maybe didn't feel like it. Mixed blessings, really. We would sometimes strip it down to where Eric would play completely unaccompanied, for quite a long time, and I remember him doing some quite incredible stuff, quite amazing. But that wasn't recorded." **JACK BRUCE, 2000**

fri 1 **FILLMORE AUDITORIUM** SAN FRANCISCO, CA, US. *PLUS BUTTERFIELD BLUES BAND, ELECTRIC FLAG*

sat 2 **FILLMORE AUDITORIUM** SAN FRANCISCO, CA, US. *PLUS BUTTERFIELD BLUES BAND, ELECTRIC FLAG*

sun 3 **FILLMORE AUDITORIUM** SAN FRANCISCO, CA, US. *PLUS BUTTERFIELD BLUES BAND, ELECTRIC FLAG*

mon 4 **WHISKY A GO GO** LOS ANGELES, CA, US. *PLUS THE RICH KIDS*

tue 5 **WHISKY A GO GO** LOS ANGELES, CA, US. *PLUS THE RICH KIDS*

wed 6 **WHISKY A GO GO** LOS ANGELES, CA, US. PLUS THE RICH KIDS

thu 7

fri 8 **CROSS TOWN BUS CLUB** BOSTON, MA, US.

sat 9 **BRANDEIS UNIVERSITY** WALTHAM, MA, US.

sun 10 **PSYCHEDELIC SUPERMARKET** BOSTON, MA, US. *THREE SHOWS*

mon 11 **PSYCHEDELIC SUPERMARKET** BOSTON, MA, US.

tue 12 **PSYCHEDELIC SUPERMARKET** BOSTON, MA, US. *TWO SHOWS*

wed 13 **PSYCHEDELIC SUPERMARKET** BOSTON, MA, US. *TWO SHOWS*

thu 14 **PSYCHEDELIC SUPERMARKET** BOSTON, MA, US. *TWO SHOWS*

fri 15 **PSYCHEDELIC SUPERMARKET** BOSTON, MA, US. *TWO SHOWS*

sat 16 **PSYCHEDELIC SUPERMARKET** BOSTON, MA, US. *THREE SHOWS*

sun 17

mon 18

tue 19

wed 20

thu 21

fri 22 **ACTION HOUSE** LONG BEACH, NY, US. *PLUS MOBY GRAPE, THE NEONS, ADMISSION $3*

sat 23 **VILLAGE THEATER** NEW YORK, NY, US. *TWO SHOWS 8PM & 10.30PM, PLUS MOBY GRAPE, SOUL SURVIVOURS ADM $3, $4, $5*

sun 24 **ACTION HOUSE** LONG BEACH, NY, US.

mon 25

tue 26 **CAFÉ AU GO GO** NEW YORK, NY, US. *PLUS THE PAUPERS*

wed 27 **CAFÉ AU GO GO** NEW YORK, NY, US. *PLUS THE PAUPERS*

thu 28 **CAFÉ AU GO GO** NEW YORK, NY, US. *PLUS THE PAUPERS*

fri 29 **CAFÉ AU GO GO** NEW YORK, NY, US. *PLUS THE PAUPERS*

sat 30 **VILLAGE THEATER** NEW YORK, NY, US. *EARLY SHOW*
CAFÉ AU GO GO NEW YORK, NY, US. *PLUS THE PAUPERS*

● **RECORDING** ATLANTIC STUDIOS (NEW YORK, NY, US). MID SEPTEMBER. ENGINEER: TOM DOWD. PRODUCER: FELIX PAPPALARDI. 'SITTING ON TOP OF THE WORLD' (T, M) *WOF; TWD*. 'BORN UNDER A BAD SIGN' (T, M) *WOF; TWD*. 'WHITE ROOM' (T).

* For key to recording abbreviations see page 160

OCTOBER 1967

sun	1	**CAFÉ AU GO GO** NEW YORK, NY, US. *PLUS THE PAUPERS*
mon	2	
tue	3	**CAFÉ AU GO GO** NEW YORK, NY, US. *PLUS RICHIE HAVENS*
wed	4	**CAFÉ AU GO GO** NEW YORK, NY, US. *PLUS RICHIE HAVENS*
thu	5	**CAFÉ AU GO GO** NEW YORK, NY, US. *PLUS RICHIE HAVENS*
fri	6	**CAFÉ AU GO GO** NEW YORK, NY, US. *PLUS RICHIE HAVENS*
sat	7	**CAFÉ AU GO GO** NEW YORK, NY, US. *PLUS RICHIE HAVENS*
sun	8	**CAFÉ AU GO GO** NEW YORK, NY, US. *PLUS RICHIE HAVENS*
mon	9	
tue	10	
wed	11	**FIFTH DIMENSION** ANN ARBOR, MI, US.
thu	12	**FIFTH DIMENSION** ANN ARBOR, MI, US.
fri	13	**GRANDE BALLROOM** DETROIT, MI, US. *PLUS MC5, THE THYME*
sat	14	**GRANDE BALLROOM** DETROIT, MI, US. *PLUS THE RATIONALS*
sun	15	**GRANDE BALLROOM** DETROIT, MI, US. *PLUS THE APOSTLES. LAST DATE OF CREAM'S FIRST NORTH AMERICAN TOUR*
mon	16	
tue	17	
wed	18	
thu	19	**ROMANO'S BALLROOM** BELFAST, NORTHERN IRELAND. *POSTPONED UNTIL NOVEMBER 2nd*
fri	20	
sat	21	
sun	22	
mon	23	
tue	24	
wed	25	
thu	26	**MAGOOS** GLASGOW, SCOTLAND. *DATE NOT CERTAIN*
fri	27	**CAPITAL** EDINBURGH, SCOTLAND. *DATE NOT CERTAIN*
sat	28	
sun	29	**SAVILLE THEATRE** CENTRAL LONDON, ENGLAND. *PLUS THE ACTION, THE BONZO DOG DOO-DAH BAND*
mon	30	
tue	31	

❝Maybe [the audiences on our first American tour] were surprised to find out we could play our instruments? Everywhere we played we broke the records. There are some very good groups out there – the Electric Flag and the Bloomfield band are very good indeed. But it's a different scene. They all rehearse all day and work in the evenings. They get a very rehearsed sound, whereas we are getting further out in playing things differently every night. We even did the same number twice some nights and the versions were so different we got away with it.❞ **GINGER BAKER, *Melody Maker*, 1967**

Top Gear became the most important rock music show on the BBC's new Radio 1, turning the Beeb's necessity for specially recorded sessions to its advantage by allowing groups more freedom to develop work for the programme. Cream first appeared on *Top Gear* this month. While the laidback John Peel is always associated with the three-hour Sunday-afternoon show, at first it was presented by combinations of Peel, Tommy Vance and Pete Drummond, as Cream's appearances now and in January reveal.

● **RECORD RELEASE US** OCTOBER 'SPOONFUL'/'SPOONFUL PART 2' ATCO 45.

● **RECORDING** ATLANTIC STUDIOS (NEW YORK, NY, US). EARLY OCTOBER, ENGINEER: TOM DOWD, PRODUCER: FELIX PAPPALARDI. 'PRESSED RAT AND WARTHOG' (B). 'ANYONE FOR TENNIS' (B). 'WHITE ROOM' (T).

● **RADIO** BBC AEOLIAN HALL (CENTRAL LONDON, ENGLAND) RECORDING TUE 24th FOR *TOP GEAR*, BROADCAST ON BBC RADIO-1 OCTOBER 29th. PRESENTERS: JOHN PEEL & PETE DRUMMOND, PRODUCER: BERNIE ANDREWS, ENGINEER: DAVE TATE. REPEATED ON *DAVID SYMONDS* BBC RADIO-1 MON OCTOBER 30th TO FRI NOVEMBER 3rd; AND ON *HAPPENING SUNDAY* DECEMBER 3rd BBC RADIO-1; AND ON *RHYTHM & BLUES* BBC WORLD SERVICE DECEMBER 18th. 'OUTSIDE WOMAN BLUES' *UT; BL.* 'BORN UNDER A BAD SIGN' *UT; BL.* 'TAKE IT BACK' *UT; BL.* 'SUNSHINE OF YOUR LOVE' *TL; BL.*

* For key to recording abbreviations see page 160

NOVEMBER 1967

wed	1	**BAL TABARIN** BROMLEY, LONDON, ENGLAND.	● **RECORD RELEASE US** NOVEMBER *DISRAELI GEARS* ATCO LP.
thu	2	**ROMANO'S BALLROOM** BELFAST, NORTHERN IRELAND.	
fri	3		● **RECORD RELEASE UK** FRI 3rd *DISRAELI GEARS* REACTION LP.
sat	4		
sun	5		
mon	6	**SILVER BLADES ICE RINK** STREATHAM, LONDON, ENGLAND.	
tue	7		
wed	8		
thu	9		
fri	10		
sat	11	**HIT CLUB** VEJGAARD HALLEN, ALBORG, DENMARK. *PLUS DEFENDERS, PARROTS, GO-GO*	● **TV** TV VILLAGE, STUDIO A (GLADSAXE, DENMARK) LIVE PERFORMANCE SAT 11th FOR *TOP POP* TV SHOW. 'NSU' *TL.* 'STRANGE BREW' *TL.* 'I'M SO GLAD' *TL.*
sun	12	**FALKONERTEATRET** COPENHAGEN, DENMARK. *TWO SHOWS 4PM & 7PM, PLUS STEPPEULVENE, DEFENDERS*	
mon	13	**KULTUURITALO** HELSINKI, FINLAND. *TWO SHOWS*	● **TV** PASILA TV STUDIOS (HELSINKI, FINLAND) RECORDING/MIMING MON 13th FOR FINNISH TV. 'SUNSHINE OF YOUR LOVE' *TSU.* 'WORLD OF PAIN' *TSU.* 'TALES OF BRAVE ULYSSES' *TSU.* 'OUTSIDE WOMAN BLUES' *TSU.*
tue	14	**KONSERTHUSET** STOCKHOLM, SWEDEN.	
wed	15	**KONSERTHALLEN** LISEBERG AMUSEMENT PARK, GOTHENBURG, SWEDEN. *TWO SHOWS*	
thu	16		
fri	17	**RIGOLETTO** JÖNKÖPING, SWEDEN.	
sat	18	**IDROTTSHUSET** ÖREBRO, SWEDEN.	
sun	19		
mon	20		
tue	21		● **FILM** FRENCH TV FILMING (16mm) LIVE PERFORMANCE AROUND LATE NOVEMBER AT REVOLUTION CLUB (LONDON, ENGLAND). 'TALES OF BRAVE ULYSSES' *FLV.* 'SUNSHINE OF YOUR LOVE' *FLV.* 'SPOONFUL' *FLV.*
wed	22		
thu	23	**CLUB A GO GO** NEWCASTLE-UPON-TYNE, TYNE & WEAR, ENGLAND.	
fri	24	**MARINE BALLROOM** CENTRAL PIER, MORECAMBE, LANCASHIRE, ENGLAND.	
sat	25		● **TV** STUDIO G, BBC TV LIME GROVE STUDIOS (LONDON, ENGLAND) MIMING/RECORDING SAT 25th FOR *TWICE A FORTNIGHT* SHOW 7, BROADCAST ON BBC1, DECEMBER 2nd. ALSO USED LATER IN TONY PALMER'S *ALL MY LOVING* BBC DOCUMENTARY. 'WE'RE GOING WRONG' *FLV-I.*
sun	26		
mon	27		
tue	28	**THE MARQUEE** CENTRAL LONDON, ENGLAND. *PLUS REMO FOUR, CREAM PROBABLY CANCELLED*	
wed	29		
thu	30		

It's likely that Cream did not make their Marquee booking on the 28th, due to Ginger Baker's ill health. On the same date the band was also due to record a BBC radio session for Alexis Korner's World Service programme *Rhythm & Blues*, but cancelled that too. "Cream drummer Ginger Baker collapsed when the group were recording for [the BBC's] *Twice A Fortnight* programme. Ginger is now in hospital with a suspected ulcer," said *Melody Maker*, adding a week later: "Baker will resume work with the group on Monday [11th Dec] when they fly to New York for recording. Manager Robert Stigwood said: 'After exhaustive tests it was found that Ginger was not suffering from an ulcer. He collapsed through exhaustion.'"

* For key to recording abbreviations see page 160

DECEMBER 1967

fri 1 **TOP RANK** BRIGHTON, EAST SUSSEX, ENGLAND. *PROBABLY CANCELLED*

sat 2

sun 3

mon 4

tue 5

wed 6

thu 7

fri 8

sat 9

sun 10

mon 11

tue 12

wed 13

thu 14

fri 15

sat 16

sun 17

mon 18

tue 19

wed 20 **DEBUTANTE'S BALL** UNKNOWN VENUE, CHICAGO, MI, US. *PRIVATE PERFORMANCE*

thu 21

fri 22 **GRANDE BALLROOM** DETROIT, MI, US. *PLUS MC5, BILLY C & THE SUNSHINE, SOAP*

sat 23 **GRANDE BALLROOM** DETROIT, MI, US. *PLUS MC5, BILLY C & THE SUNSHINE, SOAP*

sun 24

mon 25

tue 26

wed 27

thu 28

fri 29

sat 30

sun 31

● **RECORDING** ATLANTIC STUDIOS (NEW YORK, NY, US). TUE 12th -FRI 15th, SUN 24th. ENGINEER: TOM DOWD, PRODUCER: FELIX PAPPALARDI. 'PRESSED RAT AND WARTHOG' (T) *BL.* 'ANYONE FOR TENNIS' (T) *BL.* 'WHITE ROOM' (T).

“We use Atlantic's New York studios. It's done quicker there, we get a better sound, and there's a really hip engineer – one of the best in America.” **ERIC CLAPTON, *Beat Instrumental*, 1968**

“We're all temperamental, but Tom Dowd and Felix Pappalardi manage to get rid of that temperament. It's not even the sound we get that encourages us to record in America, just those people. The sessions are relaxed and everybody's working. We spend a long time in the studio, so we don't have to rush. We usually talk for hours before we record anything. Then we play, think, add sounds.” **GINGER BAKER, *Beat Instrumental*, 1968**

“The party in Chicago was interesting. Some billionaire had a very expensive place on the Lake Shore. People were arriving by helicopter. A lot of the second-city comedy guys – Bill Murray, Dan Ackroyd, John Belushi – gatecrashed. I met a couple of those guys years later and they said oh, that was a great gig. It was a very silly gig, but I think we got paid a lot of money. So it made Stigwood a few bob.” **JACK BRUCE, 2000**

* For key to recording abbreviations see page 160

JANUARY 1968

mon 1

tue 2

wed 3

thu 4

fri 5

sat 6

sun 7

mon 8

tue 9

● **RADIO** BBC AEOLIAN HALL (CENTRAL LONDON, ENGLAND) RECORDING TUE 9th FOR *TOP GEAR*, BROADCAST ON BBC RADIO 1 JANUARY 14th. PRESENTERS: JOHN PEEL & TOMMY VANCE, PRODUCER BEV PHILLIPS, ENGINEER: PETE CARR. 'POLITICIAN' *UT; BL*. 'STEPPING OUT' *ECC*. 'SWLABR' *UT; BL*. 'BLUE CONDITION' *TL; BL*.

wed 10

thu 11

fri 12

sat 13

sun 14 **REDCAR JAZZ CLUB** COATHAMS HOTEL, REDCAR, CLEVELAND, ENGLAND.

mon 15

tue 16

wed 17

thu 18

fri 19

sat 20 **LONDON UNIVERSITY UNION** CENTRAL LONDON, ENGLAND.

sun 21

mon 22

tue 23

wed 24

thu 25

fri 26

sat 27 **ST. MARY'S COLLEGE** TWICKENHAM, LONDON, ENGLAND.

sun 28

mon 29

tue 30

wed 31

"I remember the song 'Politician' came about at this BBC session. Eric and I started playing the riff. Because it was three tracks, we were able to lay it down and then I could improvise a vocal over that interesting riff. So the song really did come out of a BBC session. I've no idea why the Cream BBC sessions haven't been released, although I believe some of the original tapes are missing. They'd make a very interesting CD package."
JACK BRUCE, 2000

* For key to recording abbreviations see page 160

FEBRUARY 1968

66For the filming in Copenhagen they had a moratorium on dope-smoking for a day or so. Everybody was smoking loads of it, and blowing it out at the police, who were looking very glum. We were freezing our bollocks off, I remember that, sitting there miming to tracks. Was it 'World Of Pain'? Well, it certainly was. We'd do anything back then. Just ell us where we have to be. I don't think there was a lot of planning.**99** **JACK BRUCE, 2000**

66I think that long US tour, February to June 1968, led to the demise of the band, imply because you can't lock up three guys in a car for that long, and because we never had time to write. We had Bob Adcock by now as a personal roadie, and we would just go from whatever place it was – it always seemed to be somewhere in the Mid-West – arrive at the airport, rent a station wagon, and drive to the hotel, which would probably be a Holiday Inn or similar. We'd then drive to the gig, which would probably be called a Psychedelic Supermarket or something like that. It had all become a grind by that point.**99** **JACK BRUCE, 2000**

thu 1

fri 2

sat 3 **UNIVERSITY COLLEGE** CENTRAL LONDON, ENGLAND. *PLUS TWO OF EACH, MILLIONAIRES, SOUNDTREKKERS, ADMISSION 8/-*

sun 4

mon 5

tue 6

wed 7 **TIVOLI CONCERT HALL** COPENHAGEN, DENMARK. *TWO SHOWS 8PM & 9.30PM, PLUS HANSSON & KARLSSON ETC*

thu 8

fri 9 **LEICESTER UNIVERSITY ARTS BALL** LEICESTER LEICESTERSHIRE, ENGLAND. *LAST KNOWN UK DATE APART FROM RAH NOVEMBER*

sat 10

sun 11

mon 12

tue 13

wed 14

thu 15

fri 16

sat 17

sun 18

mon 19

tue 20

wed 21

thu 22

fri 23 **CIVIC AUDITORIUM** SANTA MONICA, CA, US. *FIRST DATE OF CREAM'S SECOND NORTH AMERICAN TOUR*

sat 24 **EARL WARREN SHOWGROUNDS** SANTA BARBARA, CA, US.

sun 25 **SAN FERNANDO VALLEY COLLEGE** SAN FERNANDO, CA, US.

mon 26

tue 27

wed 28

thu 29 **WINTERLAND** SAN FRANCISCO, CA, US. *TWO SHOWS, PLUS BIG BLACK, LOADING ZONE*

● **RECORD RELEASE US** FEBRUARY 'SUNSHINE OF YOUR LOVE'/'SWLABR' ATCO 45.

● **FILM** AT VOGNMANDSMARKEN (COPENHAGEN, DENMARK) MIMING MON 5th TO 'WORLD OF PAIN' ON BACK OF TRUCK FOR DANISH MOVIE *DET VAR EN LØRDAG AFTEN* ("ON A SATURDAY NIGHT"), AND IN UNKNOWN HALL (COPENHAGEN, DENMARK) MIMING TUE 6th TO 'WE'RE GOING WRONG' FOR SAME MOVIE.

● **RECORDING** ATLANTIC STUDIOS (NEW YORK, NY, US). SAT 10th-TUE 20th. ENGINEER: TOM DOWD, PRODUCER: FELIX PAPPALARDI. 'ANYONE FOR TENNIS' (T, M) *45A; GB CD; TWD*. 'PRESSED RAT AND WARTHOG' (T, M) *45B; WOF; TWD*. 'POLITICIAN' (T). 'PASSING THE TIME' (B). 'WHITE ROOM' WAH-WAH (T). 'DESERTED CITIES OF THE HEART' (B). 'AS YOU SAID' (B). 'THOSE WERE THE DAYS' (B).

* For key to recording abbreviations see page 160

MARCH 1968

fri 1 **WINTERLAND** SAN FRANCISCO, CA, US. *TWO SHOWS, PLUS BIG BLACK, LOADING ZONE*

sat 2 **WINTERLAND** SAN FRANCISCO, CA, US. *TWO SHOWS, PLUS BIG BLACK, LOADING ZONE*

sun 3 **FILLMORE AUDITORIUM** SAN FRANCISCO, CA, US. *TWO SHOWS, PLUS BIG BLACK, LOADING ZONE*

mon 4

tue 5

wed 6

thu 7 **FILLMORE AUDITORIUM** SAN FRANCISCO, CA, US. *TWO SHOWS, PLUS BLOOD SWEAT & TEARS ETC*

fri 8 **WINTERLAND** SAN FRANCISCO, CA, US. *TWO SHOWS*

sat 9 **WINTERLAND** SAN FRANCISCO, CA, US. *TWO SHOWS*

sun 10 **WINTERLAND** SAN FRANCISCO, CA, US. *TWO SHOWS*

mon 11 **MEMORIAL AUDITORIUM** SACRAMENTO, CA, US.

tue 12

wed 13 **SELLAND ARENA** FRESNO, CA, US.

thu 14

fri 15 **SHRINE AUDITORIUM** LOS ANGELES, CA, US.

sat 16 **SHRINE AUDITORIUM** LOS ANGELES, CA, US.

sun 17 **STAR THEATER** PHOENIX, AZ, US.

mon 18 **CONVENTION CENTER** ANAHEIM, CA, US.

tue 19 **THE FAMILY DOG** DENVER, CO, US.

wed 20

thu 21 **BELOIT COLLEGE** BELOIT, WI, US.

fri 22 **CLOWES MEMORIAL HALL** BUTLER UNIVERSITY, INDIANAPOLIS, IN, US.

sat 23 **BROWN UNIVERSITY** PROVIDENCE, RI, US. *CANCELLED*

sun 24

mon 25

tue 26 **CATHOLIC UNION SCHOOL** SCOTCH PLAINS, NJ, US.

wed 27 **STAPLES HIGH SCHOOL AUDITORIUM** WESTPORT, CT, US.

thu 28

fri 29 **HUNTER COLLEGE AUDITORIUM** NEW YORK, NY, US. *TWO SHOWS*

sat 30 **STATE FAIR MUSIC CENTER** DALLAS, TX, US.

sun 31 **MUSIC HALL** HOUSTON, TX, US.

* For key to recording abbreviations see page 160

“We rented recording equipment from a studio in LA and it was driven to the Fillmore in a giant Hertz truck. The truck was all decked out inside with two 8-track machines, a full console, and four speakers. Tommy Dowd was present, but the engineer for this session was Bill Halverson, a very young, incredible guy. Tom and Bill carefully set up all the mikes on stage and made preparations. I don't think the audience even knew [the recording] was going on.” **FELIX PAPPALARDI, *Hit Parader*, 1969**

“The live recordings were more or less the regular set. We wanted to have the set as we would do it on-stage. The recordings that were released are good, but like any live recordings you always think oh god, if only they'd got such and such a night. I think it was quite a brave attempt, and it's probably up to that time the best live recorded rock stuff. It was pretty representative of the band on an average night, but not on one of the nights when we seemed to take off – like the very early Fillmore gigs, for example.” **JACK BRUCE, 2000**

● **FILM** 16mm FILMING OF FILLMORE AND WINTERLAND GIGS (SAN FRANCISCO, CA, US) THU 7th-SAT 9th FOR TONY PALMER'S MUSIC DOCUMENTARY *ALL MY LOVING*, BROADCAST LATER ON BBC TV. 'I'M SO GLAD' *FLV-I*. 'TOAD' *FLV-I*.

● **LIVE RECORDING** THU 7th-SUN 10th. FILLMORE AND WINTERLAND GIGS (SAN FRANCISO, CA, US) OFFICALLY RECORDED FOR POTENTIAL COMMERICAL RELEASE. PRODUCER: FELIX PAPPALARDI, ENGINEER: BILL HALVERSON. REMIX FOR LIVE CREAM: ADRIAN BARBER. REMIX FOR LIVE CREAM VOLUME II: GENE PAUL AND KEVIN BRADY. AS FOLLOWS:

● **THU 7th** FILLMORE AUDITORIUM (SAN FRANCISCO, CA, US). FIRST SHOW: 'TALES OF BRAVE ULYSSES' *TL*. 'NSU' *TL*. 'POLITICIAN' *TL*. 'CROSSROADS' *TL*. 'ROLLIN' AND TUMBLIN'' *LC1; TWD*. 'SWEET WINE *TL*. SECOND SHOW: 'SPOONFUL' *TL*. 'SUNSHINE OF YOUR LOVE' *ECA* 'SITTING ON TOP OF THE WORLD' *TL*. 'STEPPING OUT' *TL*. 'TRAINTIME' *TL*. 'TOAD' *WOF; TWD (+ EDIT FROM FRI 8th)*; 'I'M SO GLAD' *TL*.

● **FRI 8th** WINTERLAND (SAN FRANCISCO, CA, US). FIRST SHOW *TSU*. SECOND SHOW: 'CAT'S SQUIRREL' *TL*. 'SUNSHINE OF YOUR LOVE' *TL*. 'SPOONFUL' *TL*. 'STEPPING OUT' *TL*. 'TRAINTIME' *WOF; TWD*. 'TOAD' *UR (EXCEPT INSTRUMENTAL EDIT INTO THU 7th VERSION, TWD)*

● **SAT 9th** WINTERLAND (SAN FRANCISCO, CA, US). FIRST SHOW: 'TALES OF BRAVE ULYSSES' *TL*. 'NSU' *TWD*. 'SITTING ON TOP OF THE WORLD' *TL*. 'CROSSROADS' *TL*. 'SWEET WINE' *TL*. SECOND SHOW: 'SUNSHINE OF YOUR LOVE' *LC2; TWD*. 'SPOONFUL' *TL*. 'SLEEPY TIME TIME' *LC1; TWD*. 'STEPPING OUT' *LC2; TWD (NOT SUN 10th AS SLEEVE)*. 'TRAINTIME' *TL*. 'TOAD' *TL*. 'I'M SO GLAD' *TL*.

● **SUN 10th** WINTERLAND (SAN FRANCISCO, CA, US). FIRST SHOW: 'TALES OF BRAVE ULYSSES' *LC2; TWD*. 'SPOONFUL' *WOF; TWD*. 'CROSSROADS' *45A; WOF; TWD*. 'WE'RE GOING WRONG' *UR; BL*. 'SWEET WINE' *LC1; TWD*. SECOND SHOW: 'SUNSHINE OF YOUR LOVE' *TL; BL*. 'NSU' *LC1*. 'STEPPING OUT' [WRONGLY CREDITED ON *LC2; TWD*] *TL; BL*. 'TRAINTIME' *TL; BL*. 'TOAD' *TL; BL*. 'I'M SO GLAD' *TL; BL-*

APRIL 1968

mon 1

tue 2

wed 3 **STATE UNIVERSITY OF NEW YORK** STONEY BROOK, NY, US. *CANCELLED*

thu 4

fri 5 **BACK BAY THEATER** BOSTON, MA, US.

sat 6 **COMMODORE BALLROOM** LOWELL, MA, US.

sun 7 **EASTMAN COLLEGE** ROCHESTER, NY, US.

mon 8 **CAPITOL THEATER** OTTOWA, ON, CANADA.

tue 9

wed 10 **WOOLSEY HALL** YALE UNIVERSITY, NEW HAVEN, CT, US.

thu 11

fri 12 **ELECTRIC FACTORY THEATER** PHILADELPHIA, PA, US. *POSTPONED TO APRIL 19th*

sat 13 **ELECTRIC FACTORY THEATER** PHILADELPHIA, PA, US. *POSTPONED TO APRIL 20th*

sun 14 **ELECTRIC FACTORY THEATER** PHILADELPHIA, PA, US. *POSTPONED TO APRIL 21st*

mon 15

tue 16 **PAUL SAUVE ARENA** MONTREAL, PQ, CANADA. *POSTPONED TO JUNE 11th*

wed 17

thu 18

fri 19 **ELECTRIC FACTORY** PHILADELPHIA, PA, US. *(GRANDE BALLROOM BOOKING FOR TODAY POSTPONED TO JUNE 7th)*

sat 20 **ELECTRIC FACTORY** PHILADELPHIA, PA, US. *(GRANDE BALLROOM BOOKING FOR TODAY POSTPONED TO JUNE 8th)*

sun 21 **ELECTRIC FACTORY** PHILADELPHIA, PA, US. *(GRANDE BALLROOM BOOKING FOR TODAY POSTPONED TO JUNE 9th)*

mon 22 **MASSEY HALL** TORONTO, ON, CANADA.

tue 23

wed 24

thu 25

fri 26 **THE CELLAR** ARLINGTON HEIGHTS, IL, US.

sat 27 **COLISEUM** CHICAGO, IL, US. *PLUS FRANK ZAPPA & THE MOTHERS OF INVENTION*

sun 28 **KIEL AUDITORIUM** ST. LOUIS, MO, US.

mon 29

tue 30

The band made an unscheduled return to England from 11th to 18th for a rest from the seemingly endless US tour (dates from 12th to 21st postponed). “They just worked us to death touring, almost literally at times. I think it was Canada where I kind of broke. The problem was I wanted our own really good PA. We'd go to quite large places, outdoor baseball-type stadiums some of them, and we had no PA, so they'd provide a tiny little system. It was killing my voice. I said to Ginger we need a PA, and he said we can't afford it. We had I think a number two album at that time, and so I just said well that's it, I'm going home. I went to the airport and got myself a ticket – which I probably didn't know how to do, but somehow managed. But two roadies came and almost physically carried me back. So I sort of carried on. I think that's an indication of the pressure we were under.”

JACK BRUCE, 2000

* For key to recording abbreviations see page 160

MAY 1968

wed 1

thu 2 **WISCONSIN STATE UNIVERSITY FIELDHOUSE** MADISON, WI, US.

fri 3 **THE SCENE** MILWAUKEE, WI, US.

sat 4 **THE SCENE** MILWAUKEE, WI, US.

sun 5 **NEW CITY OPERA HOUSE** ST. PAUL, MN, US.

mon 6

tue 7

wed 8

thu 9

fri 10

sat 11 **CABELL COUNTY MEMORIAL FIELDHOUSE** HUNTINGTON, WV, US.

sun 12 **MUSIC HALL** CLEVELAND, OH, US.

mon 13

tue 14 **VETERANS MEMORIAL AUDITORIUM** COLUMBUS, OH, US.

wed 15 **AK-SAR-BEN COLISEUM** OMAHA, NE, US.

thu 16

fri 17 **CONVENTION CENTER** AHAHEIM, CA, US.

sat 18 **ICE PALACE** LAS VEGAS, NV, US.

sun 19

mon 20 **EXHIBIT HALL** SAN DIEGO, CA, US.

tue 21

wed 22

thu 23

fri 24 **ROBERTSON GYM** UNIVERSITY OF SOUTHERN CALIFORNIA, SANTA BARBARA, CA, US.

sat 25 **CIVIC AUDITORIUM** SAN JOSE, CA, US.

sun 26

mon 27 **SWING AUDITORIUM** NATIONAL ORANGE SHOWGROUNDS, SAN BERNADINO, CA, US.

tue 28 **PACIFIC CENTER** LONG BEACH, CA, US.

wed 29 **EAGLES AUDITORIUM** SEATTLE, WA, US.

thu 30 **EAGLES AUDITORIUM** SEATTLE, WA, US. *AFTERNOON SHOW*

fri 31 **CALGARY STAMPEDE** CALGARY, AB, CANADA

● **RECORD RELEASE UK/US** MAY 'ANYONE FOR TENNIS'/'PRESSED RAT AND WARTHOG' POLYDOR (UK) AND ATCO (US) 45s.

● **TV** CBS STUDIOS, MIMING/LIVE FRI 17th FOR *THE SUMMER BROTHERS SMOTHER SHOW* (LOS ANGELES, CA, US), BROADCAST MAY 19th. 'ANYONE FOR TENNIS' (MIMING) *FLV.* 'SUNSHINE OF YOUR LOVE' (LIVE) *AUDIO TWD.*

"There's a terrible video of us playing tennis rackets, dressed up as New York cops, for 'Anyone For Tennis' on American TV. For some reason they wanted to start off with a close-up of frogs on salad. All this lettuce with frogs on it. Action! And the frogs of course would jump. Cut! So after about ten attempts it was, 'OK, nail the frogs!' Guy comes out with a hammer. If you look at the expressions on our faces we're so disgusted, because they'd just nailed the frogs. Eric looks like he's going to throw up, and we're all really fed up. Some mad director with his brilliant idea."

JACK BRUCE, 2000

* For key to recording abbreviations see page 160

JUNE 1968

sat	1	**SALES PAVILION** EDMONTON, AB, CANADA
sun	2	**PACIFIC COLISEUM** VANCOUVER, BC, CANADA.
mon	3	
tue	4	
wed	5	
thu	6	
fri	7	**GRANDE BALLROOM** DETROIT, MI, US. *(RESCHEDULED FROM APRIL 19th) PLUS MC5, THE CAROUSEL*
sat	8	**GRANDE BALLROOM** DETROIT, MI, US. *(RESCHEDULED FROM APRIL 20th) PLUS NICKEL PLATE EXPRESS, ST. LOUIS UNION*
sun	9	**GRANDE BALLROOM** DETROIT, MI, US. *(RESCHEDULED FROM APRIL 21st) PLUS THE JAMES GANG, THE THYME*
mon	10	
tue	11	**PAUL SAUVE ARENA** MONTREAL, PQ, CANADA. *(RESCHEDULED FROM APRIL 16th)*
wed	12	
thu	13	
fri	14	**ISLAND GARDENS** HEMPSTEAD, NY, US. *ADMISSION $3.50, $4.50, $5.50*
sat	15	**OAKDALE MUSIC THEATER** WALLINGFORD, CT, US.
sun	16	**CAMDEN COUNTY MUSIC FAIR** CHERRY HILL, NJ, US. *LAST DATE OF CREAM'S SECOND NORTH AMERICAN TOUR*
mon	17	
tue	18	
wed	19	
thu	20	
fri	21	
sat	22	
sun	23	
mon	24	
tue	25	
wed	26	
thu	27	
fri	28	
sat	29	
sun	30	

"The Camden County Music Fair was visited by several up-and-coming rock acts such as Cream and Hendrix. It held about 300 to 400 people. My ticket price was $5.50 and I sat front row, dead centre, about 20 feet in front of the band. Cream was my first concert, and I was completely derailed for the rest of my life. Clapton looked 20 feet tall in a red velvet jacket and blue trousers. The band came out of the wings to enter the stage and as Clapton walked by me he bashed my elbow with his guitar and stopped to make sure I was all right. He apologised profusely and then shook my hand before going on stage. For years I had to prove that it was hours of dedicated practice and not this brush with Clapton that gave me an edge on the other guitarists in the neighbourhood."

DON MERLINO, 2000

● **RECORDING** ATLANTIC STUDIOS (NEW YORK, NY, US). MID-LATE JUNE. ENGINEER: TOM DOWD, PRODUCER: FELIX PAPPALARDI. 'WHITE ROOM' (M) *45A; WOF; TWD*. 'THOSE WERE THE DAYS' (T, M) *45B; WOF; TWD*. 'PASSING THE TIME' COMPLETE (T, M) *TWD*. 'PASSING THE TIME' EDIT (M) *45B; WOF*. 'POLITICIAN' (M) *WOF; TWD*. 'AS YOU SAID' (T, M) *WOF; TWD*. 'DESERTED CITIES OF THE HEART' (T, M) *WOF; TWD*.

* For key to recording abbreviations see page 160

JULY 1968

“The success that Cream had was nice – and then there was this new feeling that it's going to end. The height of success that we'd had, and we were splitting. Very strange. But I had other things going on in my life. I wanted to have a kid, I wanted to have a house, the different things that people do, as opposed to living out of a suitcase. So there was that to look forward to. It was a good time, really.”
JACK BRUCE, 2000

mon 1 – sun 7

mon 8 – sun 14

mon 15 – sun 21

mon 22 – sun 29

mon 29 – wed 31

● **RECORDS RELEASE US** JULY *WHEELS OF FIRE* ATCO DOUBLE LP. ALSO AROUND JULY *SAVAGE SEVEN* SOUNDTRACK ATCO LP, INCLUDES 'ANYONE FOR TENNIS'.

AUGUST 1968

thu 1 – wed 7

thu 8 – wed 14

thu 15 – wed 21

thu 22 – wed 28

thu 29 – sat 31

● **RECORDS RELEASE UK** FRI AUG 9th *WHEELS OF FIRE* POLYDOR DOUBLE LP; PLUS A SEPARATE POLYDOR SINGLE LP (ONE HALF OF *WHEELS OF FIRE*) TITLED *IN THE STUDIO*. (THE OTHER HALF, *LIVE AT THE FILLMORE*, FOLLOWED SEPARATELY IN DECEMBER.)

SEPTEMBER 1968

sun 1 – sat 7

sun 8 – sat 14

sun 15 – sat 21

sun 22 – sat 28

sun 29 – mon 30

● **RECORD RELEASE UK** FRI SEP 6th 'SUNSHINE OF YOUR LOVE'/'SWLABR' POLYDOR 45.

* For key to recording abbreviations see page 160

OCTOBER 1968

tue 1

wed 2

thu 3

fri 4 **OAKLAND COLISEUM** OAKLAND, CA, US. *FIRST DATE OF CREAM'S THIRD (FAREWELL) NORTH AMERICAN TOUR*

sat 5 **UNIVERSITY OF NEW MEXICO** ALBUQUERQUE, NM, US.

sun 6

mon 7

tue 8

wed 9

thu 10

fri 11 **NEW HAVEN ARENA** NEW HAVEN, CT, US.

sat 12 **OLYMPIA (HOCKEY) STADIUM** DETROIT, MI, US. PLUS FRIEND & LOVER

sun 13 **COLISEUM** CHICAGO, IL, US.

mon 14 **VETERANS MEMORIAL AUDITORIUM** DES MOINES, IA, US.

tue 15

wed 16

thu 17

fri 18 **THE FORUM** LOS ANGELES, CA, US.

sat 19 **THE FORUM** LOS ANGELES, CA, US.

sun 20 **SPORTS ARENA** SAN DIEGO, CA, US.

mon 21

tue 22

wed 23

thu 24 **SAM HOUSTON COLISEUM** HOUSTON, TX, US.

fri 25 **DALLAS MEMORIAL AUDITORIUM** DALLAS, TX, US.

sat 26 **MIAMI STADIUM** MIAMI, FL, US.

sun 27 **CHASTAIN PARK AMPHITHEATER** ATLANTA, GA, US. *TWO SHOWS*

mon 28

tue 29

wed 30

thu 31 **BOSTON GARDEN** BOSTON, MA, US.

● **RECORD RELEASE US** OCTOBER 'WHITE ROOM'/'THOSE WERE THE DAYS' ATCO 45.

● **LIVE RECORDING** FRI 4th. OAKLAND COLISEUM ARENA (OAKLAND, CA, US) OFFICALLY RECORDED FOR POTENTIAL COMMERICAL RELEASE. PRODUCER: FELIX PAPPALARDI, ENGINEER: BILL HALVERSON. REMIX FOR LIVE CREAM VOLUME II: GENE PAUL AND KEVIN BRADY. 'WHITE ROOM' *LC2; TWD.* 'POLITICIAN' *LC2; TWD.* 'CROSSROADS' *UR; BL.* 'SUNSHINE OF YOUR LOVE' *UR; BL.* 'SPOONFUL' *UR; BL.* 'DESERTED CITIES OF THE HEART' *LC2; TWD.* 'PASSING THE TIME'/'DRUM SOLO' (aka 'SCATAFARAGUS') *UR; BL.* 'I'M SO GLAD' *UR; BL.*

● **LIVE RECORDING** FRI 18th-SUN 20th. FORUM AND SPORTS ARENA GIGS (LOS ANGELES AND SAN DIEGO, CA, US) OFFICALLY RECORDED FOR POTENTIAL COMMERCIAL RELEASE. PRODUCER: FELIX PAPPALARDI, ENGINEER: BILL HALVERSON. AS FOLLOWS:

● **FRI 18th** THE FORUM (LOS ANGELES, CA, US). 'WHITE ROOM' *TL.* 'POLITICIAN' *TL.* 'I'M SO GLAD' *TL.* 'SITTING ON TOP OF THE WORLD' *TL.* 'SUNSHINE OF YOUR LOVE' *TL.* 'CROSSROADS' *TL.* 'TRAINTIME' *TL.* 'TOAD' *TL.* 'SPOONFUL' *TL.*

● **SAT 19th** THE FORUM (LOS ANGELES, CA, US). 'WHITE ROOM' *TL; BL.* 'POLITICIAN' *GB.* 'I'M SO GLAD' *GB; TWD.* 'SITTING ON TOP OF THE WORLD' *GB; TWD.* 'CROSSROADS' *TL.* 'SUNSHINE OF YOUR LOVE' *TL.* 'TRAINTIME' *TL.* 'TOAD' *TL.* 'SPOONFUL' *TL.*

● **SUN 20th** SPORTS ARENA (SAN DIEGO, CA, US). 'WHITE ROOM' *TL.* 'POLITICIAN' *TL.* 'I'M SO GLAD' *TL.* 'SITTING ON TOP OF THE WORLD' *TL.* 'SUNSHINE OF YOUR LOVE' *TL; BL.* 'CROSSROADS' *TL; BL.* 'TRAINTIME' *TL; BL.* 'TOAD' *TL; BL.* 'SPOONFUL' *TL; BL.*

“After the San Diego gig I got put in jail. I'd gone to Mexico with some roadies and my wife. We climbed a hill and befriended some shepherds, one of whom was wearing a Royal Navy cap. We never found out why. They invited us to their local bar, a corrugated-iron shed in the hills, and we were drinking for a long time. We got completely out of it. Coming back, we got to the border and as I was drunk I hid the car-keys. It all ended up very messy. The police tried to take us to jail. I'm saying: 'I'm number one in the charts, let us go!' All these hippie kids came along and redecorated the police station with flowers. And eventually I got out because we had the gigs. I remember that the Texas dates that followed were wild.” **JACK BRUCE, 2000**

* For key to recording abbreviations see page 160

NOVEMBER 1968

"At Madison Square Garden they brought the Kennedy kids to meet us, and you'd get paraplegics to touch. It didn't fit very well with my ideals. We became a sort of show, something that people came to see rather than to listen to. It all sounds a bit precious now, but at the time there were some ideals going around, about changing the world for the better, and I got caught up in that, I guess. We did get platinum discs presented to us at the Garden. I remember bringing mine back to England, proudly, and they wanted me to pay duty on it. Typically British. I did once take down one of our gold discs to see if it would actually play, and it was Louis Armstrong backwards."
JACK BRUCE, 2000

"I remember a soundcheck at one of the big gigs on that final US tour, I went with Eric right up to the very furthest-away seats you could go to, and there were these tiny little dots on stage where we would be. And I said to Eric, 'Fucking hell! We've come a long way from the Twisted Wheel.'" **JACK BRUCE, 2000**

fri 1 **THE SPECTRUM** PHILADELPHIA, PA, US.

sat 2 **MADISON SQUARE GARDEN** NEW YORK, NY, US.

sun 3 **CIVIC CENTER** BALTIMORE, MD, US.

mon 4 **RHODE ISLAND AUDITORIUM** PROVIDENCE, RI, US. *TWO SHOWS 6.30PM, 9.30PM, LAST DATE OF FINAL US TOUR*

tue 5

wed 6

thu 7

fri 8

sat 9

sun 10

mon 11

tue 12

wed 13

thu 14

fri 15

sat 16

sun 17

mon 18

tue 19

wed 20

thu 21

fri 22

sat 23

sun 24

mon 25

tue 26 **ROYAL ALBERT HALL** CENTRAL LONDON, ENGLAND. *TWO SHOWS, PLUS YES, TASTE, FINAL CREAM DATE*

wed 27

thu 28

fri 29

sat 30

● **RECORDING** WALLY HEIDER STUDIOS (LOS ANGELES, CA, US). EARLY NOVEMBER. STUDIO PERSONNEL UNKNOWN. 'JACK'S TUNE' (BASIS OF 'DOING THAT SCRAPYARD THING') *UR*. 'GINGER'S TUNE' (BASIS OF 'WHAT A BRINGDOWN') *UR*. 'ERIC'S TUNE' (BASIS OF 'BADGE') *UR*.

● **RECORDING** IBC STUDIOS (CENTRAL LONDON, ENGLAND). LATE NOVEMBER. PRODUCER: FELIX PAPPALARDI, ENGINEER: DAMON LYON-SHAW. 'BADGE' (M) *45A; GB; TWD*. 'DOING THAT SCRAPYARD THING' (M) *GB; TWD*. 'WHAT A BRINGDOWN' (M) *45B; GB; TWD*.

● **FILM** ROYAL ALBERT HALL (CENTRAL LONDON, ENGLAND). FILMING TUE 26th FOR CINEMA-RELEASE MOVIE (COL), AND BBC TV'S *OMNIBUS* (B&W) BROADCAST SUN JAN 5th 1969 BBC1. DIRECTOR TONY PALMER. FIRST SHOW: 'WHITE ROOM' *FCV; SBV; CEV*. 'POLITICIAN' *TL*. 'I'M SO GLAD' *TL*. 'SITTING ON TOP OF THE WORLD' *TL*. 'CROSSROADS' *TL*. 'TOAD' *TL*. 'SPOONFUL' *TL*. 'SUNSHINE OF YOUR LOVE' *TL*. 'STEPPING OUT' *TL*. SECOND SHOW: 'WHITE ROOM' *TL; BL*. 'POLITICIAN' *FCV; SBV*. 'I'M SO GLAD' *FCV; SBV*. 'SITTING ON TOP OF THE WORLD' *FCV; SBV*. 'CROSSROADS' *FCV; SBV; CEV*. 'TOAD' *FCV; SBV*. 'SPOONFUL' *FCV; SBV*. 'SUNSHINE OF YOUR LOVE' *FCV; SBV; CEV*. 'STEPPING OUT' *TL; BL*.

* For key to recording abbreviations see page 160

JANUARY 1993

fri 1

sat 2

sun 3

mon 4

tue 5

wed 6

thu 7

fri 8

sat 9

sun 10

mon 11

tue 12 **EIGHTH ROCK & ROLL HALL OF FAME** CENTURY PLAZA HOTEL, LOS ANGELES, CA, US.

wed 13

thu 14

fri 15

sat 16

sun 17

mon 18

tue 19

wed 20

thu 21

fri 22

sat 23

sun 24

mon 25

tue 26

wed 27

thu 28

fri 29

sat 30

sun 31

"The Rock and Roll Hall of Fame honours the legendary performers, producers, songwriters, disc jockeys and others who have made rock and roll the force in our culture that it is. For a decade and a half, the Rock and Roll Hall of Fame Foundation has been nominating and electing those figures, and honouring them at an annual ceremony that has become one of the most celebrated events of the year, and certainly one of the hottest tickets in rock. In sometimes poignant, sometimes hilarious speeches, artists toast their peers and forebears in rock, followed by rollicking, once-in-a-lifetime performances that make history as much as pay tribute to it… Once inducted, the artists are further honoured when they are featured in the Museum's Hall of Fame exhibit, which includes a computerised "juke box" containing virtually every song of every performer inductee; etched-glass signatures of the inductees; a film on three huge screens recounting their careers and music; and a display of artefacts from the current year's inductees."

DESCRIPTION OF THE ROCK AND ROLL HALL OF FAME, 2000

● **REHEARSAL/RECORDING** UNKNOWN STUDIO (LOS ANGELES, CA, US). MON 11th. 'SUNSHINE OF YOUR LOVE' (SEVEN TAKES) *BL*. 'BORN UNDER A BAD SIGN' (TWO TAKES) *BL*. 'CROSSROADS' (THREE TAKES) *BL*. 'UNTITLED INSTRUMENTAL' (ONE TAKE) *BL*.

● **TV** EIGHTH ROCK & ROLL HALL OF FAME, CENTURY PLAZA HOTEL (LOS ANGELES, CA, US), INDUCTION AND LIVE PERFORMANCE WED 12th FOR CABLE CHANNEL BROADCAST. 'SUNSHINE OF YOUR LOVE' *UR; BL*. 'BORN UNDER A BAD SIGN' *UR; BL*. 'CROSSROADS' *UR; BL*.

* For key to recording abbreviations see page 160

CREAM DISCOGRAPHY

These are the original UK and US single and LP releases, in chronological order. (Many, many reissues have appeared over the years, and the records have been released in various combinations in many other countries; all are beyond the scope of this discography.) Of the many Cream compilations that have been issued, only two are listed here: *Best Of Cream*, which was the first of its kind; and *Those Were The Days*, the most comprehensive of its kind. Bootlegs are illegal and are not listed.
Record type (single or LP) is followed by relevant title(s). Release date(s), record label(s) and catalogue number(s) are then given, and the composer(s) is/are shown in brackets for each song. Concert source is listed for live recordings. Please play loud.

Single 'Wrapping Paper' *(Jack Bruce/Pete Brown)*/'Cat's Squirrel' *(traditional arr. S Splurge)*
October 7th 1966 UK: Reaction 591007

Single 'I Feel Free' *(Jack Bruce/Pete Brown)*/'NSU' *(Jack Bruce)*
December 9th 1966 UK: Reaction 591011
January 1967 US: Atco 6462

LP *Fresh Cream*
December 9th 1966 UK: Reaction 593 001 mono, 594 001 stereo
March 1967 US: Atco 33-206 mono, SD 33-206 stereo (minus 'Spoonful', plus 'I Feel Free')
'NSU' *(Jack Bruce)*
'Sleepy Time Time' *(Jack Bruce/Janet Godfrey)*
'Dreaming' *(Jack Bruce)*
'Sweet Wine' *(Ginger Baker/Janet Godfrey)*
'Spoonful' *(Willie Dixon)* on UK release only
'I Feel Free' *(Jack Bruce/Pete Brown)* on US release only
'Cat's Squirrel' *(traditional arr. S Splurge)*
'Four Until Late' *(Robert Johnson arr. Eric Clapton)*
'Rollin' And Tumblin'' *(Muddy Waters)*
'I'm So Glad' *(Skip James)*
'Toad' *(Ginger Baker)*

Single 'Strange Brew' *(Eric Clapton/Gail Collins/Felix Pappalardi)*/'Tales Of Brave Ulysses' *(Eric Clapton/Martin Sharp)*
May 26th 1967 UK: Reaction 591015
July 1967 US: Atco 6488

Single 'Spoonful' *(Willie Dixon)*/'Spoonful Pt 2'
around October 1967 US: Atco 6522

LP *Disraeli Gears*
November 3rd 1967 UK: Reaction 593 003 mono, 594 003 stereo
November 1967 US: Atco 33-232 mono, SD 33-232 stereo
'Strange Brew' *(Eric Clapton/Gail Collins/Felix Pappalardi)*
'Sunshine Of Your Love' *(Jack Bruce/Pete Brown/Eric Clapton)*
'World Of Pain' *(Gail Collins/Felix Pappalardi)*
'Dance The Night Away' *(Jack Bruce/Pete Brown)*
'Blue Condition' *(Ginger Baker)*
'Tales Of Brave Ulysses' *(Eric Clapton/Martin Sharp)*
'SWLABR' *(Jack Bruce/Pete Brown)*
'We're Going Wrong' *(Jack Bruce)*
'Outside Woman Blues' *(Arthur Reynolds arr. Eric Clapton)*
'Take It Back' *(Jack Bruce/Pete Brown)*
'Mother's Lament' *(traditional arr. Ginger Baker/Jack Bruce/Eric Clapton)*

Single 'Sunshine Of Your Love' *(Jack Bruce/Pete Brown/Eric Clapton)*/'SWLABR' *(Jack Bruce/Pete Brown)*
February 1968 US: Atco 6544
September 6th 1968 UK: Polydor 56 286

Single 'Anyone for Tennis' *(Eric Clapton/Martin Sharp)*/'Pressed Rat And Warthog' *(Ginger Baker/Mike Taylor)*
May 1968 UK: Polydor 56 258
May 1968 US: Atco 6575

LP *The Savage Seven* soundtrack
around July 1968 US: Atco SD 33-245 includes 'Anyone For Tennis' *(Eric Clapton/Martin Sharp)*

LP *Wheels Of Fire*
July 1968 US: Atco SD 2-700 double-LP
August 9th 1968 UK: Polydor 582 031/2 double-LP mono, 583 031/2 double-LP stereo, 582 033 *In The Studio* single-LP mono, 583 033 *In The Studio* single-LP stereo
December 1968 UK: Polydor 582 040 *Live At The Fillmore* single-LP mono, 583 040 *Live At The Fillmore* single-LP stereo
In The Studio
'White Room' *(Jack Bruce/Pete Brown)*
'Sitting On Top Of The World' *(Chester Burnett)*
'Passing The Time' *(Ginger Baker/Mike Taylor)*
'As You Said' *(Jack Bruce/Pete Brown)*
'Pressed Rat And Warthog' *(Ginger Baker/Mike Taylor)*
'Politician' *(Jack Bruce/Pete Brown)*
'Those Were The Days' *(Ginger Baker/Mike Taylor)*
'Born Under A Bad Sign' *(Booker T Jones/William Bell)*
'Deserted Cities Of The Heart' *(Jack Bruce/Pete Brown)*
Live At The Fillmore
'Crossroads' *(Robert Johnson)* from Winterland March 10th 1968
'Spoonful' *(Willie Dixon)* from Winterland March 10th 1968
'Traintime' *(Jack Bruce)* from Winterland March 8th 1968
'Toad' *(Ginger Baker)* from Fillmore March 7th 1968

Single 'White Room' *(Jack Bruce/Pete Brown)*/'Those Were The Days' *(Ginger Baker/Mike Taylor)*
October 1968 US: Atco 6617
January 1969 UK: Polydor 56 300

Single 'Crossroads' *(Robert Johnson)*/'Passing The Time' *(Ginger Baker/Mike Taylor)*
February 1969 US: Atco 6646

LP *Goodbye*
March 1969 UK: Polydor 583 053
March 1969 US: Atco SD 7001
'I'm So Glad' *(Skip James)* from The Forum October 19th 1968
'Politician' *(Jack Bruce/Pete Brown)* from The Forum October 19th 1968
'Sitting On Top Of The World' *(Chester Burnett)* from The Forum October 19th 1968
'Badge' *(Eric Clapton/George Harrison)*
'Doing That Scrapyard Thing' *(Jack Bruce/Pete Brown)*
'What A Bringdown' *(Ginger Baker)*

Single 'Badge' *(Eric Clapton/George Harrison)*/'What A Bringdown' *(Ginger Baker)*

CREAM DISCOGRAPHY

April 1969 UK: Polydor 56 315
April 1969 US: Atco 6668

Single 'Sweet Wine' *(Ginger Baker/Janet Godfrey)*/'Lawdy Mama' *(traditional arr. Eric Clapton)* version 2
August 1969 US: Atco 6708 US only

LP *Best Of Cream*
July 1969 US: Atco SD 33-291
November 1969 UK: Polydor 583 060
'Sunshine Of Your Love' *(Jack Bruce/Pete Brown/Eric Clapton)*
'Badge' *(Eric Clapton/George Harrison)*
'Crossroads' *(Robert Johnson)*
'White Room' *(Jack Bruce/Pete Brown)*
'SWLABR' *(Jack Bruce/Pete Brown)*
'Born Under A Bad Sign' *(Booker T Jones/William Bell)*
'Spoonful' *(Willie Dixon)*
'Tales Of Brave Ulysses' *(Eric Clapton/Martin Sharp)*
'Strange Brew' *(Eric Clapton/Felix Pappalardi/Gail Collins)*
'I Feel Free' *(Jack Bruce/Pete Brown)*

LP *Live Cream*
April 1970 US: Atco SD 33-328
June 1970 UK: Polydor 2383 016
'NSU' *(Jack Bruce)* from Winterland March 10th 1968 (edited version)
'Sleepy Time Time' *(Jack Bruce/Janet Godfrey)* from Winterland March 9th 1968
'Sweet Wine' *(Ginger Baker/Janet Godfrey)* from Winterland March 10th 1968
'Rollin' and Tumblin'' *(Muddy Waters)* from Fillmore March 7th 1968
'Lawdy Mama' *(traditional arr. Eric Clapton)* version 2 (not live)

LP *Live Cream Volume II*
March 1972 US: Atco SD 7005
June 1972 UK: Polydor 2383 119
'Deserted Cities Of The Heart' *(Jack Bruce/Pete Brown)* from Oakland October 4th 1968
'White Room' *(Jack Bruce/Pete Brown)* from Oakland October 4th 1968
'Politician' *(Jack Bruce/Pete Brown)* from Oakland October 4th 1968
'Tales Of Brave Ulysses' *(Eric Clapton/Martin Sharp)* from Winterland March 10th 1968
'Sunshine Of Your Love' *(Jack Bruce/Pete Brown/Eric Clapton)* from Winterland March 9th 1968
'Stepping Out' *(James Bracken)* from Winterland March 9th 1968

CD box-set *Those Were The Days*
September 23rd 1997 UK/US: Polydor 539 000-2
In The Studio 1
'Wrapping Paper' *(Jack Bruce/Pete Brown)*
'I Feel Free' *(Jack Bruce/Pete Brown)*
'NSU' *(Jack Bruce)*
'Sleepy Time Time' *(Jack Bruce/Janet Godfrey)*
'Dreaming' *(Jack Bruce)*
'Sweet Wine' *(Ginger Baker/Janet Godfrey)*
'Spoonful' *(Willie Dixon)*
'Cat's Squirrel' *(traditional arr. S Splurge)*
'Four Until Late' *(Robert Johnson arr. Eric Clapton)*
'Rollin' And Tumblin'' *(Muddy Waters)*
'I'm So Glad' *(Skip James)*
'Toad' *(Ginger Baker)*
'Lawdy Mama' *(traditional arr Eric Clapton)* version 1
'Strange Brew' *(Eric Clapton/Gail Collins/Felix Pappalardi)*
'Sunshine Of Your Love' *(Jack Bruce/Pete Brown/Eric Clapton)*
'World Of Pain' *(Gail Collins/Felix Pappalardi)*
'Dance The Night Away' *(Jack Bruce/Pete Brown)*
'Blue Condition' *(Ginger Baker)*
'Tales Of Brave Ulysses' *(Eric Clapton/Martin Sharp)*
'SWLABR' *(Jack Bruce/Pete Brown)*
'We're Going Wrong' *(Jack Bruce)*
'Outside Woman Blues' *(Arthur Reynolds arr. Eric Clapton)*
'Take It Back' *(Jack Bruce/Pete Brown)*
'Mother's Lament' *(traditional arr. Ginger Baker/Jack Bruce/Eric Clapton)*
In The Studio 2
'White Room' *(Jack Bruce/Pete Brown)*
'Sitting On Top Of The World' *(Chester Burnett)*
'Passing The Time' *(Ginger Baker/Mike Taylor)* alternate version
'As You Said' *(Jack Bruce/Pete Brown)*
'Pressed Rat And Warthog' *(Ginger Baker/Mike Taylor)*
'Politician' *(Jack Bruce/Pete Brown)*
'Those Were The Days' *(Ginger Baker/Mike Taylor)*
'Born Under A Bad Sign' *(Booker T Jones/William Bell)*
'Deserted Cities Of The Heart' *(Jack Bruce/Pete Brown)*
'Anyone For Tennis' *(Eric Clapton/Martin Sharp)*
'Badge' *(Eric Clapton/George Harrison)*
'Doing That Scrapyard Thing' *(Jack Bruce/Pete Brown)*
'What A Bringdown' *(Ginger Baker)*
'The Coffee Song' *(Tony Colton/Ray Smith)*
'Lawdy Mama' *(traditional arr. Eric Clapton)* version 2
'You Make Me Feel' *(Jack Bruce/Pete Brown)* rehearsal
'We're Going Wrong' *(Jack Bruce)* demo
'Hey Now Princess' *(Jack Bruce/Pete Brown)* demo
'SWLABR' *(Jack Bruce/Pete Brown)* demo
'Weird Of Hermiston' *(Jack Bruce/Pete Brown)* demo
'The Clearout' *(Jack Bruce/Pete Brown)* demo
'Falstaff Beer Commercial' *(Ginger Baker/Jack Bruce/Eric Clapton)*
Live 1
'NSU' *(Jack Bruce)* from Winterland March 9th 1968 (unedited version)
'Sleepy Time Time' *(Jack Bruce/Janet Godfrey)* from Winterland March 9th 1968
'Rollin' And Tumblin'' *(Muddy Waters)* from Fillmore March 7th 1968
'Crossroads' *(Robert Johnson)* from Winterland March 10th 1968
'Spoonful' *(Willie Dixon)* from Winterland March 10th 1968
'Tales Of Brave Ulysses' *(Eric Clapton/Martin Sharp)* from Winterland March 10th 1968
'Sunshine Of Your Love' *(Jack Bruce/Pete Brown)* from Winterland March 9th 1968
'Sweet Wine' *(Ginger Baker/Janet Godfrey)* from Winterland March 10th 1968
Live 2
'White Room' *(Jack Bruce/Pete Brown)* from Oakland October 4th 1968
'Politician' *(Jack Bruce/Pete Brown)* from Oakland October 4th 1968
I'm So Glad' *(Skip James)* from The Forum October 19th 1968
'Sitting on Top Of The World' *(Chester Burnett)* from The Forum October 19th 1968
'Stepping Out' *(James Bracken)* from Winterland March 9th 1968
'Traintime' *(Jack Bruce)* from Winterland March 10th 1968
'Toad' *(Ginger Baker)* from Fillmore March 7th/8th 1968
'Deserted Cities Of The Heart' *(Jack Bruce/Pete Brown)* from Oakland October 4th 1968
'Sunshine Of Your Love' *(Jack Bruce/Pete Brown)* from CBS Studios for *Summer Brothers Smother Show* May 17th 1968

Page numbers in italics indicate illustrations. *Titles In Italics* are albums, radio & TV shows, publications. Titles in 'Single Quotes' are songs. Page numbers for song entries with an "r" next to them (eg "161r") indicate information on official studio recordings listed in the Cream Diary. Page numbers for song entries with a "c" next to them (eg "180c") indicate information on official live concert recordings listed in the Cream Diary.

ACKNOWLEDGEMENTS

The author would like to offer heartfelt thanks to Jack and Margrit Bruce, Ginger Baker, Pete Brown, Ben Palmer, Ray Williams, Tom McGuinness, Tony Bacon and Nigel Osborne for their kind help and co-operation in drawing together this tribute to Cream, and to Eric Clapton for his inspiration and good vibes.

The publisher would like to thank: René Aagaard; Jeffrey M. Aarons; Hans Bäckström; Keith Badman; Ginger Baker; Julie Bowie; Jack Bruce; Margrit Bruce; Chuck Buckner; Bjørn Eirik Dahl; John Farnan; Howard Fields; Steven Gatto; Manuel Gonzalez Jr.; Don Green; George Hiatt; Cheryl Hopes (Manchester City Libraries); John Hudson (Mayfair studio); Mikael Jansson; Mark Kemmerle; Michael Krawczyk; Jim Laverty; Alan Lefton; George McManus (Polydor Records); Don Merlino; Baron Von Muller; David Nathan (National Jazz Foundation Archive); Olli Oksala; Claus Rasmussen; Heinz Rebellius; Rock & Roll Hall Of Fame; Harry Shapiro; Andrew Simons (National Sound Archive, British Library); Bengt Skogberg; Phil Smee (Strange Things); Tapani Taka; Chris Taylor; Tom Thatcher; Jeff Watt; Matthew Wheeler (Polydor Records); Charlie Whitney; Michael Wright.

Special thanks to Graeme Pattingale, Bob Elliott and John Walasko, who provided a carefully researched basis from which the Cream Diary section was developed; and to René Aagaard, who did a great deal to help the accuracy of the discography.

INTERVIEWS Most of the quotes in the main text are from Chris Welch's original interviews with Ginger Baker (1966-68 and 2000), Pete Brown (2000), Jack Bruce (1966-68 and 2000), Eric Clapton (1966-68), Tom McGuinness (2000), Ben Palmer (2000) and Ray Williams (1998). Quotes in Geoff Nicholls' piece on Ginger Baker in chapter 2 come from his interview with Baker conducted in June 2000. Quotes from Jack Bruce in the Cream Diary section are from interviews by Tony Bacon conducted in August and September 2000.

PHOTOGRAPHS Supplied by the following (number indicates page): Jacket: Eric Clapton (front) Chuck Boyd/Redferns; Cream (rear) Pictorial Press. 8/9 Robert Whitaker/Strange Things. 13 Susie MacDonald/Redferns. 19 Jeremy Fletcher/Redferns. 20 Val Wilmer. 21 Jeremy Fletcher/Redferns. 23 Michael Ochs Archives/Redferns. 26 top Rick Richards/Redferns. 27 Val Wilmer. 28/29 Val Wilmer. 30 Strange Things. 35 Strange Things. 36 Harry Shapiro. 37 Harry Shapiro. 42 Pictorial Press. 43 Strange Things. 45 Susie MacDonald/Redferns. 49 Val Wilmer. 50 Robert Whitaker/Strange Things. 51 Chuck Boyd/Redferns. 52 David Redfern/Redferns. 53 Chuck Stewart/Redferns. 54 Chuck Boyd/Redferns. 55 Michael Geary. 58 Pictorial Press. 59 Pictorial Press. 62 Robert Whitaker/Strange Things. 63 top Pictorial Press. 65 Robert Whitaker/Strange Things. 66 Michael Geary. 69 Susie MacDonald/Redferns. 70 Pictorial Press. 79 Brian Shuel/Redferns. 81 Gems/Redferns. 82/83 all three Pictorial Press. 88 Val Wilmer/Redferns. 90 Tony Gale/Pictorial Press. 91 Pete Brown. 92 Strange Things. 93 Pete Brown. 94 Strange Things. 95 Strange Things. 96 Pictorial Press. 100 Nikpop/Redferns. 102 Pictorial Press. 106 Chuck Stewart/Redferns. 107 Chuck Stewart/Redferns. 108/109 all four Robert Whitaker/Strange Things. 116/117 Hans Bäckström. 122 Michael Geary. 124/125 Michael Ochs Archives/Redferns. 129 Bob Gruen/Pictorial Press. 132 Chuck Boyd/Redferns. 141 both Chuck Boyd/Redferns. 143 Michael Geary. 145 Chuck Boyd/Redferns. 147 Pictorial Press. 148 Susie MacDonald/Redferns. 159 Keith Morris/Redferns.

Other illustrated items including advertisements, guitars and cases, magazines, newspapers, posters, programmes, records and record sleeves came from the collections of: René Aagaard; Tony Bacon; Balafon Image Bank; Eric Clapton; Bjørn Eirik Dahl; Howard Fields; Manuel Gonzalez Jr.; Dave Gregory; National Jazz Foundation Archive; National Sound Archive, British Library; Nigel Osborne; Todd Rundgren; Harry Shapiro; Tom Thatcher. We are very grateful for the help of all these individuals and institutions.

Special thanks to René Aagaard for the big box of goodies; and to Howard Fields for constant assistance.

BIBLIOGRAPHY

Tony Bacon *London Live* (Balafon 1999).
Pete Frame *Complete Rock Family Trees* (Omnibus 1993).
Ken Garner *In Session Tonight – The Complete Radio 1 Recordings* (BBC 1993).
Steve Hoffman *Sleevenotes to DCC release of Fresh Cream.*
John Platt *Disraeli Gears* (Schirmer 1998).
Mark Roberty *Clapton: The Complete Chronicles* (Pyramid 1991); *Eric Clapton – The Complete Recording Sessions 1963-1995* (St Martin's Press 1996); *Eric Clapton: The New Visual Documentary* (Omnibus 1990).
Michel Ruppli *Atlantic Records: A Discography 1947-1974* (Greenwood 1979, 4 vols).
Chris Welch *Cream: Strange Brew* (Castle 1994).
Chris Scott Wilson *Redcar Jazz Club* (Redcar & Cleveland Borough Council 1996).

Periodicals: Beat Instrumental; Hit Parader; Jazz News; Melody Maker; Music Maker; New Musical Express; Rolling Stone.

The caption on page 87 should state that *Fresh Cream's* first UK release was on the Reaction label, not Polydor.

"Bands with small line-ups managed because of the volume we played at. It compressed everything: harmonics were created that wouldn't normally be there, and you literally heard music that wasn't there. You heard noise within the noise." *Pete Townshend on Cream, 1997*